# The American History Series

SERIES EDITOR
John Hope Franklin, *Duke University*

Thomas K. McCraw
HARVARD UNIVERSITY

# American Business Since 1920: How It Worked

## Second Edition

WILEY Blackwell

A John Wiley & Sons, Ltd., Publication

This edition first published 2000, 2009.
©2000, 2009 Harlan Davidson, Inc.

Harlan Davidson, Inc. was acquired by John Wiley & Sons in May 2012.

*Registered Office*
John Wiley & Sons Ltd, The Atrium, Southern Gate, Chichester, West Sussex, PO19 8SQ, UK

*Editorial Offices*
350 Main Street, Malden, MA 02148-5020, USA
9600 Garsington Road, Oxford, OX4 2DQ, UK
The Atrium, Southern Gate, Chichester, West Sussex, PO19 8SQ, UK

For details of our global editorial offices, for customer services, and for information about how to apply for permission to reuse the copyright material in this book please see our website at www.wiley.com/wiley-blackwell.

The right of Thomas K. McCraw to be identified as the author of this work has been asserted in accordance with the UK Copyright, Designs and Patents Act 1988.

Library of Congress Cataloging-in-Publication Data

McCraw, Thomas K.
    American business, since 1920 : how it worked / Thomas K. McCraw.—2nd ed.
        p. cm.— (The American history series)
Includes bibliographical reference and index.
    ISBN 978-0-88295-266-6
    1. Industries—United States—History—20th century. 2. Corporations—United
States—History—20th century. 3. United States—Commerce—History—20th
century. 4. Labor—United States—History—20th century. 5. United States—
Economic conditions.
I. Title.
    HC106.82.M39 2009
    338.097309'04—dc22

                          2008043302

Cover illustration: Boeing 727 passenger liners under construction. Used with permission of The Boeing Company.

This book is for the McCarrons:
Liz, Rob, Eliza, and Catey

# FOREWORD

Every generation writes its own history for the reason that it sees the past in the foreshortened perspective of its own experience. This has surely been true of the writing of American history. The practical aim of our historiography is to give us a more informed sense of where we are going by helping us understand the road we took in getting where we are. As the nature and dimensions of American life are changing, so too are the themes of our historical writing. Today's scholars are hard at work reconsidering every major aspect of the nation's past: its politics, diplomacy, economy, society, recreation, mores and values, as well as status, ethnic, race, sexual, and family relations. The lists of series titles that appear on the inside covers of this book will show at once that our historians are ever broadening the range of their studies.

The aim of this series is to offer our readers a survey of what today's historians are saying about the central themes and aspects of the American past. To do this, we have invited to write for the series only scholars who have made notable contributions to the respective fields in which they are working. Drawing on primary and secondary materials, each volume presents a factual and narrative account of its particular subject, one that affords readers a basis for perceiving its larger dimensions and importance. Conscious that readers respond to the closeness and immediacy of a subject, each of our authors seeks to restore the past as an actual present, to revive it as a living reality. The individuals and groups who figure in the pages of our books appear as real people who once were looking for survival and fulfillment. Aware that historical subjects are often matters of controversy, our authors present their own findings and conclusions. Each volume closes with an extensive critical essay on the writings of the major authorities on its particular theme.

The books in this series are primarily designed for use in both basic and advanced courses in American history, on the undergraduate and graduate levels. Such a series has a particular value these days, when the format of American history courses is being altered to accommodate a greater diversity of reading materials. The series offers a number of distinct advantages. It extends the dimensions of regular course work. It makes clear that the study of our past is, more than the student might otherwise understand, at once complex, profound, and absorbing. And it presents that past as a subject of continuing interest and fresh investigation.

For these reasons the series strongly invites an interest that far exceeds the walls of academe. The work of experts in their respective fields, it puts at the disposal of all readers the rich findings of historical inquiry, an invitation to join, in major fields of research, those who are pondering anew the central themes and aspects of our past. Going beyond the confines of the classroom, it reminds the general reader no less than the university student that in each successive generation of the ever-changing American adventure, from its very start until our own day, men and women and children were facing their daily problems and attempting, as we are now, to live their lives and to make their way.

*John Hope Franklin*

# CONTENTS

# INTRODUCTION

## Themes

There have been four potent trends in American business since 1920, and you should try to keep all four in mind as you read this book. None proceeded without temporary setbacks, but all kept moving forward:

1. *The relentlessness of change.* This has been a characteristic of all capitalist economies. But it applies with special force to the United States, where it's even accurate to speak of relentlessly accelerating relentlessness. After 1920 the tempo of economic change grew faster, and then faster still. No generation in human history has experienced more rapid and relentless change than has your own—that is, you yourself, the reader of this book. And no other has witnessed such intense competition among businesses, both domestic and global.

2. *A growing empowerment of consumers and entrepreneurs.* Here the main driving force was the increase in per-capita incomes *by a factor of six* from 1920 to 2009. This unprecedented rise in the nation's affluence was accompanied by a profound shift in the nature of jobs. In 1920, 60 percent of the labor force worked on farms or in mines and factories. By 2009, the 60 percent had dropped to 13 percent. That shift, from three of every five workers to one of every eight, was nothing short of revolutionary.

Together these two big changes—sharply rising incomes and radical redeployments in jobs away from production and toward services—brought tremendous gains in both consumer power and entrepreneurial opportunity. Consumer empowerment rose sharply with the coming of cars and trucks early in the twentieth century, as the automobile gave millions of people a new and thrilling sense of liberation. Cars and especially trucks also brought a wide range of opportunities to start new businesses.

Consumers and producers were also tremendously affected by the growth of electronic media. AM radio started in the 1920s, followed in the 1940s by FM stations and black-and-white TV. Color television debuted in the 1960s, HDTV and digital cable in the 1990s and early 2000s. The Internet was born in the 1980s as a small government project. In the 1990s the World Wide Web arrived, and the privatization of the Net in 1995 set off an explosion of undreamed-of opportunities.

Still another empowering force was the emergence of women and minorities into important roles as consumers and entrepreneurs. Here the essential catalyst was the passage of new federal laws, mostly during the 1960s, after decades of intense effort. These laws brought dramatic gains in civil, voting, and employment rights.

3. *An increasing tension between centralized and decentralized decision making in business, and the general triumph of decentralization.* Constant decision making lies at the heart of business. Every hour of every day, millions of decisions are made within companies. But by whom? On what basis? In whose interest?

During and after the 1920s, as many companies grew ever larger, tensions about decision making became increasingly complicated. The best-run firms began to develop effective ways to push authority downward to the person best informed to make a particular decision—regardless of where in the hierarchy that person might rank. This was a gradual and often painful lesson for businesses to learn, as many parts of this book will show. Companies that failed to learn the lesson not only suffered, but often perished.

4. *Progress toward controlling the dark side of business, so that the system didn't destroy itself from within.* Inside companies, people are continuously pushing the envelope. They often find themselves drawing near the line of legality and sometimes crossing it. All businesses, and financial ones in particular, habitually move into gray areas of the law. Dog-eat-dog pressures ("our competitors are going to do it, so we must do it too") tempt people to find and use every loophole they can, hoping not to get caught but sometimes taking the chance. This is a characteristic not just of business, of course, but of humanity itself. New laws and regulations emerge only after the exposure of serious problems, and almost never in anticipation of them.

In economies and societies that embrace constant change, governments must always play catch-up in their efforts to regulate business. Too much regulation can kill a company or even an industry, but so can too little. In the years since 1920, U.S. regulators have done a fairly good job, though with major variations from one period to another. On the whole, regulators in all branches of government during this period deserve not a grade of A or F, but something closer to a B– or C+. In the 1930s and 1960s, regulators did their jobs unusually well. By contrast, for the 1920s, the 1950s, and the initial decade of the twenty-first century, the government hardly even attempted to play catch-up.

## The Story Told Here

This book usually takes the vantage point of people working within companies rather than the external perspectives of consumers, governments, or other groups. It focuses on the entrepreneur, the firm, and the industry. It shows from the inside how businesses operated. Even so, the book by necessity contains a good deal of social and cultural history.

The years since 1920 are logically divisible into five periods: the 1920s, the 1930s, the years of the New Deal and World War II (1933–45), the period 1945–73, and 1973 to the present. These intervals vary in length and some overlap others, but each has a unity that will become evident as the book proceeds.

Part I, which comprises the first five chapters, follows the five periods listed above, but the narratives of each chapter sometimes extend to other eras in order to present an uninterrupted analysis of a particular industry or person. For example, airplanes were built in all five periods, but the main story of airplane manufacturing is told in the chapter that includes World War II, when aviation came of age. Similarly, the electronics pioneer David Sarnoff did significant work in four of the five eras, but he appears in the chapter that covers 1945 to 1973, the years when television became widely available to American consumers.

By the twenty-first century, about 4.5 million corporations were doing business in the United States, along with 16.4 million non-farm proprietorships and 1.6 million partnerships. Obviously, only a few of these millions of enterprises can be examined here. The chronological chapters in Part I begin with a brief survey of general social and economic trends. Then, to provide deeper analysis, each chapter comes to focus on an illustrative firm. The companies chosen for this purpose are Ford, General Motors, Procter & Gamble, Boeing, RCA, and McDonald's. Each has an exciting and sometimes riveting story.

The history of American business also includes some vital aspects not easily covered through a chronological approach. Part II of the book, therefore, contains three topical chapters: one on workforce diversity, one on the financial system, and one on information technology—as exemplified in the stories of Amazon.com, eBay, and Google.

## Past and Present

In 1920, almost everyone in the United States lived very differently from the way we do now. In that year half of all Americans lived on farms or in very small towns. Many communities lacked railroad tracks or paved highways to connect them with the rest of the country. About 25 percent of the labor force still farmed, compared to 1.6 percent today. Most Americans, except for immigrants, never traveled more than about 150 miles from where they were born.

Only a third of the nation's homes had electricity in 1920. The tasks of cooking, cleaning, and doing laundry and other housework took almost 70 hours a week. Today, after one of the greatest social changes in human history, that number has plunged to about 15 hours—because of the advent of electric refrigerators, microwave ovens, washers, dryers, vacuum cleaners, dishwashers, garbage disposals, and easily available fast food and take-home meals.

Obviously, nobody in 1920 had a TV, computer, or cell phone, let alone an iPod Touch, an Xbox, or a BlackBerry. Nobody text-messaged, e-mailed, or purchased items online. Nobody patronized McDonald's, Starbucks, the Olive Garden, or any other restaurant "chain." Nobody flew on a commercial airline, used a credit card, or drew cash from an ATM. Nobody even went to a mall or supermarket. (The shopping cart, hardly a high-tech device, wasn't invented until 1937.) Because the need for a paying job was so urgent, most people never graduated from high school. Instead they took full-time jobs when they reached their middle teens. Only 1 person out of 30 completed four years of college, compared with 1 of 4 today. And 1920 was not very long ago—indeed, many people born in that year are still alive.

In 1920 the care of children, the sick, and the elderly almost always took place in the home. The development and use of antibiotics lay decades in the future. Deaths from pneumonia, tuberculosis, cholera, diphtheria, measles, influenza, and typhoid fever ran at more than ten times the current rates. Nor was it easy to control the size of families. Birth control pills hadn't been invented, reliable condoms were difficult to find, and abortions were illegal. In many areas sanitary conditions were still premodern. Only 1 in 5 households even had an indoor flush toilet.

Most of these conditions true for Americans in 1920 still exist for the majority of the world's people today. But even in many "rich" countries, household conveniences came slowly. In 1960, the year John F. Kennedy was elected president, 96 percent of American homes had electric refrigerators, as compared to only 41 percent of French homes and 30 percent of British and Italian homes. Nor, of course, did refrigerators and other modern products just appear out of nowhere. They had to be invented, developed, manufactured, and marketed by the business systems of the world. And in most industries, American companies led the way.

## American Business and the World

In 1920 the United States was already producing more agricultural and industrial goods than any other country, and its people were enjoying the highest per-capita income. Today, as noted earlier, this income has grown to six times the figure for 1920. Measured against human experience over the whole of recorded history, such a level of affluence for so many people has no precedent. Thus, despite its faults—and there are many—the most significant fact about American business since 1920 has been its outstanding economic performance. This generalization applies to almost all types of businesses, whether small, medium, or large, and whether high- or low-tech. The biggest interruption of business growth was the Great Depression of the 1930s.

The American Dream of rags to riches did not come true for everyone, of course, but it came true for enough people so that masses of others were motivated to try. The spirit of entrepreneurship exhibited by so many Americans was predicated on the belief that an energetic and hard-working person actually could become prosperous. The potential for business success was far higher in the United States than elsewhere, and the widespread perception of opportunity attracted hordes of immigrants and unleashed immense economic energy. On a per-capita basis, Americans started more businesses, saw more of them fail, and then started still more new ones than the citizens of any other country.

Best of all, one person's success did not necessarily mean another's failure. This was a truth that proved hard for critics of capitalism to accept. As the German socialist Karl Liebknecht said in 1907, "The basic law of capitalism is you or I, not both you and I." But he was wrong. Even though millions of individuals and companies failed, American business was and still is a positive-sum game. As consumers' purchasing power increased, more and more entrepreneurs and firms flourished. At its best, a market economy becomes a virtuous circle, each round of prosperity stimulating the start of another round.

The virtuous circle seldom surrounds a pretty sight or peaceful scene, however. Business can be, and usually is, quite a stormy affair. The Harvard economist Joseph Schumpeter (1883–1950), one of the keenest analysts of capitalism who ever lived, liked to argue that internal turbulence epitomizes modern business. Capitalism itself, wrote Schumpeter, is a process of transformation. It "incessantly revolutionizes the economic structure from within, incessantly destroying the old one, incessantly creating a new one." The market shows no mercy. Constant competitive turmoil is one of the defining traits of capitalist economies, and it has certainly been true of American business since 1920.

Schumpeter's metaphor for this process, a "perennial gale of creative destruction," was more emblematic of the U.S. economy than of any other. The sweeping out of old products, old enterprises, and old organizational forms by new ones became a hallmark of the American business system. Schumpeter and others called the agents of creative destruction *entrepreneurs*, a French word meaning business adventurers. In the absence of a good English equivalent, the word gained wide currency.

## A Matter of Size

With the exception of RCA, which no longer exists as an independent firm, all of the companies analyzed in Part I of this book are now big businesses. But each one began small. Most originated as entrepreneurial startups that became big because they had a winning formula.

Their large size is also a function of the kinds of industries in which they operate. In automobiles, airplanes, consumer electronics, oil, chemicals, and a few other industries (most of them requiring large capital investments), firms that survived the competitive struggle over a long period almost always grew big. This was true not only in the United States but also in other countries where these kinds of industries flourished. But—and this point is crucial—it was true only for certain types of business. In the great majority of industries, such as printing, furniture, jewelry, pubs and restaurants, housepainting, plumbing, carpentry, and repair services of all kinds, even successful companies seldom grew into big businesses. Only a few thousand of the millions of enterprises now operating in the United States are truly large. In neither the United States nor any other country does most of the labor force work for a "big business," which is usually defined as one having more than 1,000 employees.

Large companies buy from and sell to networks of small and medium-sized suppliers and subcontractors, so businesses of different sizes deal with one another constantly. In most of these relationships the big firms naturally have the preponderance of power. But *big* and *small* are relative terms. Even very big tire companies have little bargaining power against the automobile giants (whether American, Japanese, or German), which squeeze prices of "original equipment" tires to the barest minimum. So tire manufacturers must make almost all of their profits on sales of replacement tires to consumers. And the growing prominence of megastores—most notably Wal★Mart—has revolutionized the power relationship between retailers and even very large consumer-products companies.

Patterns such as these, which have appeared in all industrialized countries, are easier to understand now than they were in 1920. Many of the old political debates on the relative merits of big versus small business therefore look a little curious in retrospect. They resemble ancient but wrongheaded arguments about the nature of the cosmos, and poorly informed debates over medical treatment before the discovery of germs. (Is the sun or the earth the center of the universe? Should we bleed the patient a lot or just a little?)

Is big business better than small business—in efficiency, treatment of workers, and ethical behavior? As a general proposition, this question is illogically framed and has no correct answer. It all depends on the nature of the industry, the companies and leaders involved, government policy, and many other factors specific to the situation. Still, there's no question that businesses can grow too big; or that their executives are often paid far too much money; or that lobbyists actually write legislation advantageous to large corporate clients. All of these things have happened many times in American history, starting with the railroads in the 1850s. But the key issue is how long the electorate will tolerate such abuses without forcing the government to correct them. Because of competitive pressures and the pursuit of profits, business will almost never correct wrongdoings on its own accord.

## The Key Internal Problem

In doing business inside a company of whatever size, the hardest thing to manage is usually this: the balance between the necessity for centralized control and the equally strong need for employees to have enough autonomy to make maximum contributions and derive satisfaction from their work. To put it another way, the problem is exactly where within the company to lodge the power to make different kinds of decisions.

This issue is not confined to business, of course. It applies to any organization of two or more people. Even in a group as small as the family, it arises every day. And the way in which it does or does not work itself out can be a stubborn problem—and a vivid memory to anyone recalling the frustrations of childhood. Must the family eat together every night? Should the parent or the adolescent child set the appropriate hour of curfew? Should the adults choose what kinds of clothing may be worn to school, or is that decision better left to the children? There is no universal answer to these questions. No single rule will guarantee the best result every time, or in all families.

In military organizations, the issue of decision making at different ranks (there are 23 in America's military services, far more than in most businesses) has even more pitfalls than it does in families. Military hierarchies are so rigidly defined that even a small deviation from the rules can lead to prosecution and court-martial.

Decision making in the business world stands about halfway between the family and the military. Its balance between centralized and decentralized control has to be continuously evaluated and adjusted so that incentives remain properly aligned for the overall good of the company, up and down the hierarchy. The better a company is organized, the more naturally a decision gravitates to the spot where the best information on the particular issue is available.

This book illustrates the historical struggles with decision making and relative decentralization through stories of extraordinarily capable entrepreneurs and the organizations they led: Henry Ford and his competitor Alfred Sloan at General Motors during the 1920s; Neil McElroy at Procter & Gamble in the 1930s; Ferdinand Eberstadt at the government's Controlled Materials Plan during World War II; David Sarnoff at RCA in the 1950s and 1960s; and Ray Kroc and his McDonald's franchisees in the late twentieth century and early twenty-first. The ultimate in decentralized decision making began during the late 1990s and continues to the present day, with the explosion of online information and communication. That phenomenon is illustrated here by the stories of Jeff Bezos of Amazon.com; Meg Whitman, CEO of eBay from 1998 to 2008; and Sergey Brin and Larry Page, co-founders of Google.

## The American Business Achievement

In most academic books on American history, assertions of high achievement have been out of fashion for four or five decades, and with good reason. From about 1800 until the 1960s, U.S. history was usually taught as an uninterrupted march of progress. George Washington never told a lie. Slavery would have died out without the need for a bloody civil war. Women had it better here than elsewhere. The United States never took unjust military action. All of these teachings were either totally inaccurate or highly questionable, and perpetuating them ill served the interests of students and of the nation as a whole.

Starting in the 1960s, the pendulum of interpretation swung the other way. History began to be taught with fuller coverage of the ugly aspects of the American experience, including the plagues of racism, sexism, imperialism, and warped distribution of incomes. In the case of business, many critics properly pointed out that capitalist success of the American sort had an obnoxious underside in its unbridled pursuit of money. A society obsessed with business was not likely to be refined or genteel, and American capitalism at its worst promoted a vulgar egocentrism that emphasized the materialistic self to the detriment of the spiritual. It elevated individual rights at the expense of familial and community duties. It tended to make some people fabulously rich while others remained dirt poor. Its endless advertising assailed the senses and affronted the soul. It despoiled the environment and contributed to global warming.

The degree to which economic progress was *inevitably* accompanied by these negative aspects is not wholly understood, even by experts. Many of the issues remain controversial. But the really bad news about the current condition of humanity applies not to the United States but to those large parts of the world where living standards still teeter on the brink of starvation. Against this background, the stark fact that American business has improved the material life of millions of people is beyond dispute. And despite the negatives, few informed people would wish to reverse the situation.

This book analyzes, from the inside, how the American business achievement since 1920 came about. We begin with motor vehicles, the key consumer durable of the so-called Second Industrial Revolution.*

---

* The idea of separate industrial revolutions is not explicitly emphasized in the text of this book, but underlies its whole approach. For North America and Western Europe, the following dates apply; for most other areas of the world, the same phenomena appeared at somewhat later dates.

In the period of the First Industrial Revolution, which lasted from about the 1760s to the 1840s, steam engines powered by coal began to replace human and animal energy, and people began to work by the clock for the first time in history. Large factories arose in textiles and a few other industries, and the mass-produced output of those industries became much less expensive to consumers.

In the era of the Second Industrial Revolution, stretching from the 1840s to about the 1950s, transportation and communication were radically altered, first by the railroad, telegraph, telephone, and radio, and then by the automobile, truck, and airplane. Electric motors and internal combustion engines furnished vital new sources of power for factories, vehicles, and equipment. Mass marketing was added to mass production. Big businesses appeared, giving rise to sophisticated new forms of management.

A Third Industrial Revolution began in the 1940s and 1950s and is still changing the course of business and everyday life. Its main features have been an emphasis on information technology and knowledge work, and a shift to services as a source of employment for more people than the combined total of all other economic sectors (agriculture, mining, construction, and manufacturing). In the Third Industrial Revolution, science-based businesses such as electronics, synthetic chemicals and pharmaceuticals, and computer hardware and software have led economic growth. Meanwhile the world economy has become radically more "globalized."

# CHAPTER ONE

# Decentralization in the 1920s: GM Defeats Ford

## Cars and Trucks

During the first half of the twentieth century, the industry that best symbolized the genius of American business was motor vehicles, in particular the personal automobile. Even before the start of World War II, the car came to be regarded almost as a necessity, just as televisions and cell phones would later be perceived as near essentials of modern life.

The production of inexpensive cars depended on a prosperous mass market, and preferably a growing one. In 1900, as cars first appeared on the scene, the United States was already the richest market in the world, and it was growing very fast. Motor vehicles, an insignificant industry in 1900, became by the 1920s the country's largest. The industry's connections with suppliers of steel, rubber, and glass, plus its close relationship with oil production, made the car the single most important product of the twentieth century. By the 1970s about one-sixth of all business firms in the United States were participating in some way in the manufacture, distribution, service, or operation of cars and trucks. Meanwhile, governments on all levels played their usual game of catch-up. They built roads and bridges, registered motor vehicles, licensed drivers, installed traffic lights, set speed limits, and expanded police forces, especially state troopers. The catch-up continues to this day, with fuel-efficiency standards and air-bag mandates.

During the 1920s, the car became the center of the national consumer economy, and until the successful Japanese challenge of the 1970s it remained a pre-eminently American-made product. By the mid-1920s, an astonishing 80 percent of all cars in the world were located in the United States, where there was one automobile for every 5.3 people. By comparison, in both Britain and France there was one for every 44. For many people everywhere, driving came to be a means of escape, a way to express personal freedom. The word *automobile* itself expresses the exhilarating idea of autonomous mobility. That idea quickly became a reality, in one of the biggest leaps toward a sense of individual freedom in world history. This is probably why so many people still love their cars today, even though they hate pollution and traffic congestion.

Commercially, trucks were also liberating. People who own just one truck can become small-scale entrepreneurs. They can move shipping containers to distant markets, deliver to customers' homes, move furniture when families relocate, carry refrigerated items from place to place, or set up small businesses in painting, carpentry, and home-plumbing repair. Modern online commerce depends on UPS, FedEx, and owner-operated trucking companies. Drivers who haul cargo long distances often choose to work (or must work) very long hours. But even today many truckdrivers own their own rigs and set their own schedules. In the 1920s, all of this represented a grand set of new business possibilities and fresh opportunities for decentralized decision making. Today the volume of goods transported by trucks is almost unbelievable. The advent of containerized shipping during the 1970s brought with it immense tractor-trailers, the double- or even triple-rigged trucks that can be seen on most major highways.

The first cars and trucks were built in Europe during the 1880s and 1890s, and by 1899 about 30 American companies were producing an annual total of 2,500 automobiles. Like most new industries, this one was led by a few bold entrepreneurs—such people as Ransom Olds, James Packard, the Dodge brothers, and Walter Chrysler. The two greatest giants in the American automobile industry were Henry Ford, who soon became the best-known manufacturer of anything anywhere, and Alfred P. Sloan, Jr., who built General Motors into the world's largest industrial corporation. The contest between Ford and Sloan is one of the epic stories in the history of business, and a near-perfect example of the superiority of decentralized decision making.

## Henry Ford (1863–1947)

Ford grew up on his family's farm in Dearborn, Michigan. Even as a boy he was an incurable tinkerer, and he amused himself by taking clocks apart and putting them back together. At the age of sixteen he began working in a Detroit machine shop, then moved on to a dry-dock firm. From there he took a job at a machinery company, and next at an electric utility, where he became chief engineer. Ford's first car was an impractical "quadricycle" he built in 1896. His first two automaking companies failed. But his third, launched in 1903, succeeded brilliantly. Ford's Model T, brought out in 1908, quickly revolutionized the entire industry.

A handsome, self-confident, fit-looking man, Henry Ford had good reason to regard himself as an oracle of mass production. In 1903, a time when cars were still being built in small numbers of diverse and expensive models, he said to one of his partners, "The way to make automobiles is to make one automobile like another automobile, to make them all alike, to make them come from the factory just alike—just like one pin is like another pin when it comes from a pin factory or one match is like another match when it comes from a match factory." Not long after his start in the business, Ford vowed to "build a motor car for the great multitude . . . constructed of the best materials, by the best men to be hired, after the simplest designs that modern engineering can devise . . . so low in price that no man making a good salary will be unable to own one—and enjoy with his family the blessing of hours of pleasure in God's great open spaces." Many people bought Ford's cars for pleasure, but some bought fleets of them for taxicabs and other new businesses, much as they did with trucks.

A good friend of Ford's observed that "Standardization is his hobby. He would have all shoes made on one last, all hats made on one block, and all coats according to one pattern. It would not add to the beauty of life, but it would greatly reduce the cost of living." Ford himself went a step further, arguing that standardization did add to the beauty of life by making diversity possible: "Machine production in this country has diversified our life, has given a wider choice of articles than was ever before thought possible—and has provided the means wherewith the people may buy them. We standardize only on essential conveniences. Standardization, instead of making for sameness, has introduced unheard-of variety into our life. It is surprising that this has not been generally perceived." Whether right or wrong in this statement, Ford was expressing the paradoxical nature of standardization, which became a defining trait of many American products as viewed by people in other countries.

As for the Model T, it was standardized in the extreme—a simple, reliable, and durable machine that could usually be repaired by its owner. When Ford decided that he had finally put together the right kind of car, he stopped work on his company's many other models. All efforts now went into making and improving the T. This was a singular moment in the history of the automobile industry, and it began a 20-year dynamic of rising sales and falling prices. Whereas the first Model T of 1908 sold for $850, the four millionth, which rolled off the line in 1920, could be purchased for $440. By the early 1920s the Ford Motor Company was producing more than half of all motor vehicles manufactured in the world. The ten millionth Model T, produced in 1925, sold at the remarkably low price of $290, and it was a much better car than earlier versions. (These prices were not seriously affected by inflation during that period. In 2009, the equivalent of $290 in 1925 was about $3,600.) Such a cycle of increased output, reduced prices, and improvement of the product had never before appeared for such a "big-ticket" item.

A major step in Ford's miracle of production was the perfection of the moving assembly line. In early 1914, this development cut the time necessary to assemble a Model T chassis by about 85 percent: from twelve and a half hours to one and a half. Writing for an engineering magazine in 1915, two visitors to the Ford factory described the assembly line and went on to speculate about the larger meaning of what Henry Ford had done:

Beyond all doubt or question, the Ford Motor Company's plant at Highland Park, Detroit, Michigan, U.S.A., at the time of this writing is the most interesting metalworking establishment in the world—because of its size (something over 15,000 names on the payroll); because it produces one single article only (the Ford motor car) for sale; because the Ford Motor Company is paying very large profits (something like $15,000,000 a year); and because, with no strike and no demand for pay increase from its day-wage earners, the Ford Company made a voluntary and wholly unexpected announcement January 5, 1914, that it would very greatly increase day-pay wage [to five dollars, more than twice the prevailing rate] and would at the same time reduce the day-work hours from nine to eight.

The combined magic of the assembly line and the five-dollar day made Henry Ford famous all over the world. He seemed to represent the potential humaneness of industrialization. Higher wages, shorter hours, a fabulous product designed to liberate masses of people from isolation—these achievements made him an international hero. His actual motives in introducing the five-dollar day had more to do with reducing the labor turnover in his plants than with any humanitarian urge. By 1914, his company needed to hire more than 50,000 workers each year to maintain a force of 15,000. This 300-percent turnover rate derived from the pressures and boredom of assembly-line work and almost complete management centralization. (Ford's methods appealed irresistibly to Soviet planners in Moscow during the 1920s.)

The five-dollar day could not change shop-floor conditions, but it could partly compensate people for the monotony of their tasks. The reduction of working hours also helped, and in the 1920s Ford went a step further and shortened the workweek from six days to five without a commensurate decrease in pay. Assembly-line production represented a dramatic contrast with the pre-industrial identification of the craftsman's product with his personal pride and sense of self. But paradoxically, the *ownership* of a car provided an offsetting sense of autonomy. Ford wanted his employees to be able to buy one of his cars, and many thousands of them did.

All of these changes received wide publicity. The company courted journalists, and Henry Ford was always good copy. By the mid-1920s, he had become the most famous American in the world. The term *Fordism* entered several languages as shorthand for standardized mass production. As the French analyst R. L. Bruckberger wrote in the 1950s, "What Marx had dreamed, Ford achieved." With the assembly line and the five-dollar day, he had made a reality of the "vast role that mechanization can play in emancipating human society" from endless toil.

Ford's celebrity brought with it daily opportunities to speak out on subjects about which he knew absolutely nothing; and he loved to pontificate. One of his biographers, David Lewis, lists some of Ford's outlandish comments, such as "This globe has been inhabited millions of times, by civilians having airplanes, automobiles, radio, and other scientific equipment of the modern era." In 1919 Ford proposed that horses, cows, and pigs be eliminated. "The world would be better off without meat." In 1925 he decided that starches and sweets were incompatible with human digestion, and in 1927 he added chickens to his list. For many years, he challenged visitors to footraces, and he especially enjoyed outrunning young newspaper reporters. He was still running footraces at the age of eighty. A friend of Ford once wrote, "His mind does not move in logical grooves. It does not walk, it leaps. It is not a trained mind. It does not know how to think consecutively. . . . He does not reason to conclusions. He jumps at them." Ford employed large numbers of African Americans, but he was deeply prejudiced against Jews, and his company-sponsored newspaper, the *Dearborn Independent,* regularly published anti-Semitic articles.

In his approach to business, Ford held to two basic principles. He would produce high-quality cars and sell them as inexpensively as possible. He liked to assert that every dollar he could chop off the price of a Model T would attract at least a thousand new buyers. Many customers, he said in 1916, "will pay $360 for a car who would not pay $440. We had in round numbers 500,000 buyers of cars on the $440 basis, and I figure that on the $360 basis we can increase the sales to possibly 800,000 cars for the year—less profit on each car, but more cars, more employment of labor, and in the end we get all the total profit we ought to make."

Although Ford was one of the richest men in the world, remarks such as these appealed to everyday people, who seemed to admire and trust him as the embodiment of the common man, somebody much like themselves. It was often said that Ford's fortune of more than a billion dollars had been earned "cleanly," unlike the wealth of "Robber Barons" such as John D. Rockefeller and Andrew Carnegie. Ford himself made no secret of his disdain for some of the trappings of capitalism. He spoke harshly of "financeering." He detested stockholders, whom he described as "parasites."

In 1919, to rid himself of any stockholder influence, he bought up all the outstanding shares of his company and took it private. This was a profound and ominous step. At a single stroke, it put the gigantic Ford Motor Company under the absolute control of one erratic "Genius Ignoramus," as biographer David Lewis calls Ford. The centralization of management had now become total. And at just that moment, Ford's company was about to confront a formidable competitor, the emerging General Motors Corporation.

## Alfred P. Sloan, Jr. (1875–1966)

Henry Ford grew up on a Midwestern farm. The man who became his great rival was a city boy from the East. Unlike Ford, Sloan believed in decentralization. He deeply valued the contributions of the many supervisors to whom he delegated major responsibilities.

The son of a prosperous merchant, Sloan spent his first ten years in New Haven, Connecticut, then moved with his family to Brooklyn. At Brooklyn Polytechnic Institute he achieved a splendid academic record, and he continued to shine academically at the Massachusetts Institute of Technology, where he studied electrical engineering. He finished his MIT degree in three years, having worked "every possible minute, so that I might be graduated a year ahead." He had been, in his own words, "a grind."

When Sloan left college ("I was thin as a rail, young and unimpressive") he took a job at the Hyatt Roller Bearing Company, a small New Jersey firm with 25 employees and $2,000 in monthly sales. The company was going through hard times, and Sloan's father helped to finance its survival and then its expansion. As Hyatt began to market products to more and more manufacturers, Sloan Jr. came to know the car industry well. He sold roller bearings to Ransom Olds, Henry Ford (his best customer), and the colorful William C. Durant.

"Blue-eyed Billy" Durant, a business visionary, had put together the General Motors Corporation in 1908, the same year in which Ford introduced the Model T. Durant was a wheeler-dealer who enjoyed buying and selling whole companies. Under his leadership, General Motors continued to grow, but it remained a loose group of separate firms that often competed with each other. Buick, the best of the lot, made money that Durant then dissipated among the less successful companies. This policy angered Buick's superb leaders, Charles Nash and Walter Chrysler, both of whom eventually walked out and set up their own firms. As Alfred Sloan put it, "Mr. Durant was a great man with a great weakness—he could create but he could not administer."

Despite this shortcoming, Durant had perceived the vital point that the industry's future lay in combining within one big firm all the diverse elements involved in the production of cars: engine and parts manufacturers, body companies, chassis works, and assemblers. Only through this kind of "vertical integration," as it came to be called, could a reliable flow of mass-produced output be achieved. The industry could then exploit its potential economies of scale: a declining cost per car as output increased. Henry Ford, who became almost obsessive in his own commitment to vertical integration, expanded from within. Durant did so by buying other companies and adding them to General Motors.

This policy of acquiring related firms took him to the door of Alfred P. Sloan, Jr. Durant wanted to include Hyatt Roller Bearing in a group of accessory companies he was putting together under the name United Motors. By this time (1916) Hyatt had grown into a prosperous enterprise with 4,000 employees. Sloan and his family now owned most of the company, and they agreed to sell it to Durant for $13.5 million (equivalent to about $280 million in 2009), half to be paid in United Motors stock. Durant decided that the president of United Motors should be Sloan himself.

Two years later, in 1918, Durant merged United Motors with General Motors and made Sloan a vice-president and member of the GM Executive Committee. Then, in 1920, a stockholders' revolt forced Durant out. Pierre du Pont, a major investor in the company and one of the shrewdest business executives in the country, took the GM presidency himself and made Sloan his chief assistant. Then 45 years old, Sloan was operating at the peak of his abilities, but he still faced daunting problems. Internally, General Motors remained an organizational mess, and Durant's maneuvers had put the firm in bad financial shape. Worst of all, as Sloan later wrote, the economic depression of 1920–21 was threatening to kill the company: "The automobile market had nearly vanished and with it our income."

With some difficulty, GM weathered the short depression, and in 1923 Sloan became president of the entire firm. He turned out to be a very different kind of businessman from either Billy Durant or Henry Ford. Whereas Durant and Ford wooed the press and welcomed media coverage, Sloan shunned personal publicity. Nor did he have much of a private life. He seemed uninterested in any subject except the welfare of General Motors. In one of the most brilliant performances in the history of business, he proceeded to turn GM around and build it into the largest company in the world.

As a writer in *Fortune* described him, Sloan "displays an almost inhuman detachment from personalities, [but] a human and infectious enthusiasm for the facts. Never, in committee or out, does he give an order in the ordinary sense, saying, 'I want you to do this.' Rather he reviews the data and then sells an idea, pointing out, 'Here is what could be done.' Brought to consider the facts in open discussion, all men, he feels, are on an equal footing. Management is no longer a matter of taking orders, but of taking counsel." An associate of Sloan's once said that he had a lot in common with the products he had made at Hyatt Roller Bearing: "self-lubricating, smooth, eliminates friction and carries the load." By shunning self-aggrandizement and empowering his junior associates, Sloan put General Motors into a very advantageous position.

## General Motors versus the Ford Motor Company

During the depression of 1920–21, Henry Ford had begun constructing an enormous new manufacturing complex at the River Rouge near Detroit. At the same time, he was taking over ownership of his company after purchasing all outstanding shares of its stock. These steps strained even Ford's bank account, and he decided to squeeze additional funds from local dealers throughout the country. At the nadir of demand for cars, he directed his 6,400 dealers to take 90,000 new cars and pay him cash for them. The price of refusal was loss of the Ford franchise. Alfred Sloan, by contrast, sympathized with GM's retailers. Through a subsidiary called General Motors Acceptance Corporation, he made it easier for dealers to finance bulk purchases, and much easier for retail customers to buy cars and trucks on credit. In this way Sloan created still another innovation that dispersed outward people's potential to master their own destinies and, if they wished, to become entrepreneurs. Meanwhile, Henry Ford was reluctant to sanction installment buying by anyone.

As Sloan recalled in his autobiography, the car business was changing fast during the early twenties. Management tools remained primitive, even at General Motors:

There was no awareness of the importance of the used-car market. There were no statistics on the different cars' market penetration; no one kept track of registrations. Production schedules, therefore, were set with no real relationship to final demand. Our products had no planned relation to one another or to the market. The concept of a line of products to meet the full challenge of the market place had not been thought of. The annual model change as we know it today was still far in the future. The quality of the products was sometimes good, sometimes bad.

Far in advance of Henry Ford, Sloan saw that the industry was becoming a trade-in business. (Eventually, used cars accounted for three units out of every four sold.) Sloan sensed that a big shift in taste was occurring, and that consumers now saw car purchases as status symbols of their own progress up the income scale. He responded by developing a complete product line. Starting with Chevrolet, designed to compete with Ford's Model T, Sloan established a series of nameplates that included—at progressively higher prices to imply higher social status—Pontiac, Oldsmobile, Buick, and, at the top, Cadillac. GM began to tout its product policy as "a car for every purse and purpose." By the mid-1920s, GM's cars were equal and often superior to Ford's, not only in styling but in basic engineering and production qualities.

Henry Ford's product policy remained much simpler: keep building a better version of one car in one color (black, a color of paint that dries very fast), and keep cutting the cost. This policy, very successful in earlier years, led to disaster during the 1920s and 1930s. Whereas in 1921 Ford's share of the domestic car market had stood at 56 percent, by 1925 it had dropped to 40 percent. During this same period, General Motors' share jumped from 13 to 20 percent.

By 1929 the two firms stood neck and neck, each selling at the colossal rate of 1.5 million cars per year. Then Ford took another big fall, and by 1937 GM's market share had shot up to 42 percent while Ford's plummeted to 21 percent. The Chrysler Corporation was now in second place at 25 percent. Just a short time earlier, Ford's company had been the undisputed king of the industry and Chrysler was not even in existence.

The key years in this fateful shift were the mid- and late 1920s, when a series of events finally drove Henry Ford to abandon the Model T. One of these was the "closed-car" movement. Most Model T's, with their very light chassis, could accommodate only a cloth roof, if they had any roof at all. Most Model T's remained open to the elements, with drivers and passengers growing weary of getting dusty and wet as they drove. Whereas in 1919 only 10 percent of new cars had been "closed" (built with metal roofs) by 1927 the figure stood at 85 percent. Another significant change was the proliferation of new models in assorted colors, a policy adopted not only by General Motors but also by Chrysler. The effect of the explosion of models and colors was multiplied still further by the advent of annual model changes. Together, all of these developments amounted to a revolution in styling and marketing—with Alfred Sloan leading the way in nearly every aspect of it.

Henry Ford responded to the welter of changes by shutting down his plants and designing a new car, the Model A. This was a radical step for so large a company, because it temporarily stopped all income without stopping all expenditures. As Sloan later wrote, few people in the industry had anticipated "so catastrophic and almost whimsical a fall as Mr. Ford chose to take in May 1927 when he shut down his great River Rouge plant completely and kept it shut down for nearly a year to retool, leaving the field to Chevrolet unopposed and opening it up for Mr. Chrysler's Plymouth." Ford's Model A, once it appeared, was a much better car than the T, but it was still just one model, not a full line of products. And like its predecessor, the Model A did not go through annual model changes. Only in 1933 did Henry Ford begin to bring out new models each year, and not until 1938 did he offer the Mercury, a mid-sized car designed to compete with GM's higher-income lines of Pontiacs, Oldsmobiles, and Buicks. The Mercury had only indifferent success, as did Ford's Lincoln, which had competed ineffectively with Cadillac since its introduction in 1929.

As these changes were unfolding, the Ford Motor Company's once stellar management team slowly disintegrated. Its best young executives, fed up with Henry Ford's autocratic methods, simply quit. Decentralization of decision making had now become a necessity for retaining the brightest managers and workers. People naturally wanted to work where their creativity and skills meant something and were appreciated. As GM and firms in other industries began to reorganize from within, an increasing number of employees could make the most of their entrepreneurial energies—whether individually or, in the case of big business, as members of groups and teams. Many of the executives who left the Ford Motor Company were snapped up by Alfred Sloan at General Motors. Henry Ford turned 70 in 1933, but long before that he had become a rigid, peevish, and arbitrary chief executive. Had his company's cars not been of high quality and his brand name so famous, his firm might have gone under during the Great Depression of the 1930s.

During the 1930s and 1940s, Sloan deliberately held GM's domestic market share under 45 percent because he did not want to attract hostile attention from antitrust authorities. This policy contributed to the survival of the Ford Motor Company during its worst years. Then, during World War II, Ford landed a great deal of defense business. The company finally rebounded in the late 1940s under the direction of young Henry Ford II, grandson of the founder. Henry II, only 26 years old when he took over, hired executives from General Motors, copied GM's organizational structure, and installed statistical controls designed by a group of "Whiz Kids" who had worked for the Army Air Corps during the war. The Whiz Kids included Robert S. McNamara, who later became president of Ford and secretary of defense under Presidents Kennedy and Johnson, and Arjay Miller, who headed Ford before becoming dean of the Stanford Business School. These two, and many others like them, were topflight managers to whom Henry Ford II delegated the necessary degree of authority. He thereby decentralized decision making at the Ford Motor Company just as Alfred Sloan had done at GM some 25 years earlier.

Nonetheless, no one questioned who had won the contest for market leadership. Beginning in 1925 and continuing for 61 consecutive years (until 1987), General Motors' profits exceeded Ford's. This represented an extraordinary record of competitive supremacy—one unmatched in American business history for big-ticket consumer products and perhaps any other kind of product.

## The Lessons of the Car Wars

What can one learn from this battle? For one thing, that "first-mover advantages" of the kind enjoyed by Henry Ford are powerful but do not constitute a formula for permanent supremacy. In business, almost nothing is permanent, and the market severely punishes those who will not or cannot adapt. General Motors itself absorbed tremendous wounds during the closing decades of the twentieth century, when it became almost as rigid and ingrown as the Ford Motor Company had been 50 years earlier. And by the early twenty-first century, the very survival of the American Big Three automakers—Ford, GM, and Chrysler—lay in question. All three had been completely outmaneuvered by Toyota, one of the most decentralized and worker-empowered companies in the world.

During the 1920s, Henry Ford had grasped part of the lesson of the relentlessness of change in business, but not in its entirety. Certainly he understood the principle of creative destruction on the manufacturing side. "Not a single item of equipment can be regarded as permanent," he wrote. "Not even the site can be taken as fixed. We abandoned our Highland Park plant—which was in its day the largest automobile plant in the world—and moved to the River Rouge plant because in the new plant there could be less handling of materials and consequently a saving. We frequently scrap whole divisions of our business—and as a routine affair."

But as clearly as Ford understood the imperatives of production, he turned a blind eye to those of marketing. He refused to see that marketing, in every aspect from product policy to styling to advertising to sales, is as important to success as is manufacturing. He had little respect for the tastes of consumers, whom he (correctly) regarded as fickle. Irrespective of what they wanted, Ford thought he knew what they needed. He could not bring himself to admit that in a market economy the consumer really does reign supreme, and that for an organization to act otherwise is to invite disaster.

What are the lessons of the American car wars with regard to decision making? As emphasized earlier, the key problem within any organization of whatever size—a family, church, school, business, army, or nation—is how to allocate authority: which decisions are best made at the top, in the middle, or at the bottom?

If all decisions are made at the top, then sooner or later two things will happen. First, the quality of decision making will deteriorate. No single person, not even a Henry Ford, can have enough information to make the right choice on every issue—there is too much to know and conditions constantly change. Second, employees not directly in touch with the process of decision making will grow bored with routine, their potential contributions lost to the organization.

If, on the other hand, all decisions are pushed to the lowest levels authority will degenerate, cooperation will falter, and anarchy will prevail.

Therefore, the pivotal challenge of modern management lies in finding the right balance between centralization and decentralization, and in continually adjusting the mix in response to changing circumstances. The critical levers are the use of information and the fixing of decision making at the point at which the best information is available on the issue at hand. For this reason the design of the organization becomes crucial.

Henry Ford, who resisted even contemplating such matters, debunked the whole idea of organizational design. Sometimes his scorn became gleeful:

There is no bent of mind more dangerous than that which is sometimes described as the "genius for organization." This usually results in the birth of a great big chart showing, after the fashion of a family tree, how authority ramifies. The tree is heavy with nice round berries, each of which bears the name of a man or of an office. Every man has a title and certain duties which are strictly limited by the circumference of his berry. . . . And so the Ford factories and enterprises have no organization, no specific duties attaching to any position, no line of succession or of authority, very few titles, and no conferences.

This kind of policy is not necessarily inappropriate. In Ford's time it could bring good results, especially in small organizations. It still can today, especially in entrepreneurial startups. But once a company grows beyond a couple of hundred employees, organizational design cannot be ignored. Successful firms in automobiles and a few other capital-intensive, mass-production industries almost invariably grow large. General Motors eventually employed almost a million workers.

The tradition in business before the 1920s, at Ford and most other companies, was to organize the firm not according to its many *products* (the Model T, the Ford truck, the engine, the sparkplug, and so on) but according to just three *functions:* purchasing of raw materials, manufacturing, and selling. The responsibility of executives who oversaw these functions extended to each of the company's many products, however different they were from one another.

When things went bad under such a system, it was impossible to pinpoint the responsibility for a particular problem—that is, to know whom to fire. And if an entire industry suffered a downturn like automobiles did during the depression of 1920–21, no one knew how to respond. It was primarily this situation that gave Alfred Sloan his idea about how he should reorganize General Motors. As he later wrote, the depression brought "just about as much crisis inside [the firm] and outside, as you would wish for, if you like that sort of thing."

In response to the crisis, Sloan developed a new organizational design that became known as the "multidivisional structure." Whereas the Ford Motor Company had one boss (Henry Ford) and a mostly undifferentiated mass of underlings, Sloan devised for GM a system with dozens of product divisions within the company, each one organized under a semi-autonomous chief executive. This person was given what came to be called "bottom-line responsibility" for the operations of a single division, and therefore had to be concerned with both the manufacturing and marketing of a particular product. With this heavy responsibility came broad authority, which was decentralized throughout the company, division by division.

In creating GM's multidivisional structure, Sloan worked out a way to deal with human relationships that was just as ingenious for business organization as was Ford's assembly line for production. What Ford did for physical machines, Sloan did for human beings. Just as Ford's greatest innovation was the systematic assembly of separate mechanical parts into one Model T, Sloan's was the fusion of separate human talents into one organizational whole.

Viewed in retrospect, the idea of having semi-autonomous product divisions within one big company sounds simple. (So does the assembly line.) But in the 1920s it was an intellectual breakthrough of the first order. Sloan himself, as bright as he was, struggled for a long time to reach the right solution. In a long internal GM document dated 1921 and labeled "Organization Study," Sloan and his associates wrote the following:

1. The responsibility attached to the chief executive of each [divisional] operation shall in no way be limited.
2. Certain central organization functions are absolutely essential to the logical development and proper control of the Corporation's activities.

Years later, as he was working on his autobiography, Sloan looked back on these two sentences and realized that "the language is contradictory." A typical business executive "usually asserts one aspect or another of [organization] at different times, such as the absolute independence of the part, and again the need of co-ordination, and again the concept of the whole with a guiding center." Thus, the puzzle of centralization versus decentralization "is the crux of the matter," and "interaction . . . is the thing." Centralization had to be mixed with decentralization according to the issue being decided.

The multidivisional structure made such a mixture possible. Among its other virtues, the new structure in effect turned one large company into groups of smaller-scale entities. (Toyota later did this in almost every way imaginable, with dazzling success.) It provided incentives for numerous managers to work together in a spirit of cooperation as they moved up the corporate ladder.

Wherever possible, Alfred Sloan exerted his own influence by persuasion rather than by fiat. He put in place a series of cross-divisional committees and saw to it that high-ranking executives served on multiple committees of different makeups. In this way he forced all managers of importance within the company to communicate regularly with one another. He did this with resolute attention to the key puzzle he was trying to solve: "How could we exercise permanent control over the whole corporation in a way consistent with the decentralized scheme of organization? We never ceased to attack this paradox." Good management, Sloan concluded, must reconcile two opposing forces. It must combine "decentralization with coordinated control."

Coordinated control came primarily through financial reporting and capital allocations. Sloan worked hard on these issues, and GM soon became one of the most sophisticated of all American companies in its use of budget targets and financial ratios (inventory turnover, fixed versus variable costs, profit as a percentage of sales, and so on). Within its factories, GM made continual adjustments along the production lines based on what the numbers were telling top managers at headquarters. As Sloan summed up his approach, "From decentralization we get initiative, responsibility, development of personnel, decisions close to the facts, flexibility. . . . From co-ordination we get efficiencies and economies. It must be apparent that co-ordinated decentralization is not an easy concept to apply." Over the next several decades, and particularly after World War II, GM's multidivisional structure (also developed at almost exactly the same time during the early 1920s at the Du Pont chemical company) was emulated by hundreds of other companies throughout the world.

Sloan's autobiography, the source of many of the quotations above, is one of the two or three most important books on business management ever written. Still, it does not represent the last word on the subject. Conditions continuously change, so there can never be a "last word." As Sloan himself knew, the essence of management is persistent attention not only to what goes on inside an organization but also to altered circumstances in the external environment: changes in consumer preferences, the rise of new technologies, swings in the business cycle, shifts in government policy, and new patterns of international trade.

The only alternative was chaos—which is the state that reigned at the Ford Motor Company during the 1920s and 1930s. Information flows at Ford grew confused and irregular. Managers could not seem to identify problems or pinpoint responsibilities. Budgeting procedures fell so far behind that overburdened accountants actually began using scales to *weigh* piles of invoices rather than add up the numbers written on each sheet. The company had become a victim of its own success: it had grown too large to manage in the way Henry Ford insisted on managing it.

Alfred Sloan, by contrast, continually adapted, adjusting his company's structure in response to external and internal pressures. Under his direction, as *Fortune* put it, General Motors "escaped the fate of those many families of vertebrates whose bodies grew constantly larger while their brain cavities grew relatively smaller, until the species became extinct . . . because Mr. Sloan has contrived to provide it with a composite brain commensurate with its size."

In historical retrospect, the contrast between Henry Ford and Alfred Sloan illuminates a characteristic irony in American business and in the national culture as a whole. Many strands of American tradition romanticize the solitary hero and underrate the necessity for cooperation through structured organization. *Individualism* is prized, while *bureaucracy* remains a dirty word. In this sense Henry Ford, with his unschooled solo genius and bombastic opinions about everything, was the more typically "American" personality. That is probably why his name appears before Sloan's on many lists of great business executives. (Ford was also the first billionaire crackpot, another recognizable American type.) But it was Sloan, the quiet, persuasive, decentralizer—the trained engineer and systematic organization man—who better epitomizes most American business triumphs of the twentieth century.

Today, of course, both Ford and General Motors have long since been overtaken by the superior management styles of foreign firms, principally Japanese. For GM, the pioneer decentralizer, this defeat has been particularly ironic. The new champion, Toyota, has often paid lip service to Henry Ford. But it has actually won on the racecourse of decentralization designed by Alfred Sloan.

# CHAPTER TWO

# Brand Management in the 1930s: Decentralization at Procter & Gamble

## The Great Depression

General Motors continued to operate at a profit even during the 1930s, the most impoverished decade in American history. GM never failed to pay a dividend on shares of its stock—but only because it laid off thousands of workers as car sales declined. Despite his greatness as a manager, even Alfred Sloan could not figure out how to deal wisely with labor unions. GM continued to make money, but it badly mishandled negotiations with the rising United Automobile Workers, as did Ford and Chrysler.

Overall, the Great Depression of 1929–41 hit the American economy like a sledgehammer. Unemployment, which had stood at about 3 percent in 1929, soared to 25 percent in 1932, by far the highest figure up to that time and still a record. Whole sectors of the economy went into precipitous decline: mining, agriculture, construction, finance. Vital industries shriveled: banking, lumber, cement, steel. Millions of families became poor and a few people actually starved to death. Thus, some of the century-long themes set forth in the introduction to this book, such as rising incomes and the increasing empowerment of entrepreneurs, were temporarily interrupted. But most other trends, including the decentralization of decision making and the growing influence of consumers, maintained their momentum.

The Great Depression was so severe that most history books treat the 1930s as a catastrophic decade for the American business system. That judgment is largely accurate, but not entirely so. Although hundreds of thousands of small companies went bankrupt during the thirties, even more new firms emerged to take their places. Most were small companies in labor-intensive sectors such as food service and retailing. In 1929, for example, there were about 1.5 million stores in the United States, and by 1939 almost 1.8 million. Many were tiny establishments of the mom-and-pop variety, a high proportion of which soon perished with the rise and rapid spread of self-service chain supermarkets. Nonetheless, the continual appearance of new companies was testament to the resiliency of the business system, even during the worst depression in the nation's history.

## The Types of Firms That Prospered

Several existing companies that had been small at the beginning of the 1930s expanded significantly by its end. IBM, for example, mushroomed in response to the demands for data processing that grew out of new government programs. After the passage of the Social Security Act in 1935, the federal government had to maintain a file on almost every employee in the country. This need generated a big market for IBM's electro-mechanical punch-card systems, the forerunners of modern computers. Thomas J. Watson, Sr., IBM's paternalistic chief and one of the greatest businessmen of the twentieth century, minimized layoffs despite the economic downturn of the early 1930s. (In a dramatic gesture, Watson also made a very deep cut in his own salary.) During most of the lean years, Watson continued to manufacture punch-card equipment in spite of diminishing demand. As a result, he was ready with a stockpile of machines when government orders began to pour in. By the end of the decade, IBM was poised for a spurt of even faster growth to meet the great demands of World War II.

During the first four years of the depression, real Gross National Product dropped by 31 percent. Investment fell by an almost unbelievable 87 percent, as people stopped building new houses and businesses ceased buying new equipment. The government's responses to the stock-market crash, to bank failures, to crises in major industries, and to widespread unemployment brought a series of strong actions under President Franklin D. Roosevelt. (Those actions—the catch-up by government in its oversight of the business system—are a story for the next chapter.)

Whereas investment fell by 87 percent, consumption dropped only 19 percent, and there was a simple reason why: different kinds of decision making are involved for consumption as compared to investment. Decisions to invest come primarily from business executives. When forecasts for demand are low, they usually decide to put less money into new plants and to let their inventories dwindle. Consumption decisions, on the other hand, are made by almost everybody. People must eat every day, and they have other needs that can't easily be postponed. Many families went from year to year without buying new houses, new cars, or even new clothes. But they could not stop eating, doing the laundry, or washing dishes.

Nor did they stop seeking entertainment. Throughout the depression Americans flocked to movie theaters, where tickets cost an average of 20 cents apiece. (During the 1930s a typical working person in the United States earned less than $1,000 per year.) Each week, theaters sold about 80 million movie tickets, a per-capita rate ten times that of today. After an early dip during the worst years of the depression, the film industry maintained a healthy level of profits throughout most of the 1930s, in part because it was vertically integrated.

A few holding companies such as Metro-Goldwyn-Mayer owned or controlled studios, distributors, and theater chains, coordinating them in such a way as to shut out independent artists and theater owners. These practices were later judged to be illegal under U.S. antitrust law. But meanwhile, the big studios maintained strict controls over production budgets—keeping even the most famous actors, directors, and writers under tight contracts. During the 1930s Hollywood churned out 5,000 feature films, a huge multiple of the rate of releases today. Most 1930s films were made on shoestring budgets, but many of them were superbly entertaining. In the view of numerous critics, several 1930s films have never been surpassed as representatives of the art form. These include *The Wizard of Oz* and *Gone with the Wind,* both of which were expensive productions for their time but cheap by today's standards.

Even though consumers had much less disposable income during the thirties, most Americans could still afford to go to the movies, and many of them could still purchase expensive items that had come to be regarded as necessities. About 10 million families, for example, managed to purchase new refrigerators. These Frigidaires, Norges, Kelvinators, and Kenmores made daily food shopping unnecessary and therefore saved people lots of time and transportation costs. Indoor flush toilets, manufactured by companies such as Crane, Kohler, and Standard, could be found in 60 percent of American homes by 1940, as compared to only 20 percent in 1920. And as volumes of sales increased, the prices of refrigerators and other household conveniences steadily declined.

## Procter & Gamble

The experience of the country's leading consumer-products company illustrates the characteristic of the Great Depression in which consumption dropped by much less than investment. It also demonstrates that a truly well-run firm can innovate and prosper even during the worst of times.

"P&G," as Procter & Gamble came to be called, was founded in 1837 in Cincinnati by two immigrants: William Procter, a candlemaker from England, and James Gamble, a soap-boiler from Ireland. Their new company prospered, and by 1859 it had 80 employees and annual sales of more than $1 million (equivalent to about $26 million in 2009).

Fifteen decades later, in the early twenty-first century, Procter & Gamble was one of America's largest companies, with 140,000 employees worldwide and huge annual sales (over $70 billion in 2008). More than half of its sales came from abroad. P&G was the world's biggest advertiser (spending over $5 billion annually), and the largest producer of branded household goods and other consumer items. Its many brands led the field in about half of all categories in which the company participated.

P&G's long and colorful history reflects many traits of America's own social and cultural history. These include the nation's persistent entrepreneurship, its mania for consumer products, its preoccupation with youth and physical beauty, and its tradition of hucksterism. To this last category Procter & Gamble contributed the phenomenon of the "soap opera," which made its debut in 1933 on a national radio network.

Fundamentally, P&G is now and always has been a marketing company. The key marketing event in its early history came in 1878, when an employee forgot to turn off his soap-mixing machine when he left for lunch. While he was gone, the mixer beat additional air into the soap. Soon the company began receiving requests for this new "floating soap," and Harley Procter, who had succeeded his father William as head of the firm, realized that a unique sales opportunity lay before him. At this time almost all soap was made in bars, and Harley believed that his company could exploit the advantages of a floating bar. People sitting in a bathtub or washing clothes in a basin could easily find their soap atop the water rather than having to fish around for it underneath the surface.

Harley Procter proceeded to change the product's name from "P&G White Soap" to "Ivory," a word he took from Psalm 45 of the Old Testament ("All thy garments smell of myrrh, and aloes, and cassia, out of the ivory palaces, whereby they have made thee glad"). He then persuaded the company's board of directors to spend an unprecedented amount of money in advertising the virtues of Ivory. The first ad, published in 1882 in a weekly religious magazine, was targeted to consumers, not to wholesalers or retailers as was the usual practice. Beginning in the 1890s, Harley Procter promoted Ivory under the slogans "It Floats" and "99 and 44/100 percent pure." (He had commissioned a chemical analysis that disclosed the information, trivial except for purposes of marketing, that Ivory contained slightly fewer impurities than most other soaps.) These two slogans, endlessly repeated in the company's ads, became familiar to nearly everyone in America for the next three generations.

In 1896, P&G ran the first color ad that ever appeared in a U.S. magazine. The company hired its first advertising agency in 1900 to promote both Ivory and Lenox, a yellow laundry bar. In ads Ivory was often pictured with babies, as a not-so-subtle suggestion that it was mild to the skin. Later this claim led the company to market Ivory as a dishwashing soap as well—easy on the hands of people slogging through piles of dirty dishes in kitchen sinks.

Meanwhile, during the 1880s, Procter & Gamble built "Ivorydale," a huge new factory located in a Cincinnati suburb. In 1901, P&G integrated backward into the pressing of cottonseed oil, one of the main ingredients of soap. In 1903 and 1904, Procter & Gamble built new plants in Kansas City and at "Port Ivory" on Staten Island in New York. In 1905 P&G converted itself from a partnership to a corporation and began to export in large volume. By the 1930s the company was marketing 200 branded items worldwide, including 140 soaps.

Throughout the twentieth century, P&G's main competition came from Colgate-Palmolive and Lever Brothers, the subsidiary of a British firm (today the giant Anglo-Dutch company Unilever, which remains P&G's chief competitor worldwide). All three companies advertised heavily because they needed mass markets in order to exploit the economies of scale in production and distribution that made low prices possible.

Soaps were simple to produce, and most were chemically almost identical. But to manufacture bars in enormous quantities and sell them for a few pennies each was not simple at all. Branding and efficient advertising thus became essential to success. And once the leading brands were established, the expense of introducing a new one posed a formidable entry barrier for would-be competitors.

Lever Brothers, with its Lux Soap and Lux Flakes laundry soap, offered very tough competition for Ivory. Colgate weighed in with soaps called Palmolive and Cashmere Bouquet. Procter & Gamble itself, building a portfolio of brands step by step, introduced Ivory Flakes in 1919 to compete with Lux Flakes. Then, in 1927, P&G purchased from a St. Louis manufacturer both Oxydol laundry soap and Lava, a hand soap containing pumice for better scrubbing action. Lava sold widely, appearing in almost every auto repair shop in the country. Mechanics ended each workday by vigorously scrubbing their hands and forearms with Lava. Both Lava and Oxydol became strong brands, the latter turning into one of the company's biggest moneymakers.

Meanwhile, P&G kept adding still more soaps to its list of brands. Dreft, the first synthetic detergent for all-around household use, was added in 1933, during the worst part of the Great Depression. Drene, P&G's first liquid shampoo (1934), proved too potent, stripping so much oil out of consumers' hair that the company had to mix in a "conditioning" agent. For many people, conditioners then became still another semi-essential product.

## The Character of the Firm

By the 1930s Procter & Gamble had developed a curious corporate culture, many aspects of which were still in evidence decades later, at the close of the twentieth century. P&G in the thirties was a stodgy, tradition-bound, parochial firm—stiff and formal, almost military. Job applicants were given batteries of exams, including psychological tests. These tests persisted long into the future. As a play on the "GMAT," the standardized test for admission to MBA programs, applicants began to refer to the "P&GMAT." Male P&G managers, even at middle and low levels, wore dark suits and white shirts. People taking entry-level jobs were assumed to be signing on for an entire career. All promotions were made from within. The company discouraged unionization and segregated its cafeteria by gender.

P&G cut costs in every way its managers could think of. The company would pay for washing salespeople's automobiles only once a month. Every employee with a car, including the large traveling salesforce, was instructed to park on the street rather than in fee-charging lots. Elevators at the Cincinnati headquarters could not be used for trips of only one floor. Security was tight.

The company fancied itself as having many secrets. It zealously guarded plans for advertising campaigns, new product introductions, and statistics on sales and profits.

Top management remained so entrenched that the company resembled a medieval fiefdom, and P&G's founding families continued to hold most of the voting stock. Over the 41 years from 1907 to 1948, only two men served as CEO. The first, "Colonel" William Procter, was a descendant of the founder and an officer in the Ohio National Guard. He was a shy, humorless man, but a rock-solid character with a social conscience. Like Alfred Sloan at General Motors, he almost never gave a direct order, preferring to manage by persuasion. His protégé and successor, Richard Redmont "Red" Deupree, complemented him perfectly. Deupree was an extroverted, cheery-eyed manager with a keen instinct for marketing.

The company's culture reflected the personalities of both Procter and Deupree. Even though P&G remained a hidebound organization, it was widely acknowledged to be the nation's most innovative marketer of consumer products and one of the quickest firms in any industry to respond to external changes. P&G was also well known for its corporate conscience. In 1886 it became one of the first large firms in the nation to grant employees a half-day off every Saturday. Under Colonel Procter's leadership it pioneered in disability and retirement pensions (1915), the eight-hour day (1918), and, most important of all, guaranteed work for at least 48 weeks per year (1920s). This last policy was extremely unusual in American business; in an era without unemployment benefits, it made—almost by itself—P&G an attractive place to work.

Except under conditions of economic depression, secure year-round employment might have been easy for Procter & Gamble to manage, because the market for soap and other household goods was steady as opposed to seasonal. But other aspects of the business made year-round employment quite difficult. In particular, fluctuations in the price of raw materials caused problems because they indirectly broke up the seasonal regularity of wholesale purchases of P&G's products by big distributors.

Before the 1920s, wholesalers who marketed P&G's brands to retailers would stockpile products during periods when raw materials were cheap and P&G's wholesale prices for finished goods therefore low. Wholesalers would then draw down their inventories when the prices P&G had to pay for cottonseed and other raw materials went up. Thus, P&G's shift to guaranteed year-round employment forced the company to reorganize its distribution system. In 1920, it started bypassing wholesalers altogether and selling directly to retailers. For a variety of reasons this kind of change occurred in many other industries as well, and the declining power of wholesalers became a powerful trend in American business throughout the twentieth century. This strategy became known as "cutting out the middleman," and it constituted yet another form of management decentralization and consumer empowerment.

During the 1930s, Procter & Gamble's executives, like most other businesspeople, were very concerned about the deteriorating state of the national economy, but P&G withstood the depression extremely well. Like Thomas J. Watson at IBM, President Red Deupree voluntarily cut his own salary. P&G kept layoffs to a minimum and temporarily reduced wages by 10 percent (a figure that matched the national *deflation* of the early depression.) Somehow, the company managed to show a profit even during the hardest years of the 1930s, and in 1937 it had the best year since its founding, with $200 million in sales and $27 million in profits (about $3 billion and $410 million in 2009 equivalents). Among P&G's many brands, the big moneymakers were Ivory, Oxydol, and Crisco, a synthetic shortening.

P&G had introduced Crisco in 1912 after years of research on the hardening of vegetable oil. The company was confident that consumers would prefer Crisco to lard, which sometimes smelled bad and had inconsistent cooking qualities. P&G spent a fortune on advertising, flooding the print media with ads. Soon Crisco became a household word, and its sales grew larger year after year.

In soap, P&G during the 1930s moved well ahead of its competitors, achieving more than twice the total U.S. market share of either Lever Brothers or Colgate-Palmolive. The three together accounted for about 80 percent of all domestic sales of soap, with P&G alone at just under 50 percent. Each year during the late 1930s, the company produced about 600,000 tons of soap and 195,000 tons of Crisco shortening, both of which it sold in bulk to laundries and restaurants as well as in small packages to consumers. At that time, the company's annual costs were roughly $90 million for raw materials, $23 million for payroll—and a whopping $15 million for advertising (in 2009 equivalents, $1.3 billion, $335 million, and $218 million).

## Building the Market

Procter & Gamble advertised in almost every way imaginable at the time. It spent about half its ad budget on radio dramas, which became known as soap operas because of P&G's sponsorship. For other promotions P&G dreamed up endless contests, many calling for the completion of sentences beginning with phrases such as "I like Ivory Soap because . . ." The company spent lavishly on prizes: cash, watches, refrigerators, cars, rugs, radios, vacuum cleaners, and stockings. P&G also conducted door-to-door giveaways of coupons for reduced prices on soap. Beyond providing incentives to consumers, each new campaign offered a convenient excuse for P&G's thousands of salespeople to visit retailers. Once inside the store, the salespeople could brief retailers on P&G's latest marketing initiative and urge them to augment current inventory in anticipation of bigger demand.

In situations like this, the modern relationship between mass production and mass marketing reached something close to blissful synthesis. Commenting on the cultural aspects of mass marketing in general, the economist Joseph Schumpeter once remarked, "It was not enough to produce satisfactory soap. It was also necessary to persuade people to wash." P&G's competitor, Lever Brothers, invented the initials "B.O." (though not, of course, body odor itself) as a problem remediable by its Lifebuoy soap. Warned by ominous radio commercials, millions of anxious consumers soon began lathering up their armpits with Lifebuoy at least once a day. Later, an immense follow-up market developed for underarm deodorants, followed by yet another huge market for antiperspirants. All of these products, sold under brand names now familiar in most of the world, were spotlighted for intense competition: among P&G (Secret), Unilever (Degree), Gillette (Right Guard), and other big companies.

On another major front, Lever Brothers introduced in 1936 a vegetable shortening called Spry, a product designed to compete with P&G's wildly successful Crisco. After a hush-hush buildup, Lever sprang Spry onto America's consciousness with a nationwide giveaway of one-pound cans. Lever advertised Spry as being "extra-creamed," a meaningless term intended to imply that its texture was more uniform than that of Crisco.

In a quick counteroffensive, Procter & Gamble declared Crisco to be "double-creamed," an equally meaningless slogan. Lever then responded that Spry was "triple-creamed," thereby triggering P&G's rejoinder that Crisco was "super-creamed." After several months of competing salvos about creaming, Spry reached sales about half those of Crisco. This was a very impressive performance for a new product in so short a time.

But the campaign as a whole helped both companies. Crisco's own sales increased because the sensational advertising war convinced numerous consumers of the superiority over lard of any vegetable shortening regardless of brand. This kind of pattern, in which heavy competitive advertising increased the overall size of the market, occurred again and again with consumer goods throughout the country (and then the world), especially for products of modest cost. This was one of the major ways in which business practices affected the evolution of popular culture.

## Soap Operas

For nearly a century, most of the huge advertising budgets for P&G's products has been spent on radio and TV commercials. The company's forays into electronic media had started in the 1920s, with radio programs such as *Sisters of the Skillet* and *Crisco Cooking Talks*. The soap opera made its epic debut in 1933 with the heart-rending melodrama, *Ma Perkins*. Ma was a compassionate widow whose lengthy list of friends brought to her sympathetic attention every type of human predicament. The show ran on NBC radio as *Oxydol's Own Ma Perkins*, and attracted a wide audience. Afterward came *The Road of Life*, sponsored by Ivory soap; *The Guiding Light* (Duz laundry detergent, another long-time P&G product); *Young Doctor Malone* (ultimately sponsored by Joy dishwashing detergent, a product introduced in 1950); *Backstage Wife* (Cheer, 1950); and *Life Can Be Beautiful* (Tide, introduced in 1946 and still the best-selling detergent in the world).

By the late 1930s, Procter & Gamble was paying for five hours of programming on network radio every weekday. Most of this colossal amount of airtime was devoted to P&G's 19 soap operas, each lasting 15 minutes. All 19 programs offered lessons of domestic wisdom dispensed by appealing characters wending their way through life's multitudinous trials. The target audience was women between the ages of 18 and 50, the group that purchased most household goods; but a large number of men tuned in as well.

In the late 1940s, P&G began to adapt its soap operas to the new medium of television. The first projects did not turn out well. *Ma Perkins* flopped, deeply saddening her many fans. Another offering, *The First Hundred Years*, failed to last even one year. But then P&G struck it rich with a 15-minute serial, *Search for Tomorrow*, produced by the advertising firm of Leo Burnett. A few years later, P&G became the first soap-opera sponsor to produce half-hour serials (1956, *Edge of Night, As the World Turns*), and, after that, the first to expand to a full hour (*As the World Turns*, 1975). At one point during the mid-1950s, P&G had 13 different soap operas on television.

As TV networks and cable companies often do today, P&G began to raid some of its own successful programs for characters to populate a new series. (*Somerset* was spun off from *Another World*, as scriptwriters caused half a dozen characters to move to a new city). Then, during the 1970s, several talented producers and writers left the P&G stable to do spicier shows such as *General Hospital* and *The Young and the Restless*. Now exempted from P&G's strict guidelines for wholesomeness, these soaps became heavily laden with sex. They also contained occasional violence, which usually took place off-screen. Eventually the combination of sex and violence became the winning formula for almost all such programs, including P&G's own.

The company's most enduring soap operas have been *As the World Turns,* which in 2006 celebrated its 50th year on television, and *The Guiding Light,* which started on radio in 1937, moved to television in 1952, and ran continuously into the twenty-first century. This record (70+ years and counting) far surpassed that of any other serial or program in the history of electronic media. *The Guiding Light* featured the estimable Reverend Dr. John Ruthedge, who imparted comforting messages through his eloquent sermons. Dr. Ruthedge kept a lamp burning in his window (the guiding light itself) to reassure townspeople that he was always at home, available for wise counsel on any type of problem they might encounter.

Also at home day and night was Procter & Gamble. Its products were always there for the consumer, who was given scant opportunity to overlook them. The soap opera's contribution to American culture was debatable at best, but its effectiveness as a sales vehicle remained beyond question. The editors of *Advertising Age* proclaimed P&G's marriage with the soap opera as "the longest-running and most successful media strategy in U.S. advertising history."

## Neil McElroy's Epiphany about Brands

After its successes with Ivory and Crisco, P&G developed a new business technique called "brand management." Because it focused attention on a *product* rather than a business *function,* brand management turned out to be a revolutionary idea, very similar to the multidivisional structure introduced by Alfred Sloan at General Motors. It also had the same tendency to decentralize decision making.

Sometimes the birth of a business innovation is impossible to date with precision, but not this time. The shift to brand management began on May 13, 1931, with an internal memorandum written by Neil McElroy (1904–72), an athletic-looking junior executive who had come to P&G after his graduation from Harvard in 1925. While working on the advertising campaign for Camay soap, McElroy became frustrated with having to compete not only with soaps from Lever and Palmolive, but also with Ivory, P&G's own flagship product. In his now-famous memo, he argued that more specific attention should be paid to Camay, and by extension to other P&G brands as well. In addition to putting a particular executive in charge of each brand, there should be a substantial team of people devoted to thinking about every aspect of its production and marketing. This dedicated group would spend its entire energies on one brand and it alone. Each new unit would include a brand assistant, several "check-up people," and others with very specific tasks.

The concern of these managers would not be P&G as a company, but the *brand* of each individual product, which they would manage as if it were a separate business. In this way the special qualities of every brand would be distinguished from those of every other. In ad campaigns, Camay and Ivory would be targeted to different consumer markets, and therefore would become less competitive with each other. The goal was not to sell a bar of Camay *or* Ivory to a particular household, but bars of both Camay *and* Ivory. Over the years, "product differentiation," as businesspeople came to call it, developed into a key element of manufacturing and especially of marketing.

Neil McElroy's memo of 1931 ran to three pages, a bold violation of President Deupree's model of the "one-page memo." This was a P&G custom that had become well known in management circles. But the contents of McElroy's memo made such good sense that they were approved up the corporate hierarchy and endorsed with enthusiasm by Deupree himself.

Thus was born the modern system of brand management. It was widely emulated, and in one form or another is still followed in the twenty-first century by consumer-products companies throughout the world. Typically, brand managers have been energetic young executives marked for bright futures within a company. All of Procter & Gamble's own CEOs after Deupree had brand-management experience. This group included Neil McElroy himself, who headed the company after Deupree retired in 1948, and who in 1957 became secretary of defense under President Eisenhower.

Brand management as a business technique was one of the signal innovations in marketing during the twentieth century. It epitomized the persistent trend in American business of balancing centralized oversight with decentralized decision making, based on determining who in the company has the best information about the decision at hand. Executives at the top would make the strategic decisions about which brands to introduce, acquire, or divest. But they would then delegate to brand managers the specifics of marketing each product.

## Doc Smelser and the Market Research Department

Neil McElroy's formula for success was: "Find out what the consumers want and give it to them." Procter & Gamble went to extreme lengths to do both. It hired hundreds of women to bake, wash dishes, and do laundry in their own homes, and then report the results to P&G. This kind of market research became the hallmark of the company's approach to the development of new products and the continuous effort to improve existing ones.

For many years, the leader of the market-research effort was D. Paul "Doc" Smelser, a small, feisty, serious man who often came to work dressed in sporty suits and ties. (This was not a tradition at P&G, which was known for its executives' conservative attire.) The cerebral Smelser had earned a Ph.D. in economics from Johns Hopkins, hence the nickname "Doc." He started at P&G in a new unit for the purpose of analyzing futures markets for cottonseed oil and other commodities.

Doc soon armed himself with reams of statistics not only about raw materials but also about consumer products. He liked to walk up to senior P&G executives and ask them, out of the blue, questions such as "What percentage of Ivory soap is used for face and hands and what percentage for dishwashing?" Often nobody had the slightest idea. Thus Doc was able to convince top management that P&G, as a company, was totally ignorant of some basic elements of how its products were being used—and therefore of how they should be marketed.

Doc Smelser's embarrassing questions raised some very big issues, and P&G responded quickly in addressing them. In 1925 the company created a formal Market Research Department and put Doc in charge of it. For the next 34 years, until his retirement in 1959, Doc built this group into the most sophisticated unit of its kind in the world. He and his staff of researchers (ultimately several hundred strong) developed systems of asking audiences a series of very detailed questions. In tabulating the answers, they discovered almost everything that could possibly be learned about how P&G's products and competing items were being used, and what consumers liked or disliked about them. In the process, they also learned about new ways to market them. Doc was especially well informed about the reach of P&G's advertising media. He grew fond of surprising managers of radio stations by informing them of precise statistics about the size of their audiences, statistics they themselves did not possess.

One of Doc's shrewdest innovations was his creation of Procter & Gamble's corps of door-to-door interviewers. This group consisted mostly of young women who had graduated from college and therefore possessed "the maturity to travel alone," as one of their supervisors put it. A criterion for the successful applicant was that she be attractive but not inordinately so. Doc wanted members of his force to project a nonthreatening image—wholesome but not glamorous. This, he believed, would create a bond between interviewer and interviewee, and thereby facilitate candid conversations.

Doc's interviewers fanned out into neighborhoods all over the country. They went from house to house armed with an imposing array of questions about laundry, cooking, dishwashing, and every other activity for which P&G marketed a product or was thinking of introducing one. Interviewers were instructed to wear a conservative dress, high heels, gloves, and a hat. As they knocked on doors and talked with consumers, they were to carry only a purse—certainly no lists or forms to fill out. The visits could then seem more casual, even though all conversations were designed to extract copious and detailed data. Interviewers were expected to have total recall, and after their friendly visits would hurry back to their cars and record what they had learned. During Doc's 34 years with P&G, a total of 3,000 women and, eventually, a fair number of men worked as field researchers.

In the 1960s, the company began to phase out this group. Cheap long-distance telephone rates had made it possible to conduct mass surveys more cost-efficiently. By the 1970s, Market Research at P&G was doing about a million and a half telephone or mail-in interviews a year. When the company became a heavy television advertiser, it instituted its "DAR" (Day After Recall) method for measuring the impact and memorability of TV commercials. With the help of its many advertising agencies, P&G used focus groups and other opinion-sampling techniques to adapt its products to changing needs and tastes and to sharpen its commercial messages.

In time, every major consumer-products company in the world had to conduct market research in order to prosper. But Procter & Gamble was the leader, and it remained so into the twenty-first century. The biggest changes at P&G after Doc Smelser's time were in the growing number of the company's brands, the broadening of its markets worldwide, and the even greater sophistication of its market research—made possible by computerization and the Internet.

In the early years of the new century, the brands that P&G offered made up a very long list of names it had made famous (or was keeping famous, since many had been acquired by purchase). These brands included soap and laundry products such as Ivory, Safeguard, Tide, Cheer, Downy, Mr. Clean, Bold, Bounce, Cascade, Joy, and Dawn; cotton-based goods such as Bounty, Charmin, Pampers, Luvs, and Tampax; food and beverage brands such as Folger's, Pringles, and Iams pet foods; health care items including Vicks 44, NyQuil, Prilosec, and Pepto-Bismol; personal-care products such as Crest, Oral-B, Scope, Secret, Sure, Pantene, Head & Shoulders, Olay, CoverGirl, Max Factor, Clairol (acquired in 2001), Wella (2003), and Gillette (purchased in 2005 for $57 billion, P&G's largest acquisition ever). Gillette brought into the fold not only a series of shaving-related products, but also Duracell batteries and other items. In all, P&G's list of brands is so long (about 300, and changing constantly) that it raises the question of how many people in the 180 countries in which the company operates go through a week or even a day without using at least one of its products.

## The Phenomenon of Brands

In the way the word *brand* is understood today, it has a short history of just over a hundred years. It is closely tied to the rise of print and electronic media and the gradual onset of self-service shopping. The modern practice of joining brands with heavy advertising began in the nineteenth century, with products such as Singer Sewing Machines and patent medicines such as Dr. Miles' elixir. The biggest breakthrough came with inexpensive foods and household goods that could be branded and packaged for individual consumers: Nabisco's Uneeda Biscuit, Heinz's Ketchup, Gillette's Safety Razor. Eventually there developed in marketing circles a saying that "brands drive out commodities." That is, once a brand gains a strong foothold, an unbranded product cannot compete as long as the branded item is maintained at high quality and reasonable cost.

By the early twentieth century, Ivory soap and its competitors Lifebuoy and Palmolive had driven out thousands of generic soaps produced locally. They had also displaced homemade soap. The branded soaps were so cheap and reliable that the time and drudgery that families saved from not having to make their own soap came as a much-appreciated relief. The same was true of canned foods offered by Heinz, Campbell, Libby, and other companies.

Some brands quickly disappeared, despite heavy advertising and high quality. Others hung on precariously, their market shares rising and falling for no apparent reason. A few went straight to the top and stayed there for decades. Brands that ranked first in their product lines in the 1920s and are still number one include Ivory soap, Wrigley's chewing gum, Coca-Cola soft drinks, Goodyear tires, Gillette razors, Campbell's soup, Nabisco crackers, and Del Monte canned fruit.

To maintain supremacy over such a long period, any branded item must first remain useful. (Nobody today knows the brand of the best buggy whip.) Second, the quality of the product must continue to be high, or it will be overtaken by competing items. Third, because consumers promptly reject a brand that fails to deliver expected value, companies must pay close attention to who is buying the brand and for what reasons. That's why P&G's Market Research Department under Doc Smelser and others played such a vital role.

The whole idea of brand management implies that the company's fundamental task is usually not to maximize sales in the short run but rather to develop long-term consumer loyalty. That kind of loyalty not only sustains a strong market for the company's existing products but also facilitates the introduction of new ones.

The goal of brand loyalty is not easily accomplished, in part because not all consumers have the same attitude toward brands. Some develop deep psychological attachments, incorporating brands into their self-images. These kinds of consumers sometimes flaunt the brands they purchase like badges, to announce what types of people they are: Ralph Lauren, Donna Karan, Gucci, Prada, and so on. Consumers in a second category, which probably comprises the majority who buy branded goods, are simply saving time by choosing items about whose quality they can be confident. Whether or not a branded article is of the highest quality isn't the whole issue, since cost is also a factor. The key here is consistency in value received for money spent. A residual number of consumers, making up perhaps a third of all purchasers, don't seem to care much about brands one way or the other. But enough do care to make it worthwhile for companies to be sensitive to even the subtlest trends in market reaction to their brands. This attention, by itself, is evidence of the continuing growth in the power of consumers throughout the twentieth century and the early twenty-first.

During the 1970s and 1980s, career-obsessed managers in several American companies began to exploit the brands under their control for short-term profit gains. They did this by raising prices too high (General Motors cars), reducing the quality of the product without cutting its price (Halston clothing), and unwisely "extending" or "stretching" the brand itself (Frito-Lay Lemonade, Crystal Pepsi). Starting in the 1990s, some companies assigned "brand equity managers" to monitor the behavior of brand managers and prevent them from dissipating brand value through short-term profit-maximization.

Not all extensions or stretchings of brands were ill advised, of course. Procter & Gamble stretched Ivory "horizontally" across similar products, from bar soap to Ivory Flakes and Ivory Snow, and on to Ivory Shampoo and Ivory Dishwashing Liquid, all with great success. Many firms carried out effective "vertical" brand stretching to different products and services. The Disney company moved from movie cartoons to comic books, then to theme parks, feature films, toys, retail stores, Broadway shows, and international tour guiding.

It is difficult for people working in companies like Procter & Gamble to judge just how far a given brand can be stretched, either horizontally or vertically. It's also hard to specify in dollar terms what a particular brand is worth. Similarly, it's impossible to tell at what point advertising expenditures exceed the amount necessary to keep a brand healthy—and become money poured down the drain. There is little question that much of the total amount spent on advertising serves no useful purpose. But exactly how much is unknowable, and a company that fails to spend enough can face serious consequences.

During the "leveraged buyout" movement of the 1980s, a more precise notion of the value of brands began to emerge. The occasion was the multi-billion-dollar purchases of companies such as RJR Nabisco, much of whose value was embedded not in physical or financial assets but rather in its brands, such as Ritz Crackers, Oreo Cookies, and A-1 Steak Sauce. So the selling price of such a company's common stock could go up rapidly once the company itself was put "in play"— the bidding war driven in part by the firm's possession of brands. Many companies began to assign explicit values to their brands, actually listing them as assets on their balance sheets.

Occasionally, brands have been purchased by other makers of similar products. Electrolux, a Swedish company, produced and sold a variety of kitchen appliances under brands once manufactured and marketed by other firms: Westinghouse, Kelvinator, Frigidaire, White, and Gibson. Then, too, brands are often retained even if companies themselves are acquired, in whole or in part, by their competitors. The French tire company Michelin purchased Uniroyal's and BFGoodrich's tire operations, and the Japanese firm Bridgestone acquired Firestone. When "globalization" took off in the 1990s, it soon became evident that international companies could not assume that their brands had the same value across cultures, or even that particular brands conveyed the same meaning to consumers everywhere.

Meanwhile, several prominent brands, such as Kleenex, Scotch Tape, and Jell-O, had become almost synonymous with their product categories. In a few extreme cases, if a company did not take sufficient care to protect itself, this kind of success could actually destroy legal rights to a brand name. That happened with such former brands as thermos, linoleum, aspirin, yo-yo, and cellophane—all of which are names that now can be used by generic manufacturers.

Like most other elements of business, brand management will continue to be as much art as science, calling for difficult judgments on the part of producers and especially marketers. Consumers can be persuaded to try new products, but in a competitive economy they can't be exploited successfully for very long. As consumers' range of choices became greater, their collective power over decisions made within companies grew commensurately. The ultimate source of such innovations as Doc Smelser's market research and Neil McElroy's brand management was precisely this growth in consumer power. It turned out to be one of the most important trends affecting American business throughout the twentieth century and into the twenty-first.

## People as Brands

Sometimes, the idea of brands has been carried to peculiar lengths. Famous names of entrepreneurs such as Henry Ford, Estée

Lauder, and Ralph Lauren had long been used in marketing their firms' products. Then, late in the twentieth century and even more so in the twenty-first, advertisers began to speak of famous individuals as "brands." This was particularly true of athletes and authors: Michael Jordan, Peyton Manning, Maria Sharapova, Tiger Woods, Tom Clancy, Danielle Steele, Stephen King, J. K. Rowling. Celebrities of all kinds began to think of themselves as brands. Many not only endorsed other products but also set up their own product lines: fragrances, clothing, sports equipment.

Occasionally the process became bizarre. The premature deaths of Marilyn Monroe, Elvis Presley, and Princess Diana were spoken of as "good career moves" promoting ever-increasing demands for memorabilia. Even Monroe's worst movies became "classics." Graceland, Presley's home in Memphis, attracted more paying visitors with each passing year. For many devotees of the Presley brand, the anniversary of his death on August 16, 1977, became not only a day of mourning but also a day to buy something—anything—connected with him. And in the case of Diana, the "People's Princess," the date of her own death (August 31, 1997) seemed to many people an almost sacred occasion. Its tenth anniversary in 2007 was marked by an avalanche of new books, magazine articles, medallions, coins, plates, and other "tributes"— none free of charge, of course. In these cases the line between consumer empowerment and consumer exploitation, which has never been very clear, became indistinguishable. "I often wonder," Joseph Schumpeter once wrote in his diary, "if there is any cause that ever arose and had success that was not business for somebody." Schumpeter was ruminating not on what he regarded as a deplorable situation, but rather on a characteristic of capitalism.

## Updating P&G's Corporate Culture

Of course, brand management by itself is no permanent solution to the problems of business organization in any type of company. There can be no permanent solutions in business, since conditions are forever changing. Toward the close of the twentieth century and the start of the twenty-first, Procter & Gamble took major steps to modernize its culture. Many of these changes came in response to external shifts in the business environment, exemplified by a sharp plunge in the share price of the company's common stock during the year 2000. Thereafter, P&G began to reverse its historic policy of extreme secrecy, opening up both within the company and outside it. Top management encouraged employees to dress casually, and—in a complete turnabout from its traditions of secrecy—actually created blogging software for its employees, many of whom avidly began their own blogs. P&G shifted its approach to research and development from a "Not Invented Here" prejudice against external ideas to what it called "Connect and Develop"—inviting new proposals from every available source. Most important, it adapted its core strategies to the forces of globalization. In apparent response to these new policies, the company's stock price recovered and attained new peaks. Meanwhile, numerous young alumni and alumnae of P&G gravitated toward senior management jobs at Silicon Valley Internet firms, where their superior marketing skills were in short supply. One of the best examples was Meg Whitman, who served as CEO of eBay from 1998 to 2008 and became a member of Procter & Gamble's board of directors.

In 2007, P&G began a major reorganization of the entire company by dividing its global businesses into three major categories: household care, beauty care, and health and well-being. (Its Anglo-Dutch competitor Unilever took similar steps.) In an important signal of women's increasing clout, P&G appointed Susan Arnold president of Global Business Units, the company's number-two executive position. The titles of many other officers exemplified the ways in which P&G and other global companies reshaped their structures so as to decentralize decision making even more. The firm created about two dozen new senior management positions, such as Group President, North America; Group President, Asia; Group President, Central and Eastern Europe, Middle East, and Africa; Group President, Global Fabric Care; Group President, Global Personal Care; President, Global Hair Care, and—very significantly—President, Global Wal★Mart Team.

Wal★Mart, which by this point was America's largest corporation, came to wield unprecedented authority over the pricing and shelf-space of consumer products. Its policies profoundly affected thousands of supplier companies, several hundred of which opened offices adjacent to or even within Wal★Mart's headquarters in Bentonville, Arkansas. Wal★Mart's unprecedented power forced even big producers such as Procter & Gamble to pay constant attention to the giant retailer's every move. Among many other consequences—not all of them beneficial to the nation's economy—the spectacular rise of Wal★Mart and other low-cost retailers epitomized the rising empowerment of consumers. That trend, along with the decentralization of decision making, is one of the major themes of this book, and both are embodied in the story of Procter & Gamble.

*Right: Henry Ford and his first car, the "quadricycle" of 1896.* From the collections of Henry Ford Museum & Greenfield Village and Ford Motor Company.

*Below: The first Ford "factory," on Mack Avenue in Detroit, 1903.* From the collections of Henry Ford Museum & Greenfield Village and Ford Motor Company.

*Opposite top: Henry Ford and his son Edsel with the original quadricycle and the 15 millionth Model T, late 1920s.* Baker Library, Harvard Business School and Ford Motor Company.

*Opposite bottom: Ford's immense River Rouge industrial complex, whose construction began in the 1920s. Iron ore and hundreds of other raw materials went into "The Rouge," and completed cars came out.* From the collections of Henry Ford Museum & Greenfield Village and Ford Motor Company.

*Top: Ford assembly line workers polishing freshly painted auto bodies, early 1930s.* From the collections of Henry Ford Museum & Greenfield Village and Ford Motor Company.

## PONTIAC

𝒯HE New Pontiac Big Six, built by Oakland, exemplifies the value offered in General Motors products—providing a car of exceptional beauty, performance, comfort and size at prices ranging from $745 to $895

*Opposite top: The brilliant Alfred P. Sloan, Jr., of General Motors, still thin as a rail at age 52. This picture was taken in 1927, the year in which competitive pressure from General Motors finally forced Henry Ford to shut down his giant factories and retool for his new Model A. Corbis/Bettmann-UPI.*

*Opposite bottom: The 1929 Pontiac, created by Sloan and his team to complete the GM line of nameplates on an ascending scale of price and prestige: first Chevrolet, next Pontiac, then on to Oldsmobile, Buick, and, at the top, Cadillac--"a car for every purse and purpose," as GM's 1929 "Spring Showing" trade catalogue advertised the line. The original Pontiac advertisement was in full color: the car silver with red trim, the flowers pink, yellow, and lavender. GM automobiles were available in many colors and with annual model changes to encourage consumers to trade in as well as upgrade. Sloan's emphasis on this kind of aspirational marketing, in addition to his internal reorganization of the company, led to GM's defeat of Ford in the epic battle for market share. Courtesy of General Motors Corporation and Baker Library, Harvard Business School.*

*Top: The 25 millionth Chevrolet, which rolled off the line in 1940. Alfred Sloan is in this picture, but, typically, so are many other members of GM's management team, plus a number of workers. Sloan is in the front row, second from right. Corbis/Bettmann.*

*Red Deupree, the longtime president of Procter & Gamble who cut his own salary during the early years of the Great Depression.* Courtesy of The Procter & Gamble Company.

*10.tif The resourceful Doc Smelser, who headed P&G's elite Market Research Department for 34 years.* Courtesy of The Procter & Gamble Company.

*Top: One of Doc Smelser's 3,000 door-to-door interviewers, calling on a consumer as part of P&G's ceaseless market research, 1940s.* Courtesy of The Procter & Gamble Company.

*Bottom: A large cast delivering P&G's soap opera "The Guiding Light" over NBC radio, circa 1940. This program began in 1937, moved to television in 1952, and was still on the air during the first decade of the 21st century.* Courtesy of The Procter & Gamble Company.

*Left: Neil McElroy, whose now famous memo of 1931 inaugurated Procter & Gamble's strategy of "brand management," a technique later adopted by scores of consumer-products companies throughout the world.* Courtesy of The Procter & Gamble Company.

*Bottom: During World War II, P&G like many other consumer-products companies produced munitions as well. Here a P&G employee inspects shells that have just been loaded with powder.* Courtesy of The Procter & Gamble Company.

# CHAPTER THREE

# The New Deal and World War II, 1933–1945: Decentralizing Regulation and War Mobilization

## Roosevelt, the New Deal, and Regulation

Despite the success of standout firms such as Procter & Gamble, the big movie studios, and a few specialized businesses, the Great Depression posed an unprecedented economic challenge to the United States. President Franklin D. Roosevelt, elected in 1932, was a career politician who knew much less about business than had his predecessor, Herbert Hoover. Nonetheless, Roosevelt became one of the most important figures in the history of American capitalism—for the time had come for public regulation to catch up to business practice and it was FDR who oversaw these sweeping changes.

Although Roosevelt professed faith in the country's economic system, he insisted that important parts of it be altered, and he led a fight that blunted its excesses and thereby strengthened it. In line with the larger business trends of the century, the reforms put in place by FDR's "New Deal" empowered investors and informed consumers by making corporate behavior much more transparent. But there was a great deal more to Roosevelt's stewardship of the economy than this: notably the many forms of decentralized management that characterized the new financial regulations and, later, the nation's monumental effort in mobilizing for World War II.

The Roosevelt "revolution" of the 1930s embodied not just an economic movement; it also achieved a partial political settlement of some long-festering issues. These included the excessive power of business vis-à-vis workers and consumers, as well as ingrained injustices toward women, the elderly, the poor, the disabled, and racial and ethnic minorities. While the New Deal did not solve any of these problems, it did ameliorate them.

Workers gained a significant degree of new influence during the 1930s because of changes in federal law and the increasing power of labor unions. Whereas only 7 percent of the nation's nonagricultural workforce had been unionized in 1930, that number had more than doubled by 1940, tripled by 1945, and peaked during the 1960s. (After that, union membership began a gradual decline because of the replacement of many union jobs by automation, the rise of industrial competition from abroad, growing anti-union sentiment at home, and the general shift of the workforce from manufacturing to the less easily unionized service sector.)

The gap in income distribution, which had been extreme in the 1920s, narrowed during the New Deal and even more so just afterward. From the mid-1930s until the mid-1980s, U.S. society in general was overwhelmingly middle class. The relative equalization of incomes that began in the 1930s derived in part from demographic trends and changes in the nature of work. But it also owed much to new laws and other government actions instituted during the Roosevelt administration. The most important of these were Social Security, unemployment compensation, the minimum wage, support of labor unions, and the graduated income-tax system.

The attitude of many American businesspeople toward Roosevelt's policies, after a brief honeymoon during 1933, became one of downright hostility. Bankers, other financiers, and managers of big business were especially belligerent. Many of them regarded the New Deal as a grab for power by unscrupulous Democratic party politicians. Even sophisticated executives such as Alfred Sloan and Pierre du Pont exhibited an almost irrational hatred of Roosevelt, and they poured part of their fortunes into campaigns to unseat him. Several anti-Roosevelt groups, such as the American Liberty League, were so transparently dominated by the du Ponts and other moneyed families that their efforts actually enhanced Roosevelt's standing with voters. In a context of economic depression, it was easy for FDR and other savvy politicians to make common cause with the masses and array themselves against what Roosevelt called "economic royalists" and "organized money." Indeed, so popular was FDR with the American people that they elected him to an unprecedented third term—then, in 1944, to a fourth.

The New Deal did not actually revolutionize the American economy, as both its supporters and enemies liked to assert. The business system retained the same overall structure in 1940 that it had in 1930. Yet government supervision did increase markedly in the interim, as industries such as trucking, airlines, and interstate gas and electric utilities came under federal regulation. Other industries already regulated, including railroads, banking, telecommunications, and broadcasting, came under tighter scrutiny. Some New Deal measures turned out to be inappropriate in the long run for the industries concerned and were repealed during later deregulation movements. But as a whole, the regulatory acts pushed through in the 1930s made the economic system much more legitimate in the eyes of the American people.

In the long run, the most significant New Deal business reform was a complex series of laws designed to reshape the nation's capital markets. This legislation affected not only firms in the banking and securities industries, but also the thousands of companies whose shares were traded on stock exchanges. The Securities Act of 1933 and the Securities Exchange Act of 1934 required that all such companies issue to stockholders and deliver to the government detailed annual reports. These reports contained copious amounts of previously secret information, which had to be laid out in prescribed form and certified by independent accountants. Legislation of 1938 extended the requirements to all "public" companies whose shares were freely bought and sold, whether or not they were listed on stock exchanges.

While a few firms, such as United States Steel, had been voluntarily issuing reports to shareholders for several decades, and railroads and utilities already were required to submit annual reports to regulatory commissions, for most other firms the 1930s legislation brought a completely new world of doing business in the sunshine. In addition to numerous other figures, companies now had to disclose precise data on their sales, profits, and salaries and bonuses paid to officers and directors. Without these laws, the many corporate scandals that lay in the future—insider trading, back-dating of stock options, accounting frauds, and gigantic compensation packages for CEOs—would never have seen the light of day.

In the face of much kicking and screaming from business (then, as now, a conditioned reflex to almost any proposal for regulation), the securities laws were drafted with meticulous care by some of the smartest people in the country. These laws placed the burden of execution primarily on the private sector, thereby decentralizing enforcement far and wide—and avoiding the need for a large, centralized public bureaucracy. Because of their rigorous requirements, which included criminal penalties for violations, the securities laws provided much new business for attorneys working for private firms. The laws created even more work for professional accountants, whose numbers skyrocketed to meet the new legal mandate for independent audits of balance sheets and income statements.

The securities laws had especially beneficial effects on those who had opposed them most stridently—stock-exchange officials and investment bankers. One can see just how bad the crisis in the financial sector had been from a quick look at a few statistics. For the year 1933, at the nadir of the Great Depression, new corporate issues of securities totaled only $161 million, about one-fiftieth the figure for 1929. The number of shares traded on the New York Stock Exchange languished at less than half a billion for the year 1932, one-third the 1929 figure.

By comparison, more than one billion shares were traded on a single day in 1997, the first time that had ever occurred; thereafter, this kind of daily trading volume became routine. Trading on this scale would never have been possible without the foundation laid down by the reforms of the New Deal and strengthened in subsequent years. The many elements of this intricate and decentralized regulatory system formed a solid basis for confidence on the part of investors. The new system helped the capital markets not only to recover, but to achieve new levels of prosperity and world leadership. In securities regulation the government deserved an A+, a grade that held until the 1980s, when the financial system began to change in radical ways described later in this book. But even today the groundwork so carefully laid in the 1930s survives mostly intact.

Meanwhile, new federal price-support systems reshaped the conduct of commercial agriculture, practically ending the depression that had begun in that sector during the early 1920s. And under the National Industrial Recovery Act of 1933, similar systems were instituted for hundreds of other industries. The early thirties were a time of serious deflation (falling prices), and federal price supports were imposed in hopes of stopping the downward spiral. The general plan was to use "codes of fair competition" to maintain standard prices for products made by different companies in the same industry. But, for a variety of reasons, these codes seldom worked well. The sticking points included the difficulty of classifying product lines, the disparate cost structures of big firms as opposed to small ones, and the impossibility of setting prices that manufacturers, distributors, and consumers would all judge to be "fair." Even if agreement had been possible, too many opportunities existed for firms to differentiate their products and thereby evade the codes. Nor could even the best cost-accounting systems set "fair" standard prices in advance of the actual demand for specific items. Therefore, the government's effort to support prices was abandoned for many industries even before 1935, when the Supreme Court declared the National Industrial Recovery Act of 1933 unconstitutional. The pro-union provisions of the act were quickly re-established and strengthened in the National Labor Relations Act of 1935.

After the passage of the crucial Fair Labor Standards Act of 1938, which established stronger ground rules for maximum hours and minimum wages, the New Deal began to run out of steam. By this time the country's attention had shifted to ominous events unfolding in Europe and Asia. As Roosevelt put it, "Dr. New Deal" was now obliged to become "Dr. Win the War." World War II began in Europe in September 1939, and the United States entered it officially after the Japanese attack on Pearl Harbor in Hawaii on December 7, 1941.

## The World Conflict, 1939–1945

In its effect on American business, as in many other ways, World War II was the most significant event of the twentieth century. Its ramifications were almost endless. Because of the pressing need to develop high-tech weapons, and also to deal with the heavy toll of casualties and sickness, the war either created or gave new momentum to industries that would become the most important of the late twentieth and early twenty-first centuries. These industries were so different in nature from those of the Second Industrial Revolution (steel, automobiles, and electrical equipment) that they formed the core of a Third Industrial Revolution, rooted in scientific research and based more on knowledge work than on mechanized mass production. The new industries included advanced telecommunications and electronics (including primitive computers), aviation and aerospace, atomic energy, synthetic chemicals and pharmaceuticals, and highly sophisticated medical devices.

The war gave a profound jolt to American society in general, and therefore to businesses across all industries. About a half-dozen of these changes were momentous: the movement of masses of women to jobs outside the home; the conditioning of millions of people to a worklife in big organizations, be they corporate or military; the creation of large populations on the West Coast and in the Sunbelt; the smoothing out of the business cycle; the introduction of mass income taxation and the withholding-tax system; and, perhaps most important of all, the start of a long stretch of economic prosperity. The period from the early 1940s to the early 1970s became a kind of golden age for American business.

In wartime as in peace, the hardest problem that business organizations faced was in finding a proper balance between centralized control and decentralized decision making. In the effort to mobilize the economy for all-out war, this challenge became *the* crucial issue of management in both the public and private sector. The heart of the question was this: how could a democratic capitalist country mobilize for war without having the central government dictate all business decisions and thereby wreck the decentralized market mechanism on which the economy was based? At the other theoretical extreme, how could a laissez-faire government completely bereft of economic powers coordinate its independent industries to fight a massive war?

Every country involved in World War II confronted the problem of mobilization management, but the United States faced special difficulties. Despite the regulatory measures of the New Deal, the American government as of 1941 still had less control over its national economy than did any other major belligerent, with the possible exception of China. The task of mobilization presented the most serious administrative challenge the United States government had ever faced. Yet in the end the nation solved this problem extraordinarily well — much better than Germany or Japan, both of which overcentralized industrial control and gave too much authority to military officers.

In Germany, these officers sacrificed quantity production in favor of achieving the highest quality. The airplanes and other tools of Germany's war machine were superbly designed, but they were so diversified and nonstandardized that lengthy production runs at factories became a critical problem. In addition, the repair of German equipment on the battlefields turned into a nightmare, as thousands of spare parts remained unavailable because there were too many varieties to keep in stock. By the middle of the war, owing to interference from military people stationed at industrial plants, the German army was using 151 different models of trucks and 150 different models of motorcycles. The air force had 425 models or variants of planes in use or under construction. From a production viewpoint, this policy was nothing short of absurd, one consequence being that the productivity of aircraft workers in Germany was only half that of their American counterparts.

The other major Axis powers also fell short when it came to production. Japan's industrial mobilization, in addition to being badly managed, suffered from a shortage of essential materials. The country had few natural resources, and American submarines proceeded to sink most of the ships attempting to carry imports into Japan. And the army and aviation materials produced by Italy, the third major Axis power, amounted to less than that of the Ford Motor Company, the number-three American defense contractor. Ford made all sorts of engines. Also, in its vast Willow Run plant near Detroit it put together thousands of standardized B-24 bombers, essentially by assembly-line methods.

## The U.S. Production Miracle

During the war years American business turned out 86,000 tanks, 600,000 jeeps, 2 million army trucks, 193,000 artillery pieces, 17 million handguns and rifles, and 41 billion rounds of ammunition. Shipyards on both coasts, led in production technology by the standardized Kaiser works in California, launched 12,000 warships and merchant ships as well as nearly 65,000 smaller craft for use in coastal patrols and amphibious landings. Most of these numbers denote outputs unprecedented in world history. Even for just the ships and smaller craft, the mind's eye can't easily picture a fleet of such magnitude. Placed end to end on land, the line of vessels would stretch approximately from New York to Omaha.

Most remarkably of all, aircraft companies in the United States built almost 300,000 planes during the war years. By comparison, the leading American postwar producer of airliners, Boeing, manufactured about 6,000 passenger jets during the 30-year period from 1960 to 1990. These modern jetliners were a lot more complicated and expensive than the warplanes of the 1940s, but the fiftyfold difference in numbers, produced in one-sixth of the time, speaks for itself.

America's production of aluminum during the war increased by a factor of four, and that of magnesium, also used in aircraft, by a factor of 350. Mobilization also gave birth to the modern synthetic rubber industry, and by war's end U.S. synthetics accounted for 85 percent of the material used to make tires and other rubber products for both military and civilian use. Before the war the United States had produced almost no rubber and had been the world's largest importer of the commodity; after the war it became the largest exporter of it. All the imports were of natural rubber, all of the exports of synthetic rubber.

The war changed nearly every part of the economy in some way. Numerous manufacturing plants converted from civilian to military production, and munitions companies grew much bigger. Supplies of "highway" fuel fell by one-third during the war, as the output of aviation gasoline leaped twentyfold. The production of steel increased from 28 million tons in 1938 to 101 million by 1943, almost all of it now directed to military use.

For steel and several other materials, the biggest single shift came from diversions away from the manufacture of automobiles. Carmakers began instead to build tanks, jeeps, trucks, armored personnel carriers, and other military equipment. Almost 40 percent of the car companies' output went into aircraft and related items. Of the 813,000 aircraft engines built in the United States during World War II, the car companies made 456,000 of them. Most of these engines were very complex machines, and it was essential that they be utterly reliable. Otherwise the planes they powered would fall out of the sky.

American industrial mobilization as a whole was brilliantly successful. Without question it was the key to victory over Japan, and it was the single most important element in the Allied triumph on the Western Front in Europe. By 1944 the Americans were far outproducing the British, Germans, and Japanese combined. In perhaps the most dramatic way possible, this performance demonstrated once more the strength and resilience of the American business system and the flexibility of the U.S. government.

No part of this great achievement came easily, however, and the strain on mobilization planners was severe and relentless.

## The Struggle to Manage Mobilization

Evidence of the strain is clear from the planners' prolonged trial-and-error approach. For many months stretching from 1939 to 1942, they set up one special body after another, but only a few of these agencies worked well. Most were staffed with business executives called to Washington as "dollar-a-year men" who remained on their firms' payrolls and served without much compensation from the government. In 1939 Roosevelt set up the War Resources Board, headed by Edward Stettinius of United States Steel. In May 1940 came the National Defense Advisory Commission, which included William S. Knudsen, a production genius who in 1937 had succeeded Alfred Sloan as president of General Motors.

Many agencies created during the early years of the war had overlapping jurisdictions: the Army and Navy Munitions Board, the Supply Priorities and Allocation Board, and the War Production Board. This last body was headed by Donald Nelson, who came to Washington from Sears, Roebuck. Nelson was regarded as a peacemaker, someone who could listen to the demands of contending parties from business, government, and the military without losing his temper. The War Production Board took overall charge of industrial mobilization but continued to share its authority with other agencies and several bureaus of both the Army and the Navy. (At this time there was no independent Air Force. It was formed in 1947 out of what had been the Army Air Corps.)

Given the immense scale of mobilization, there were inevitable foul-ups and disagreements about which kinds of public and private purchasers should have a numbered "priority" to buy vital but scarce raw materials. Business executives protested against impossible targets for production. Military officers threw tantrums when their demands for munitions went unmet. Government planners, tired of refereeing, stomped out of meetings. In some of the official postwar reports issued by the government, a tone of tension creeps into what are usually the driest of bureaucratic documents. Here, for example, is a passage from an authoritative Commerce Department account entitled *The United States at War,* published in 1946:

First, it became utterly impossible to produce everything ordered at any time in [the] near future. It was an industrial impossibility. The total called for was in excess of our industrial capacity.

Second, there was a resulting collision between the various production programs and between the men who were responsible for them. . . .

Third, all semblance of balance in the production program disappeared because of the different rates of contracting and of production that resulted from the scramble to place orders. . . .

Fourth, there was terrific waste in conversion. After a tragically slow start, many a plant was changed over to war production when its normal product was more needed than its new product. . . .

Fifth, we built many new factories, and expanded many others, which we could not use and did not need. . . .

Finally, the priority system broke down because of "priority inflation." People with military contracts had the right to take more scarce materials and components than there were, so that a priority or an allocation became nothing more than a "hunting license."

Early in the war, mobilization planners had tried desperately to figure out some practical way to allocate strategic materials. They began with the "priority" classification described above. But priority status meant only that certain buyers would get preferences over the normal run of customers. It did not mean they would actually receive supplies in the volumes they requested. Nor could the system effectively differentiate between the Army, the Navy, and other authorized purchasers, all of whom might have had an equally weighted "priority" for the same materials. Even within each military service, separate bureaus competed for the same supplies. The chaos of the priority system continued until November 1942, nearly a year after the attack on Pearl Harbor.

## Decentralization through the Controlled Materials Plan

At that point the Roosevelt Administration announced a dramatic new strategy to which it gave a prosaic name: the Controlled Materials Plan. The Plan was the brainchild of Ferdinand Eberstadt (1890–1969), an investment banker of luminous intelligence who had moved to Washington to chair the Army and Navy Munitions Board. He had then become vice-chairman of the powerful War Production Board, under which the new Plan would now be administered.

Eberstadt was the son of a German Jewish father and German-Venezuelan Catholic mother. (He himself became a Presbyterian.) His parents had come to the United States before any of their children were born, settling in New Jersey. There young Eberstadt attended a private prep school before enrolling at Princeton. He made a brilliant college record, despite being temporarily expelled during his freshman year for unruly behavior. After graduation, he went to Europe to continue his studies, then during World War I served in France as a U.S. Army artillery officer. Following the war he received a degree from Columbia Law School and entered a Wall Street law firm. A bold young man whose personal bearing seemed to alternate randomly between charm and imperiousness, Eberstadt had little patience with some of the backslapping business types who were coming to prominence during the 1920s. He preferred the rarefied air of innovative corporate finance, where unintelligent people quickly perished.

Leaving the practice of law in 1925, he became a partner at Dillon, Read, an elite Wall Street investment bank. There, exploiting his foreign-language skills, he negotiated the firm's most sensitive loans to European clients, particularly German coal and steel firms. Eberstadt pursued his work with single-minded dedication. (Three of his four children were born during his periodic absences in Europe.) He had a vivid sense of his own abilities, and in 1929 he was fired by Dillon, Read after being rebuffed in his bid for a greater share of the firm's profits. In 1931 he established his own firm, F. Eberstadt & Co.

Many investment banks went under during the Great Depression, and almost no new ones attracted much business. The resourceful Eberstadt, however, quickly discovered a niche for his startup firm. His company flourished to such an extent that in 1939 he was profiled in a *Fortune* article entitled, simply, "Ferdinand Eberstadt." Because big industrial firms were already tied to established investment banks such as Goldman Sachs, Eberstadt sought clients among small- to medium-sized companies, most of which were family owned.

Inheritance-tax laws, passed by Congress at the behest of the Roosevelt Administration and replicated in many state legislatures, were forcing numerous families to sell their companies upon the death of the founding ancestor. Eberstadt's solution was for these firms to "go public" during the founder's lifetime. They would sell a large minority of common stock to the public, thereby giving the heirs money to pay inheritance taxes but at the same time allowing them to keep voting control of the firm. He called his stable of clients "little blue chips." Some of them went on to become big businesses: McGraw-Hill, Norwich Pharmacal, Victor Chemical.

Eberstadt's special gift, evident throughout his career, was an uncanny sense of how to design institutional mechanisms to meet novel situations. He also had the courage to implement them. As one of his fellow wartime planners put it, "Above all he could make decisions—very tough decisions. Even when they hurt people—influential people—he made them."

In 1942, working as vice-chairman of the War Production Board, Eberstadt was appalled at the disarray he saw. The new mobilization agencies were thwarting one another, and the military services were under such stress that their own discourse had become a continuous shriek. The pressing need was for a stern hand to guide the task of industrial mobilization.

At the same time, Eberstadt knew that any plan that did not exploit market forces could not fully tap the potential of American business. The challenge before him was to create a system that would give play to market forces, yet steer them to produce the right kinds of equipment in the right amounts, to arrive at the right places at the right times.

His solution was to pull back from all attempts at pervasive centralized direction. Dictatorial management of war production was beginning to work well enough in the Soviet Union, but it formed a very bad fit with the American market economy. Eberstadt's aim was to achieve maximum effectiveness of production and distribution at all levels, with minimal interference from the top. It was the same kind of goal articulated for peacetime business by Alfred Sloan at General Motors and Neil McElroy at Procter & Gamble.

Eberstadt acknowledged Sloan's influence on his own thinking, and with Sloan-like logic he worked out an ingenious way to decentralize decision making. He decided to guide mobilization by the rationed allocation of only three items: steel, aluminum, and copper. This technique would be powerful but simple. The Controlled Materials Plan moved away from the loose "priority" regime, which sought to allocate scores of products using a dysfunctional mechanism, and toward tight control of these three key metals, without which no important munitions company could operate. Therefore, Eberstadt reasoned, it was no longer necessary for the War Production Board to pay much attention to the many other items it had been trying to prioritize.

The ideas that animated Eberstadt were to match supply with demand and—most important—to facilitate quick shifts in allocations of the key metals from one use to another as circumstances changed. The Plan therefore called for a careful sequence of steps, all aimed at the decentralization of decision making. First, forecasters would compute the volume of the three metals that would be available over the coming months. (All three were under very high-pressure production schedules.) Eberstadt and his staff would then ask "claimant agencies" such as the Army and Navy to submit to the Plan's Requirements Committee their claims for steel, aluminum, and copper. These claims were to consist of consolidated estimates from prime military contractors such as General Motors and Boeing, who would negotiate on behalf of themselves as well as their hundreds of subcontractors.

Eberstadt's new system placed a tremendous premium on accuracy. If insufficient estimates crept into the computations at any level, from the bottom of the subcontracting chain all the way up to the claimant agency, then the schedule for manufacturing the affected item would stall for want of necessary materials. On the other hand, if inflated claims were put into the system, then the Requirements Committee, chaired by Eberstadt himself, would impose penalties, including recommendations for criminal indictments. In this way the Plan practically mandated accurate forecasting within individual firms as a matter of self-interest. The system was much like the Securities and Exchange Commission's requirements for accurate corporate reporting, with the onus for accuracy placed on the companies, under penalty of prosecution.

The prime contractors, after receiving "tickets" that entitled them to purchase a given quantity of controlled materials, would next allocate supplies to their own plants, to those of their subcontractors, and so on down the line. At subcontractor levels, thousands of managers in small businesses would calculate what they needed to fulfill their obligations, and then submit their estimates to the big prime contractors. In this way, original requests for materials were made in drafting rooms and on shop floors, where information was most current and engineers and workers best informed. At the prime contractor level, the different needs of various subcontractors would be balanced against one another, and also against the big company's own requirements for the many military products it was manufacturing. The total "claims" for materials would then be adjusted accordingly.

In one of the most important changes from the flawed "priority system," both the claimant agencies and their prime contractors were delegated the power to shift controlled materials from one use to another at levels up and down their own bailiwicks. This new "vertical" chain of authority, as it came to be called, created an internal market within each organizational jurisdiction. It thereby fulfilled one of Eberstadt's overriding aims of giving industrial mobilization "greater similarity to the normal commercial practice."

If, for example, a prime contractor wanted to switch part of its copper allocation from one project to another—say, from copper coils to copper wires—it could do so without having to ask the government's permission. This decentralization of decision making all the way down the vertical chain made the Controlled Materials Plan a much more flexible instrument than the previous "horizontal" regime. In that system, nontransferable "priorities" had been awarded across the board to thousands of contractors and subcontractors, and even to individual factories, without regard to whether total supply could keep up with total demand.

Under the new system, only a few strategic decisions would have to be made by top military and civilian planners. The officials in charge of allocating steel might see that over the next few months the Navy was going to need more of it for a specified number of ships, while the Army needed the same amount for its tanks. In this scenario, the ships would have to be constructed first, because they had to be afloat and ready to carry the tanks to overseas battlefields. Therefore, competing claims for scarce steel by ship and tank contractors must on this occasion be resolved by Eberstadt and his staff in favor of the Navy. Later on, the situation might be the reverse: tanks now, ships later, so the Army gets the steel.

Meanwhile, the Navy itself, as a claimant agency, would be forced to choose between using its steel allocation for either warships or support ships. And even within those categories, it would have to establish tradeoffs among fighting ships such as aircraft carriers, cruisers, destroyers, and submarines on the one hand, and among supporting cargo ships, troop transports, and fuel tankers on the other.

To the long list of complex problems in mobilization planning, the Controlled Materials Plan brought a stark simplicity. Although only three metals were designated, their rationing had a domino effect on hundreds of other critical materials. Strategic choices, by necessity, still had to be made at the top. But the *production* dynamic now flowed in the opposite direction, from the bottom up. The Plan represented a vast pyramid of decision making in which thousands of individual tradeoffs took place up and down through different layers of operation. Each tradeoff was made at the spot where the information necessary to select the right alternative was most likely to be available. This was administrative elegance at its best—a triumph of decentralized decision making.

Eberstadt's Controlled Materials Plan was announced in November 1942, implemented during 1943, and kept in operation for the rest of the war. It represented a distinctively American solution to the most challenging of all organizational problems. In one sense it recalled the old Hamilton-Jefferson debates of the 1790s, which also grappled with achieving the right balance between central authority and individual freedom. And like those debates, the problem of industrial mobilization was resolved by intense and often bitter bargaining.

Ferdinand Eberstadt succeeded far beyond his own expectations. But in an ironic twist, he and several other planners fell victim to one of the many shakeups deriving from the politics of war mobilization. In 1943, not long after the Controlled Materials Plan went into operation, he was relieved of his post as vice-chairman of the War Production Board. (He had refused to fire one of his loyal subordinates, and in turn was fired himself, by President Roosevelt.) But by then it didn't matter. Eberstadt's work was done, his Plan was in place, and for the remaining two and a half years of the war it hummed along like a well-oiled engine. The Plan alone, of course, cannot be credited with the production miracle of World War II, but a record quite so miraculous could not have occurred without something very much like it.

## Paying for the War

The Controlled Materials Plan guided the expenditure of several hundred billion dollars (equivalent to several trillion today). The money came from the American public through borrowing, taxes, and sales of treasury bonds to the Federal Reserve, which then authorized the printing of money to pay for the bonds. Planners borrowed in every way they could think of, from sales of high-denomination bonds to institutions and wealthy individuals, to mass sales of "War Bonds" with face values as low as $25. Some war-bond campaigns even urged children to buy special 25-cent savings stamps and paste them into a book that when full could be taken to a bank and exchanged for a bond.

Taxes paid for a little less than half of all military expenditures, and the urgent need for more money gave birth to the modern income-tax system. In 1933, less than 3 percent of the population had been covered by a tax return, either as taxpayers or dependents. Even as late as 1940, only about 7 million Americans made enough money to have to pay any income tax. But in 1942, a 5 percent "Victory Tax" was applied to all annual gross incomes exceeding $624 (equivalent to $9,000 in 2009), and this new law, almost by itself, quadrupled the number of taxpayers for that year. By the end of the war the number had multiplied by a factor of six, to 42 million. Thus, in the space of only 12 years, from 1933 to 1945, the percentage of Americans covered by a tax return (taxpayers and their dependents) grew from less than 3 percent of the population to more than 70 percent.

The most important procedural change came in 1943 with the introduction of the withholding tax. Under this system, which is now familiar to almost everyone with a job, employers deducted taxes from workers' wages on a current basis, then forwarded the money to the Internal Revenue Service. Before 1943, taxes had been sent directly to the IRS by individual taxpayers, either quarterly or annually.

Both the income tax and the idea of War Bonds were marketed to the American people through systematic appeals to their patriotism. At the start of each War Bond drive, numerous magazines would do cover stories urging citizens to buy bonds. Well-known entertainers would go on the radio with barrages of announcements endorsing bond drives and the income tax. Irving Berlin, the composer of "White Christmas" and other popular songs, wrote a tune called "I Paid My Income Tax Today." The Disney studios turned out a cartoon film in which Donald Duck computed his tax bill, marking out standard deductions for his dependent nephews Huey, Louie, and Dewey. The costs of these services were mostly donated—by studios, advertising agencies, publishers, radio networks, and show business personalities.

Throughout the public relations campaign, the new tax system was repeatedly linked to the war effort. Any mention of social programs was omitted. And ever since that time, the American system of taxation has relied on payments of income taxes by millions of individuals, as well as by corporations and other businesses. In most other industrialized countries, a much greater proportion of revenue is collected in the form of indirect value-added taxes computed and paid by firms, and through sales taxes paid by consumers at checkout counters. For the modern American tax system, as in so many other ways, World War II was the most transformative event of the twentieth century.

## Employment and the Growth of the Workforce

For many workers the 1930s and the 1940s were like night and day. The biggest problem of the Great Depression had been joblessness, but World War II brought unprecedented demands for laborers, both in uniform and out. The number of people in the armed forces increased more than thirtyfold between 1939 and 1944. And even though so many workers now wore uniforms, total civilian employment also leaped forward.

Unemployment had reached about 25 percent in 1933 and was still at a depression-level 17.2 percent in 1939. But by 1944 it had dropped to just 1.2 percent. During an interval of only 11 years, therefore, the United States recorded both the worst and best employment numbers in its history. Most people who joined the military services were young men, but the new civilian war workers came from varied demographic groups. The largest single cohort, 3 million, consisted of women aged 21 through 64.

Though these statistics have a cold and lifeless quality on paper, they symbolize staggering social changes in the lives of masses of people. Overall, 16 million men and women served in uniform during the war, 10 million of whom were drafted. The pattern of civilian employment was also transformed. Vast new munitions factories, financed mostly with federal funds, opened their doors. The average workweek in manufacturing rose from 38 hours to more than 45. Defense-related jobs increased from 9 percent of total employment to 40 percent and remained at that level until the year the war ended.

The incidence of personal travel shot upward. Recruits reporting to Army, Navy, and Marine training bases logged millions of miles by car, bus, and especially rail. Sometimes accompanied by their families, servicepeople then traveled to duty stations throughout the country, and continued on to ports of embarkation for trips overseas. At the same time, hordes of young civilians relocated to places with numerous war-related jobs, such as California, Texas, and Michigan. More than a million African Americans moved from southern farms to northern factories. Families of all races moved once, twice, half a dozen times. World War II brought the greatest internal mass migration in American history.

## Decentralized Rationing and Conscription

Meanwhile, retail business was changing fast, as thousands of small companies with no connection to war work closed their doors. Among them were service stations, garages, grocery stores, and appliance dealers. By order of the War Production Board, practically no radio sets were manufactured for civilian use during the war, and the same was true of electric washing machines, shavers, irons, toasters, stoves, mixers, waffle irons, and heating pads. The manufacture of home refrigerators, the most prized of all household appliances, dropped by 99.7 percent between 1941 and 1943. Most significant, no civilian cars were produced, the last one rolling off the assembly line in March 1942. Even the production of pianos stopped, as such companies as Steinway, Baldwin, and Kimball turned to making wooden and aluminum parts for military aircraft.

Many consumer goods were rationed: rubber, gasoline, fuel oil, nylon, work shoes, meat, sugar, coffee, fats, and oils. In an effort to conserve rubber and gasoline further, the government imposed a national speed limit of 35 miles per hour. As a means of saving fabrics for use in uniforms, tents, and parachutes, clothing companies were forbidden to make trousers with cuffs, suits with vests, or full-cut skirts. The War Production Board issued a pledge to "the women and girls of America that there will be no extremes in dress styles during this war . . . and that their present wardrobes will not be made obsolete by radical fashion changes."

The consumer-goods rationing program was run mostly by the Office of Price Administration (OPA), a new agency created to control what otherwise would have become disorderly inflation. In a capitalist economy, the control of inflation in times of ample money but a shortage of goods is impossible so long as markets are allowed to operate unfettered. But OPA and other agencies, through skillful use of their rationing and price-control powers, did a good job of minimizing price increases. These agencies were staffed with some of the country's ablest young economists.

It was absolutely essential that price control and rationing be decentralized. For rationing, the government set up 6,000 community boards across the nation, including at least one for every county in every state. All were staffed with local civic leaders, who promoted compliance by appealing to the patriotism of their neighbors. Each family was allocated so many gallons of gasoline per month, so many pounds of meat, and so much sugar and coffee, according to how many people lived in the household and the kinds of jobs held by the adults. Almost the entire population became familiar with coupons and rationing books, with their perforated stamps and tickets. Had this system been run entirely from Washington, gridlock would have resulted because the government would have been hopelessly ill informed about the needs of people living hundreds or thousands of miles away.

The same was true of the conscription system. To manage conscription, the U.S. Selective Service System relied on thousands of local draft boards to classify men as 1-A (ready to be drafted immediately) through 4-F (not physically fit for military service).

Local rationing and draft boards, therefore, represented pragmatic and extraordinarily effective methods of coordination: between the makers of broad policy at the top and the makers of specific decisions at each level downward through the organization, where the best information existed. Both rationing and the draft resembled Alfred Sloan's multidivisional structure at General Motors, Neil McElroy's brand-management system at Procter & Gamble, the SEC's regulation through private lawyers and accountants, and Ferdinand Eberstadt's Controlled Materials Plan.

Despite all the rationing and the great diversion of resources to the war effort, consumer spending actually increased during World War II. The United States was the only major combatant for which this was true. In Britain, per-capita consumer spending declined in inflation-adjusted terms by 20 percent between 1938 and 1944. In the United States it rose by 22 percent. Meanwhile, the total output of the American economy grew by far more than the 22 percent figure for consumption. Direct comparisons of wartime and peacetime statistics raise apples-and-oranges issues because of the command-economy nature of much wartime production. Nevertheless, the official numbers indicate that Gross National Product, adjusted for inflation, increased by 93 percent between 1939 and 1944. Considering that the United States had by far the largest economy in the world, an increase of this magnitude over so brief a time was just shy of unbelievable.

## Big and Small Business

The situation confronting mobilization managers remained urgent throughout the war, and they chose to rely on companies they knew to be capable of producing in volume. Usually this meant big businesses, which headed the list of the Controlled Materials Plan's prime contractors. At one point the army general in charge of buying munitions said bluntly (and with dubious accuracy), "All the small plants of the country could not turn out one day's requirements of ammunition." Although the national culture had long idealized small entrepreneurial firms, time pressures led planners to award most of the major procurement contracts to large companies. The 55 percent jump in manufacturing employment between 1939 and 1944 took place mainly in big firms. Even Procter & Gamble, a consumer-products company, put 14,000 people to work stuffing powder into artillery shell casings, thereby filling about a quarter of all the shells made in the United States during the war.

This tilt toward reliance on big business turned out to be a thorny political issue. In 1942, a Senate committee reported with alarm that three-fourths of all military procurement contracts had been awarded to only 56 of the nation's 184,000 manufacturing companies. To help finance the operation of "small businesses" (in this case defined as those employing fewer than 500 people), Congress created the Smaller War Plants Corporation, an agency that evolved after the war into the permanent Small Business Administration.

Despite such efforts, the pattern of relying on big business to propel industrial mobilization held firm. About 30 percent of all prime defense contracts went to only 10 companies: 1. General Motors; 2. Curtiss-Wright (aircraft and engines); 3. Ford; 4. Consolidated Vultee (aircraft); 5. Douglas Aircraft; 6. United Aircraft; 7. Bethlehem Steel; 8. Chrysler; 9. General Electric; 10. Lockheed (aircraft).

## Aviation

Five of these top ten contractors were aircraft firms, and still another, Boeing, ranked number 12. Also, as we have seen, General

Motors, Ford, and others produced planes and aircraft engines. The manufacture of airframes, engines, and propellers had suddenly become America's number-one industry measured by value of output, up from number 44 in 1939. Employment in the manufacture of aircraft and related equipment grew from about 80,000 workers in 1940 to 1.3 million in 1943.

The makeup of the workforce changed as well. By 1944, women constituted 40 percent of all workers in airframe plants, and 30 percent in engine and propeller plants. The image of "Rosie the Riveter," an idealized young woman employed in an aircraft factory, was stamped onto the national consciousness through songs, posters, a documentary film, and other publicity. Women were not as well paid as men to do the same work, and after the war many women were forced to relinquish their jobs or otherwise cede some of their gains. But women made a vital contribution to the mobilization effort, and in so doing broke down employment barriers of very long standing.

American production of aircraft was probably the most significant industrial feat of World War II. It surpassed even the Manhattan Project, which brought forth the atomic bomb. Aircraft production was crucial to the prosecution of the war, not only in light of the Allied bombing campaigns against Germany and Japan but also because the amphibious invasions of Europe and the Pacific islands could not even have been attempted without supremacy in the air.

The American achievement in aviation was especially noteworthy because it proceeded almost from a standing start. During the 20 years before 1939, a total of only 13,500 military aircraft had been manufactured in the United States. Yet in May of 1940, President Roosevelt called for the production of 50,000 planes per year. Critics derided his proposal as irresponsible. Charles Lindbergh called it "hysterical chatter." But against this initial background of pessimism, American companies proceeded to turn out the following totals:

1941: 26,000 aircraft
1942: 48,000
1943: 86,000
1944: 96,000
1945: 50,000

U.S. aircraft production easily overwhelmed the combined output of the Axis powers. In Germany, manufacturing peaked in 1944 at 40,000 planes, despite a ferocious effort employing thousands of imprisoned workers from the conquered nations of Europe. Japan's highest figure, 28,000, was also reached in 1944. But most of these German and Japanese planes were small single-engine defensive fighters, whereas a big percentage of the new American aircraft were large, multi-engine bombers and transports. So the dominance was far greater than would appear from the numbers alone.

In every major belligerent nation except the Soviet Union, private companies built the planes—firms such as Vickers in Britain, Messerschmitt in Germany, and Mitsubishi in Japan. Almost all of the funding came either directly or indirectly from the government of each nation. In the United States, 350 new aircraft plants sprang up across the country, large numbers of them in California and Texas. Because the Navy and the Army Air Corps bought the planes, admirals and generals as well as civilian planners had much to say about which designs from which companies would be built in what volume, and by whom. There was even intense inter-firm rivalry. Nonetheless, much cooperation went on, some of it driven by patriotism, some of it forced by government directives. Often planes designed by one firm would be built by other firms as well. And the entire effort of aircraft production benefited mightily from the operation of Ferdinand Eberstadt's Controlled Materials Plan, as it used one of the three controlled materials, aluminum, in immense volumes.

In weight of aircraft produced, the largest single manufacturer was Douglas of California, which employed 17,000 people in 1940 and 154,000 by 1943. A young MIT engineer named Donald Douglas (1892–1981) had founded this company in 1921. In

Douglas Aircraft's early years, the 1920s and 1930s, its production of planes grew slowly, then began to follow the irregular pattern that has since typified the industry as a whole. In 1939, before the war, Douglas built 314 planes. In 1944, at the height of production, it turned out close to 12,000. In 1946, right after the war ended, it sold 127 planes. Soon production recovered slightly, but it continued to fluctuate as demand for both civilian and military aircraft varied wildly from year to year.

From a business viewpoint, these production numbers seem surreal. The task of managing any kind of company with such uneven sales raises almost insuperable problems in finance, personnel, production, and marketing. Donald Douglas was a competent manager, but like most other aviation pioneers, he was better at running an entrepreneurial startup than a big business over the long term.

During the 1960s Douglas's market share was overtaken by Boeing, largely because of Donald Douglas's early reluctance to develop jet airliners. In 1967 Douglas Aircraft was absorbed in the merger that produced McDonnell-Douglas. This new company became the largest defense contractor in the United States. In 1997, as the end of the Cold War reduced the demand for its products, McDonnell-Douglas itself was acquired by Boeing.

## Boeing Airplane

The company founded by William Boeing in 1916 was the biggest winner in America's postwar aircraft sweepstakes. Bill Boeing was the son of immigrant parents from Germany and Austria. He grew up in Michigan, attended Yale, and first went to the state of Washington in search of additional resources for his father's timber company. During World War I he formed Pacific Aero Products Company, the forerunner of Boeing Airplane.

Boeing specialized in seaplanes and was known in the industry as an engineering firm adept at constructing large aircraft. It had some success during the 1920s, then, in 1929, through a series of mergers, it became part of the United Aircraft and Transportation Company. This firm represented a financier-led attempt to consolidate different parts of the industry, including passenger traffic. But like several other big industrial mergers of the late 1920s, United Aircraft did not hold together for long, and Boeing reverted to being an independent firm. Nonetheless, the merger had made Bill Boeing and other entrepreneurs immediate millionaires.

After the onset of the Great Depression, Congress began investigating business frauds in several industries, including securities and aviation. When Bill Boeing was called to the capitol to testify, he became very angry and responded by selling all his holdings in the company and withdrawing from any further role in it. Thereafter Boeing Airplane was run primarily by Philip Johnson (1894–1944), an engineer who had been recruited when he was a student at the University of Washington.

When war began in Europe in 1939, the company stood on the edge of bankruptcy. Of the first 6,000 planes ordered by the American military, Boeing received orders for only 255 tiny trainers plus 38 bombers, with a government option for an additional 42—not an auspicious start. But the bomber in question, called the B-17, turned out to be one of the most effective weapons of the war on either side. As soon as military planners realized what a jewel it was, orders poured in. Phil Johnson, as chief executive, began a frantic scramble to build more and more B-17s—first in the hundreds, then in the thousands. Employment at Boeing's Seattle factories climbed from 1,800 in 1938 to 45,000 by 1945.

By that time, the B-17 had become famous all over the world under its nickname, the Flying Fortress. In all, Boeing and other companies produced 13,000 B-17s. From 1942 to 1945, these planes flew thousands of bombing missions over Germany. Bristling with guns, they shot down two of every three German fighter aircraft lost on the Western Front. B-17s suffered heavy casualties themselves, at a rate exceeded in the U.S. military only by the Navy's submarine service. About a third of all Flying Fortresses in the European war were put out of commission by enemy fire.

By 1942, Boeing was well into the development of an even bigger plane, which turned out to be the most complicated product ever manufactured up to that time: the B-29 Superfortress. By the end of the war, Boeing-designed bombers had delivered nearly half of all the tonnage dropped by the Air Corps in Europe, and more than 99 percent of the payload in Japan. Most of the bombs dropped on Japan were carried by B-29s, including the firebombs that devastated Tokyo and the atomic bombs dropped on Hiroshima and Nagasaki.

The B-29 Superfortress was an enormous aircraft, three times the weight of the B-17. Designed specifically as a long-range bomber, it could fly almost 6,000 miles without refueling. By mid-1945, almost 4,000 B-29s had been built. When the war ended in August 1945, an additional 5,000 were still on order, because American planners had expected the conflict in the Pacific to continue until 1947. Most of those planes on order were never produced.

In 1944, CEO Phil Johnson suddenly died, and the direction of the company fell to William Allen (1900–1985), who had been Boeing's principal legal counsel. Allen's most daunting postwar challenge was simply to keep the company alive. Many other high-tech firms were sliding downhill—laying off workers, closing plants, and losing design engineers. But Allen managed to hold together the firm's superb engineering and production team, partly by redesigning Boeing's bombers as passenger aircraft.

Meanwhile, the demands of the Cold War prompted planners at the Pentagon to rethink the nation's strategy for air warfare. The result, in the late 1940s and early 1950s, was the commissioning of a series of medium-sized to very large jet bombers. Boeing, consistently looking ahead, won the competition for the government contracts to build most of these planes, and began to produce a series of ultra-modern swept-wing bombers.

Beginning in 1947, more than 1,300 B-47 Stratojets rolled off the line. Then, in 1952, came the company's eight-engine B-52 Stratofortress. Like the B-47, the B-52 was designed to carry either conventional or nuclear weapons, and it became the backbone of the Strategic Air Command. (The B-52 is the plane featured in *Dr. Strangelove*, a Hollywood spoof of the Cold War widely regarded as one of the greatest films ever made.) In all, Boeing delivered to the Air Force about 750 B-52s, and they played an important role not only in the Strategic Air Command but also during the Vietnam War, the Gulf War of 1991, and the NATO campaigns in Yugoslavia in 1999 and Afghanistan in the twenty-first century. No new B-52s had been built for several decades, but many had been modified to fly longer distances, launch cruise missiles, and minimize their detection by radar.

Overall, the technological advances that accompanied successive moves in design and production from the B-17 to the B-29 to the B-47 to the B-52—all in just over a decade—were remarkable. The B-52 weighed 12 times as much as the B-17. It could fly more than twice as fast and three times as far. These increased capabilities required a series of scientific and engineering breakthroughs not only in aviation but also in metallurgy and electronics.

Unlike innovations in some defense-related industries, much of this new technology was transferable to the civilian market. Boeing adapted well, far better than its two main competitors, Douglas and Lockheed. In 1954 Boeing launched its four-engine 707 passenger jet, which quickly became the workhorse of commercial airlines throughout the world. Still newer models rolled out in regular succession: in 1963 came the 727; in 1967 the 737, which in modified form is still a big seller; in 1969 the 747 (an immense four-engine plane, 50 percent heavier than the B-52); in 1982 the more fuel-efficient 757 and 767; in 1997 the 777, the most sophisticated airliner ever built up to that time; and in 2008 the 787, an extremely light, fuel-efficient "Dreamliner"—the first commercial plane with a "composite" as opposed to a metal structure—with passenger capacity of about 250. As early as the 1980s, Boeing had taken its place among America's leading exporters, in some years ranking number one.

## Ups and Downs

Despite Boeing's great success, its experience during the decades after World War II was anything but smooth. The aircraft business has always been cyclical, even without the wild distortions from wartime to peacetime production. Modern airplanes represent very large capital investments, and because the planes are so durable, airline companies can easily postpone new purchases, buying replacement parts as necessary to keep a plane in service for decades. Therefore, the history of the industry has been plagued by fluctuating demand, frequent cash-flow crises, and canceled or postponed orders for new planes. That is why Douglas, Lockheed, and other great companies exited the civilian market to concentrate on federally-funded defense and aerospace projects.

In the late 1960s, Boeing itself approached financial disaster because of uneven orders for the 747. In 1970, management slashed the company's workforce from 105,000 to 38,000. Since then, employment has trended upward (in 2008 it was about 150,000), mainly through augmented defense business, which the company began to emphasize in 2002. Its main military aircraft have been the huge C-17 Globemaster III transport, the Apache helicopter, and the F/A-18 and F-15 fighter jets. In addition, Boeing has produced missiles and communication satellites and has participated in both the International Space Station and—with its principal competitor Lockheed—the U.S. Space Shuttle programs. Its overall sales are divided about equally between civilian and government buyers, and it is the largest and most sophisticated aerospace company in the world.

In the international market for big airliners, Boeing's only serious rival has been Airbus Industrie, a consortium supported by public funds from several countries in the European Union. In some years Boeing sells more planes worldwide, and in other years Airbus. Competition between the two has been fierce and acrimonious. When Boeing has objected to public subsidies for its European rival, Airbus has responded by pointing out that Boeing, as America's number-two defense contractor, receives very substantial, if indirect, help from its home government.

## Postscript: The Scourge of Scandal

Without a doubt, defense procurement has helped Boeing, but in all countries this kind of business contains many seeds of corruption. Because the U.S. defense budget is so immense—now exceeding those of the next ten countries combined—those seeds that sprout yield particularly poisonous fruit. Not long after President Eisenhower left office in 1961, his fears about the undue influence of a "military-industrial complex" came true, as an apparently permanent feature of the national landscape.

Scandals involving the awarding of government contracts to defense companies became routine, and sometimes spun out of control altogether. Between 1986 and 1989, following a huge defense buildup by the Reagan administration, the FBI launched a secret probe of weapons procurement that included fraud, bribery, and illegal campaign contributions. This inquiry, called Operation Ill Wind, resulted in the convictions of twelve Navy and Air Force procurement officers and more than sixty private citizens working for defense contractors. Almost all of the nation's top defense corporations were implicated—Boeing, Lockheed, Northrop, Unisys, and many others. Collectively they paid hundreds of millions of dollars in fines. In 1988, Congress passed the Procurement Integrity Act, which slowed the rate of scandals for a time. Over the next several years, the most frequently fined company was General Electric. And after the start of the Iraq War in 2003, the questionable actions of Halliburton—a construction and oil-well equipment and services giant—were so numerous as to become routine news stories. Boeing itself became involved in a series of nightmarish scandals. Within the brief period 2003–05, these scandals caused the dismissal of two of its CEOs, the imprisonment of two other high-ranking executives, and payment of fines totalling $615 million.

In the broader sense, the interpenetration of all the major players in national defense procurement—the "revolving door" of retired military officers, civilian officials, defense contractors, lobbyists, and political candidates—had become a commonplace of public life in the United States. In the long sweep of American history, this was a major departure from tradition. Procurement scandals have cropped up during all wars, but the difference now was their magnitude and their uninterrupted routine even in peacetime. So much money was involved that scandals became an integral part of "Pentagon Capitalism," a phenomenon that derived from the momentum necessary to win World War II and the Cold War (1946–89). But neither the government nor ordinary citizens have shown the will to stop this momentum.

Despite many exceptions, the nation's nonmilitaristic tradition had remained dominant until World War II and the Cold War. Since then, so many members of Congress have become caught up in securing lucrative defense contracts for their home states and districts, not to mention campaign contributions for re-election, that the legislative branch has failed to check the excesses of the executive branch as the Founders intended. Instead, the legislature has become a codependent enabler of the executive, itself a big part of the problem. Meanwhile, the business system has been complicit—deeply complicit. But the core of the problem is political, so, as always, it is necessary for the government to reform itself and play catch-up.

# CHAPTER FOUR

# Science and R&D: Color TV, Chemicals, and Pharmaceuticals Strengthen Postwar Prosperity

## Economic Background

After the mobilizations and sacrifices of World War II, the United States entered a long period marked by three major historical developments: a civil rights revolution, an unbroken 28-year run of ever-rising prosperity, and a seemingly permanent Cold War with the Soviet Union. Throughout the struggle for civil rights and the conflict with the Soviet Union the business world provided one other constant: a relentless rise of new industries, most notably consumer electronics, chemicals, and pharmaceuticals. Underlying the success of these industries was their powerful commitment to research and development (R&D).

From the beginning of World War II until 1973, real per-capita Gross National Product grew at the very healthy compound annual rate of 3 percent. By comparison, the rate from 1890 until World War II had been only 1.2 percent; from 1973 to 2009 it was a little over 2 percent. These apparently small differences have big long-run consequences. At a compound rate of 3 percent, per-capita income will double in 24 years, whereas at 2 percent it will double in 36 years, and at 1 percent in 72 years.

A few national economies recorded even faster postwar growth rates, but on the whole the American business system outperformed all others. From the end of the war until the 1960s, output per hour worked in the United States remained more than twice that of most other industrialized nations, and many times that of developing countries. With about one-sixteenth of the world's population, the United States accounted for two-fifths of its gross production of goods and services.

Nearly every index showed a positive trend. About 40 percent of American families had owned their homes in the decades before World War II, but this number grew to 62 percent by 1970. Thus a key aspect of the "American Dream" had now come true for most of the nation's people. About 2.4 million war veterans received low-cost home loans financed through the Veterans Administration. In education, eight million former servicemen went back to school on the G.I. Bill, which provided funds for education and training. Of these, 2.3 million attended college, vastly swelling the ranks of undergraduates and further democratizing higher education. In 1947, half of the students entering American colleges were receiving support under the G.I. Bill.

New prospects for employment and family relocations near military bases during World War II caused masses of people to move into what became known as the Sunbelt. After the war, the widespread installation of air conditioning gave the region a second great boost, and the resulting shift in population worked profound changes in the social and political life of the nation. Whereas in 1940 only one American in nine had lived in what are now the three most populous states of the Sunbelt—Texas, Florida, and California (most of which lies in the Sunbelt)—one in four did by 1995.

During the 1960s, after a hundred years of net out-migration, the entire South (defined as the states of the 1861–65 Confederacy) began to attract new residents, a phenomenon that likely would not have occurred without the development of air conditioning. The population of Florida expanded so fast that by the 1990s the state ranked fourth in the nation, up from twenty-fifth in 1940. While the population of the country as a whole approximately doubled between 1940 and 2008,

Florida's jumped by a factor of ten, from fewer than 2 million to almost 20 million.

The advent of jet airliners facilitated travel to the Sunbelt by hordes of tourists, as did the new Interstate Highway System. This costly project was justified in part by a Cold War rationale. Its initial name, "Interstate and Defense," reflected the idea that another war mobilization would require a better infrastructure. The 300,000 miles of federal highways in 1945 grew to 895,000 by 1970. Much of the new construction was of four-lane, six-lane, and even eight-lane "freeways" paved in expensive concrete—the best highway system in the world.

Robust growth of the American economy was mirrored in almost every aspect of business. The end of the wartime freeze on the sale of consumer durables, together with an unprecedented new level of purchasing power, led to the release of what was called "pent-up demand." Shopping centers sprang up across the country, and retail sales multiplied. People bought tens of millions of new cars, TV sets, stereos, and air conditioners. The aggregate power of consumers took another step forward, and advertisers trumpeted the "American Way of Life" as something akin to an ideal existence.

## Social Trends

As the U.S. birth rate soared, the "baby boom" generation born between 1945 and 1960 shaped and was shaped by the civil rights movement and the feminist movement. "Boomers" showed a greater willingness to question authority than any generation before them. Consequently, many of the institutions that had long held society together—family, school, business, and government—came under deep scrutiny in campaigns led mostly by boomers. Business and government in particular were portrayed as repositories of wrongdoing and bad faith. Because of their long involvement in suppressing the rights of women, African Americans, and others, the indictment against them had more than a little plausibility.

For many boomers, hopes for change soon soured into a stark pessimism. In the 1960s, a wave of political assassinations deprived the civil rights movement of three of its most prominent leaders—Medgar Evers (1963), Malcolm X (1965), and Martin Luther King, Jr. (1968), as well as President John F. Kennedy (1963) and his brother, Senator Robert F. Kennedy (1968). In the 1970s, after U.S. government officials were shown to have lied about casualty rates in the Vietnam War (1963–75) and crimes committed at the direction of President Richard M. Nixon during the Watergate crisis (1973–74), many Americans became disenchanted with politics. Patriotism and national pride began to decline. Most people coming of age during this period found it hard to embrace their parents' notion that the United States was a wondrous and blessed place to live. Instead, an informed cynicism appeared to be the only sensible attitude.

In the face of these social changes, two conditions of overarching importance remained constant, as noted: (1) continuing economic prosperity, exemplified by an outpouring of consumer goods and the international primacy of American business; and (2) the Cold War between the United States and the Soviet Union. During the 1950s and 1960s, both nations, the world's only two "superpowers" in the wake of World War II, amassed nuclear arsenals capable of destroying the world. They approached the brink of nuclear catastrophe during the Cuban Missile Crisis of 1962.

Sometimes the Cold War became hot, as in the Soviet suppression of liberation movements in Hungary (1956) and Czechoslovakia (1968), and in the American actions during the Korean War (1950–53) and the war in Vietnam (1963–75). Those last two "limited" wars symbolically pitted the "free world" against communism, and cost the lives of about 3 million Asians and more than 100,000 Americans.

During more than four decades of Cold War (1946–89), the perception that the United States needed to maintain a giant military establishment placed heavy demands on the business system to produce great quantities of high-quality weapons. The three-way alliance of government, higher education, and business that had emerged during World War II now became entrenched. This alliance changed the internal policies of many universities and high-tech companies, and its emphasis on R&D reshaped the structure of American science and engineering.

## R&D and the Cold War

Throughout the Cold War, the most prosperous sectors of the economy besides basic consumer goods and new home construction were high-tech industries—particularly aircraft and guided missiles, electronics, and chemicals and pharmaceuticals. These three industries had obvious military relevance, a fact that confronted public officials and business executives with some hard choices. Federal administrators in charge of science policy had to decide how much expenditure on R&D would be necessary for the United States to "stay ahead" of the Soviet Union. In addition, they had to determine whether "fundamental" research—that is, work not directly connected to product development—should be conducted only in universities or in corporate research labs as well.

During most of the postwar era, it seemed essential to do fundamental research in both places. Ample federal funding was possible because of national economic prosperity, and the allocation of this money to research appeared necessary because of the ongoing struggle with the Soviet Union. Consequently, the government channeled stupendous sums to both universities and corporations. During the three postwar decades, federal funds underwrote about 70 percent of all R&D done in electronics; and of federally sponsored industrial research as a whole, 80 percent concerned military applications. In 1950, when the Korean War broke out, about 15,000 military-related research projects of all kinds were underway. By the early 1960s, this number had grown to 80,000.

It was clear that some of the nation's best research talent was gravitating toward military rather than commercial work. Many scientists and engineers preferred to devote their careers to defense-related R&D, and the government furnished the funds for companies and universities to pay them well. For better or worse, in the minds of many scientists and engineers it was more exciting to try to develop a hydrogen bomb or land a person on the moon than to invent or improve some everyday consumer product.

The nation's emphasis on military-related projects hurt the commercial divisions of some science-based companies only slightly, those of others much more seriously. Into this second category fell much of the consumer-electronics industry. Over the course of the twentieth century, its story is one of impressive and long-running success, followed by a drift into a series of distractions at the expense of discovering and responding to what consumers wanted.

## Television and David Sarnoff

Until the 1970s, U.S. firms led the world in consumer electronics. American companies brought forth a steady output of affordable radios, phonographs, and TV sets. Experts everywhere assumed that American companies would remain on top for a long time, and likely forever. But those firms lost more than just their primacy. After having gone almost unchallenged before the 1960s, they fell behind their European and Japanese competitors during the 1970s and 1980s, and succumbed altogether by the 1990s.

Both the rise and fall of the consumer electronics industry are reflected in the story of the Radio Corporation of America (RCA) and its charismatic leader David Sarnoff (1891–1971). The story suggests how intimately the American government was involved in science-based business throughout the century—as protector, promoter, regulator, and military customer. It also shows, in vivid detail, the perils of too much management centralization in the hands of one person.

In the spring of 1945, just returned from Army service, David Sarnoff gathered his top managers together and told them that "RCA has one priority: television. Whatever resources are needed will be provided." He intended that RCA be the leader in television sets, tubes, transmitters, components, and R&D. "There's a vast market out there, and we're going to capture it before anyone else."

RCA had begun its TV research in the 1920s. Then, during the depression of the 1930s, when most companies reduced discretionary spending as much as possible, Sarnoff stepped up RCA's efforts. By 1936 the firm had built a series of TV relay stations between a transmitter atop the Empire State Building in New York City and its research labs in Camden, New Jersey. In

1939, Sarnoff showcased RCA's progress with TV at the World's Fair in New York. His demonstration came off well, and an RCA subsidiary began to fill eight to twelve hours of airtime per week with televised baseball games, boxing matches, plays, and variety shows. RCA put its sets on the market at prices ranging from $395 to $675 — the equivalent of $6,000 to $10,000 in 2009.

These efforts to develop television during the 1930s proved to be premature. The average annual per-capita income in 1939 was less than $700, and very few families could afford to buy a TV set. But the fundamental problem went much deeper. TV was a *systems* innovation. It required a regular schedule of programming, mass sales of sets, industrywide standards for broadcasting and equipment, and facilities for repairing and adjusting the many things that could go wrong with home TV reception. These systems did not yet exist, and the times were not propitious for their quick development. Government regulators, seeing how fast the technology was changing, delayed until mid-1941 the setting of standards for the industry. In December of that year the United States entered World War II, and in April 1942 the government banned further commercial development of television. David Sarnoff and RCA would have to wait.

## Sarnoff's Talents

In 1975, *Fortune* inaugurated a "Hall of Fame for Business Leadership." The magazine selected 15 charter inductees, including John D. Rockefeller, Andrew Carnegie, J. P. Morgan, Henry Ford, Alfred Sloan, and ten others. One of these ten was David Sarnoff, who, as head of RCA for nearly forty years, did more than any other person to bring radio and television into the American home.

Sarnoff had risen from the deep poverty of a Jewish village in Russia. In 1895, when David was four years old, his father emigrated to New York, temporarily leaving the family behind. A few years later, once they reassembled in a $10-per-month slum tenement on New York's Lower East Side, young David went to work to help support the family. He sold Yiddish newspapers for a penny a copy and earned $1.50 per week singing as a boy soprano at a synagogue. Meanwhile, he received instruction in English, which he learned to speak with eloquence and without a foreign accent.

David dropped out of school after the eighth grade because of his family's continuing need for money. He found a messenger's job at the American Marconi Company, a subsidiary of the English firm set up by Guglielmo Marconi, the young Italian inventor of wireless telegraphy. Sarnoff soon became one of the firm's quickest "fists" at the telegraph key, and he rose rapidly within the organization. He later made it a point to shepherd Marconi around New York during the inventor's frequent visits, and the two became good friends.

At the age of 20, Sarnoff took over the Marconi station at Wanamaker's Department Store in New York, a radio facility set up to attract curious shoppers. Not long afterward, on an April night in 1912, the *Titanic* struck an iceberg in the North Atlantic and began to sink. Suddenly the air was filled with signals sent out from the sinking ship, from rescue vessels, and from amateur radio operators up and down the East Coast. The moment Sarnoff heard the news about the *Titanic*, he rushed to Wanamaker's, where he stayed at his radio for 72 hours. He was not able to accomplish much, but a story soon arose portraying a heroic young David picking up the S.O.S., making order out of the chaos of signals, and passing along critical information about who had died and who had survived.

However misleading the legend, which was concocted by Sarnoff himself and retold in many future magazine profiles, the *Titanic* disaster "brought radio to the front, and incidentally me." Congress passed a law requiring large passenger ships to install wireless communications. The business of American Marconi grew rapidly, and the company gave its young operator new responsibilities and a big pay raise. Only a few years later, barely out of his teens, Sarnoff began to transform himself into the business dandy he would remain for the rest of his life. Five feet seven with a round baby face, he wore tailored suits, a Homburg hat, and carried a walking stick.

By the time Sarnoff was 30, he had already worked in electronics for 14 years. In a 1928 speech at the Harvard Business

School, he described the role of a new kind of executive, one able to develop high-tech products and bring them to market. This new-model manager, like Sarnoff himself, would have a personal understanding of technology, a good idea of where both it and market forces were headed, and an ability to meld the two for business planning.

## The Birth of Broadcasting

Sarnoff's life coincided almost exactly with the development of radio and television. He knew every important person in the industry from Marconi onward. He often commented that he was lucky to have been born at just the right time and to have decided in his youth to "hitch my wagon to the electron."

In his early years, radio's primary role was expected to be "point-to-point" transmission, as in ship-to-ship and ship-to-shore telegraph. As the young Sarnoff sent and received these signals on behalf of American Marconi, he began to speculate that the industry's real future lay in "point-to-mass" communication, or what came to be called broadcasting. A memorandum he sent to his Marconi superiors, dated 1915, anticipated modern radio operations:

The idea is to bring music into the house by wireless . . . all the receivers attuned to the transmitting wave length should be capable of receiving such music. The receiver can be designed in the form of a simple "Radio Music Box" and arranged for several different wave lengths, which should be changeable . . . [and] supplied with amplifying tubes and a loudspeaking telephone, all of which can be neatly mounted in one box. The box can be placed on a table in the parlor or living room, the switch set accordingly, and the transmitted music received.

Sarnoff's Radio Music Box memo received little attention, mainly because the Marconi firm was so busy with defense work that it couldn't handle much else. But throughout World War I (1914–18), the radio industry was propelled forward by the urgent communication needs of armies and navies on both sides of the battle lines. Throughout Europe and in the labs of American companies such as American Telephone & Telegraph (AT&T), Westinghouse, and General Electric (GE), radio research was pursued vigorously. Because American Marconi was a foreign-owned corporation, after the war the Navy asked GE, the leading domestic electrical manufacturer, to help set up a U.S. company that could take charge of wireless communication for both business and government. That new company became RCA. The Navy contributed its own array of electronics patents to be combined with those of GE and other firms, to create for RCA a workable pool of inventions. These in turn formed the basis for future R&D in all areas of electronics.

In 1919, after prolonged negotiations, the Marconi company withdrew from the field, selling its stock for $3.5 million—the equivalent of $49 million in 2009—to the consortium of American firms (mostly GE and Westinghouse) that owned the new RCA. David Sarnoff, then in his late twenties, became one of RCA's key executives as soon as it was formed, and shortly thereafter its general manager.

During the months of deal-making that led to the creation of RCA, a Westinghouse engineer operating from his house in Pittsburgh had begun as a hobby to send out radio signals of recorded music. Soon he began receiving letters from enthusiasts who picked up the signals on their home-made "crystal sets," as early radios were called. A Westinghouse executive, sensing the market potential, asked the Department of Commerce for a license to broadcast. Thus in 1920 was born KDKA of Pittsburgh, America's first commercial station. Suddenly electronics executives in several companies realized that a rich new market might now be exploited with only a small investment.

Sarnoff viewed the emergence of KDKA with some unease. Still, he saw that Westinghouse's initiative had not yet foreclosed the opportunity for RCA and its chief parent, General Electric, to dominate the industry. Radio, like television later on, required several elements to make it commercially viable. These included sets to receive signals, a distribution structure to market the sets, stations to broadcast programs, and a reliable source of funds to produce programs. None of the elements were yet in place. So Sarnoff dusted off his Radio Music Box memo and sent it to the headquarters of GE, where it was now taken quite seriously.

Sarnoff then began to organize the first radio network, which was to be a subsidiary of RCA. Here he ran into a serious dispute with AT&T, which had started to put together its own system of stations. But AT&T, as the existing telephone monopoly, was in a disadvantageous political position, and in 1926 an arbitrator worked out a resolution along lines favorable to RCA. Under his ruling the ownership of a new firm called the National Broadcasting Company (NBC) would be divided among RCA (50 percent), GE (30 percent), and Westinghouse (20 percent). AT&T would exit broadcasting, and its affiliated stations would go to RCA and be networked under the name NBC Red. RCA's existing stations, together with those of Westinghouse and GE, would become NBC Blue. All of the new affiliates would tap a central feed in New York, then use telephone lines leased from AT&T to carry signals to distant stations from which they could be broadcast over local airwaves. (In 1941, at the request of the U.S. government, RCA divested NBC Blue, which then became the basis for ABC, the American Broadcasting Company. NBC Red became simply NBC.)

In the mid-1920s a competing network, the Columbia Broadcasting System (CBS), had been organized under the leadership of a young entrepreneur named Bill Paley, and the number of radio stations began to increase rapidly. The country had only one station in 1921, but 2,800 by 1950. By 1990, boosted by the rapid spread of FM stations, the total reached 9,400.

## RCA's Continuous Rise

David Sarnoff proved especially adept at absorbing insights from wars and other major events. The lesson he took from World War I was that a central authority—in this case the U.S. Navy—could impose order on a chaotic new industry. By asserting its power and helping to get the required legislation, the Navy had been able to allocate radio frequencies, sponsor R&D, and sort out conflicting claims of inventors.

But, given America's nonstatist traditions, it seemed inappropriate for the government to assume complete charge of radio, as happened in many other countries. Somehow, a nongovernmental organization would have to take over the Navy's role in radio after the end of World War I. It was largely for this purpose that RCA had been organized. Its selection as inheritor of the Navy's technology typified the flexibility of business-government relations that had been evident throughout American history. The arrangement took what had been a government monopoly and lodged it in the hands of a new company owned by a consortium of private firms that otherwise would have competed with each other.

During the 1920s the potential for great profits attracted hundreds of companies and entrepreneurs to radio, as always happens with major innovations, like automobiles in the 1900s and the Internet in the 1990s. Radio sets at first sold for prices ranging from $25 to $500 (roughly $300 to $6,000 in 2009). By 1923 more than 200 manufacturers of radio sets and 5,000 makers of components had entered the market. From 1923 to 1934, more than a thousand additional companies began to manufacture sets, but 90 percent of them failed or were absorbed by competitors. For its part, RCA marketed sets, parts, and vacuum tubes, all of which were manufactured by its parent GE.

RCA had been created in part to manage communications from ship to shore and from American stations to those overseas. Its other function was to sell radio equipment made by GE. By the mid-1920s, however, it was encountering a whirlwind of other business problems, all of which had to be managed simultaneously. Sarnoff found himself under intense pressure. Competitors were unhappy with RCA's exclusive pool of electronics patents from its parent companies and the Navy. Federal regulators believed that RCA was trying to monopolize the electronics industry. And certain executives at GE regarded RCA as an uppity child and Sarnoff himself as a brazen young Jew encroaching on what had long been a preserve of white Anglo-Saxon Protestants. Sarnoff's salvation came from his own obvious talents and the patronage of Owen D. Young, the officer of General Electric who had selected him to be RCA's general manager back in 1921. Young was also a nationally prominent lawyer whose name was often mentioned as a potential presidential candidate.

It was testament to Sarnoff's abilities that he managed this situation with such resourcefulness that both he and RCA came out on top. He solved the maelstrom of problems by taking three strategic steps:

1. He brought order to the broadcasting side of the business by organizing NBC, the first network.

2. On the manufacturing side, he worked out a plan not to fight those who infringed RCA's patents but instead to license these patents to all comers on a non-exclusive basis. This would remove the temptation to infringe in the first place, and at the same time provide RCA with an income stream from royalties. From the mid-1920s until the patents began to expire (and new ones came along regularly), almost all American radios were manufactured under RCA licenses. Sarnoff plowed much of the royalty income back into R&D.

3. The third strategic step was achieving independence from RCA's corporate owners. Throughout the 1920s, Sarnoff became more convinced that RCA must break free so that it could act faster in the face of changing technology. As he said years later, "We were submerged under too many layers of electrical company management."

He could never have detached RCA from its parents by himself, but at just the right moment he received decisive assistance from the government. In 1930, the Antitrust Division of the Justice Department brought a lawsuit against RCA, General Electric, Westinghouse, and AT&T. The suit charged that the original patent pool, plus the crosslicensing agreements, leased telephone lines, and other arrangements were illegal under the Sherman Antitrust Act. In November 1932, the defendant companies, guided by Sarnoff, submitted a proposal that became the basis for a consent decree granted by the government—just one week before the antitrust trial was scheduled to begin.

Under the terms of this decree, RCA would become independent and could begin to make its own tubes and radios. GE and Westinghouse would pledge not to compete in radio manufacturing for two and a half years, after which they could produce sets under license from RCA. In the meantime, they would distribute their entire holdings of RCA common stock to their own share-holders. They would have no representation on RCA's board, and RCA itself would retain control of the crucial patent pool.

These terms were just what Sarnoff wanted. In this case as in earlier (and later) ones, he showed himself a master at winning from the government conditions favorable to his company. He had long spoken of the need for "unification" of the electronics indus-try, and now he had the proper instrument—an unfettered RCA. In 1933 he moved the firm's New York headquarters to Rockefeller Center, which had just been built in the city block surrounded by 49th and 50th Streets and Fifth and Sixth Avenues. He then set up a plush office on the 53rd floor of the newly christened RCA Build-ing. The company, after having lost money during the two worst years of the Great Depression, in 1934 earned $4.2 million on sales of $79 million (about $68 million profits on $1.3 billion sales in 2009 equivalents). Sarnoff then began in earnest to promote televi-sion research. RCA had reached the verge of success when World War II intervened and forced a temporary moratorium.

## Television Flourishes

During World War II, Sarnoff spent most of his time in London, serving as General Dwight D. Eisenhower's adviser on commu-nications in connection with the invasion of Europe. When the war ended in 1945, the government lifted its restraints on com-mercial TV, and Sarnoff resumed his all-out campaign. In 1946 RCA sold 10,000 TV sets. In 1947 it sold 200,000, four-fifths of the U.S. total. Fifteen television stations were operating by this time, some owned by large electronics companies, others independent. Nearly all stations used RCA cameras and equip-ment. NBC was broadcasting from New York and building new stations in Cleveland, Chicago, and Los Angeles. Most consum-ers at this time found it necessary to erect outdoor antennas atop their roofs in order to get reasonably good reception, and even then sets could pick up only three or four stations. Further prog-ress seemed slow at the time, but once TV broadcasting gained a foothold, it grew quickly:

| Year | Number of U.S. Stations | Percentage of Households Served |
|------|------------------------|--------------------------------|
| 1940 | None | None |
| 1950 | 100 | 9% |
| 1960 | 580 | 83% |
| 1970 | 680 | 95% |

During most of the post–World War II period, sales of electronics products grew twice as fast as GNP, but the primary reason was not the emergence of television. Instead it was the intensification of the Cold War. Whereas products developed and manufactured for the military accounted for less than 20 percent of electronics-industry revenues in 1950, by 1970 the number reached almost 50 percent. Military planners continuously pushed the frontiers of R&D in order to maintain a technological edge over the Soviet Union. Many companies vied for well-paying defense contracts, but much of the work was so complex that only leading firms such as RCA, GE, and Raytheon could meet the stringent requirements.

David Sarnoff was himself an ardent cold warrior. He missed few opportunities to excoriate communism, which he associated with pre-industrial life. During the 1950s he proposed that RCA donate millions of tiny phonographs to be parachuted into the Soviet Union, along with recordings in Russian narrating the wonders of capitalism. The proposal was rejected by the government, but it exemplified Sarnoff's identification of RCA and himself with America's Cold War crusade.

## Color TV

Television images originally were produced only in black-and-white tones, but Sarnoff had long known that it was possible to broadcast in color, and his commitment to this goal came to border on monomania. When RCA resumed work on color TV after World War II, it found the technological problems of its all-electronic system daunting. Throughout the 1940s, RCA's rival CBS had been experimenting with a partly electronic technology that filtered transmission signals through a mechanical spinning disk inside the

TV set so as to produce a color image. The RCA team regarded this method as archaic, and it was stunned when the Federal Communications Commission (FCC) in 1950 accepted the CBS system as the industry standard.

RCA appealed this decision in federal court, but in the meantime it was rescued by external events. As World War II had done in the 1940s, the Korean War focused the electronics industry on defense needs. The National Production Authority, a mobilization agency, invoked a ban on the manufacture of color TV sets that held until 1953. In that year, after renewed hearings, the FCC approved new standards based on the all-electronic RCA system.

Having won the acrimonious battle of the standards, Sarnoff expected a surge in the mass production and marketing of color sets. Wall Street agreed, and the price of RCA common stock quickly rose by 44 percent. As it turned out, almost everyone was too optimistic. Like radio and black-and-white TV before it, color television was a systems technology. Getting it into operation was not just a matter of tooling up to manufacture and sell color sets—color broadcasts had to be planned, color cameras installed, transmission facilities upgraded, and legions of repair technicians trained. In the end, it took the industry about 15 years to move from black-and-white to color broadcasting.

RCA began volume production of color sets in 1954, offering a model with a 12 1/2-inch screen at a price of $1,000 (equivalent to about $7,800 in 2009). In the mid-1950s, 21-inch black-and-white sets were selling for less than $300. Meanwhile, production difficulties with the color picture tube, the most complicated consumer good ever manufactured up to that time, resulted in a rejection rate of about two-thirds during factory inspections. Sarnoff had predicted sales of 75,000 color sets in 1954, 350,000 in 1955, and 5 million in 1958. In fact, few sets were sold at all in 1954 and only 5,000 in 1955.

The price of a color TV was simply too high for the quality of the pictures home viewers saw on their screens. Sets were very hard to tune. Colors bled together, especially for programs not broadcast live. Despite Sarnoff's claims about the "compatibility" of RCA color receivers, pictures broadcast in black-and-white appeared fuzzy on color sets. In 1956, *Time* pronounced color TV the year's "most resounding industrial flop," and quoted RCA's competitors as saying that the introduction had been premature. For Zenith, Westinghouse, and other companies, a strategic retreat was the obvious course. For RCA, however, the road was less clear, and Sarnoff faced what he later called "the toughest battle of my life."

In an unusual step, RCA's board of directors in 1956 gave its 65-year-old chief executive a new ten-year contract, even though the company was currently losing money and was being forced by market conditions to halve the price of its color TV sets. That reduction triggered a $150 million antitrust suit by Philco, alleging that "unreasonably low" prices signaled a bid by RCA to monopolize the market. Meanwhile, RCA's precious pool of 10,000 TV-related patents was again under assault in antitrust litigation brought by the Justice Department.

Sarnoff was a combative person, and his life-long habit had been to fight any challenge with ruthless tenacity. This time, however, because of intense government pressure, he decided to bow out of the lawsuits. In 1958 RCA paid off Philco, and, in a landmark step, settled with the Justice Department by making most of RCA's patents available to domestic competitors at little or no cost. RCA then tried to recoup its lost domestic royalties by licensing its patents to European and Japanese companies. Every major Japanese TV-manufacturing firm became a licensee. By the 1970s RCA's annual royalty income from consumer-electronics patents reached $100 million, most of it from color-TV technology. This money—the equivalent of $580 million in 2009—went straight to the bottom line as pure profit.

During the early 1960s, RCA had improved its picture tubes through a crash R&D effort, and TV color images had become sharper in home reception. RCA's subsidiary NBC did everything it could to help, broadcasting more and more programs in color. Because of these efforts, in the 1960s color TV finally began to take off, and all major domestic manufacturers plunged into the market. In 1961 even Zenith, a long-time nemesis of Sarnoff, ordered 50,000 of RCA's color picture tubes. RCA was equipping many other competitors as well, at a profit of $35 (about $250 in 2009) for every picture tube sold. It was also selling production and transmission equipment to TV stations all over the country. The 5-million-set sales year Sarnoff had predicted for 1958 finally materialized in 1965.

## Progress and Missteps

In addition to its integrated manufacturing businesses in radio, TV, and audio recording, RCA maintained extensive R&D labs. The company also produced electronic systems for guided missiles and other military hardware under defense contracts. It was an article of faith with Sarnoff that RCA be involved in all things electronic, and that it remain on the cutting edge of R&D. Usually it did, but not always.

Ultimately, Sarnoff's R&D licensing strategy worked to RCA's disadvantage, especially in foreign markets. The company did a substantial overseas business in industrial products as well as in licensing, but Sarnoff decided not to market aggressively or manufacture consumer items abroad because he didn't want RCA to compete with its R&D licensees. (In the case of the large Japanese market he had little choice, since local officials had all but closed the country to both imported consumer electronics and to foreign firms' manufacturing plants.) So RCA mostly confined its sales and its factories to North America, unlike dozens of other big American companies that exported their products and built plants overseas.

This practice also differed from the strategies of European and especially Japanese firms. Companies such as Sony, Matsushita (Panasonic), Hitachi, and Mitsubishi exported their goods from Japan in great volume. Under the umbrella of a protected home market, they constructed world-class facilities, charged high prices within Japan, and sometimes sold at lower prices abroad. They took full advantage of the freer postwar trading system that had evolved under American foreign-policy leadership. To penetrate the rich U.S. market, they exploited the efficient American distribution network, selling through Sears and other mass retailers. Eventually they built manufacturing plants in many countries, including the United States.

In the end, competition from across the Pacific destroyed much of RCA's radio and TV-set business, and along with it almost the entire American consumer-electronics industry. In 1955, American manufacturers' share of the U.S. radio set market stood at 96 percent. Then came a competitive surge from Japan, which was experiencing its "miracle" economic recovery after World War II. As inexpensive Japanese radios poured into the United States, the market share of domestic U.S. producers began a steady decline—to only 30 percent by 1965, and then to almost zero by 1975. The same pattern was duplicated in later years, first with black-and-white TVs, then with color sets.

RCA lagged both domestic and foreign competitors in developing other important products that emerged during the 1950s. Although RCA had led the world in vacuum-tube technology, it made no breakthroughs in transistors. These revolutionary devices were invented at AT&T's Bell Labs in 1947 and developed during the 1950s and 1960s by Texas Instruments, Motorola, Sony, and other firms. The transistor was only a tiny fraction of the size of a vacuum tube but could perform the same work, using much less energy. Transistors also were resistant to shock and could be installed in large numbers on printed circuit boards. First used in hearing aids, transistors were then introduced into car radios during the mid-1950s, and within two years they had become the industry standard.

Without the transistor, a whole series of electronics applications based on printed circuits and microchips would never have been possible. The most conspicuous such use, of course, was in the computer, which as long as it relied on vacuum tubes remained the size of a small truck. RCA's obstinacy toward transistors derived partly from its huge investment in the manufacture of tubes. It was now in the fatal position of staying ahead in the wrong technology.

## Disasters

Sometimes RCA failed because it *did* enter a new business. The company committed one of its gravest blunders when it dived into the computer industry during the 1950s and 1960s. Here RCA possessed the requisite technical skills but fell short in manufacturing and particularly in marketing. Consequently, it suffered a very public humiliation at the hands of IBM. When RCA finally exited the computer business in 1970, it was forced to write off about a quarter of its net worth.

But the actual penalty went even deeper. Because it had squandered 40 percent of its researchers' total time on computers, RCA had neglected R&D in other areas. As the engineer who headed the company's labs later said, "We shot a whole generation of research and engineering on computers, and starved the real cow—color television—to do it." RCA had pioneered color TV in the greatest long-term effort in the company's history. Yet at the very moment of its triumph, it not only lost the computer war to IBM but also began to surrender its lead in TV technology to other companies.

The 1960s became the age of the conglomerate in American business, and RCA plunged wholeheartedly into this ill-fated adventure. First it acquired the publisher Random House, rationalizing the move as a natural expansion into "communications," albeit in nonelectronic form. The next major acquisition came after David Sarnoff had passed the CEO's reins to his son Robert, and in retrospect it seems a bizarre choice: the Hertz rent-a-car company. Robert Sarnoff then oversaw RCA's purchase of Coronet carpets, the Banquet Foods frozen-dinner company, a golfing-attire firm, and many other enterprises with no connection to electronics.

By the late 1960s, the glory of the color-TV triumph was beginning to fade within the RCA labs, even though much additional work remained to be done. Because of its blockbuster-obsessed corporate culture, the company downplayed further R&D efforts in color TV and began to look for another breakthrough product. How else, its R&D leaders reasoned, could the company's 6,200 scientists and engineers be usefully employed? Yet RCA was now in a more vulnerable position than at any time since the 1930s. Not only were other American firms challenging its lead in color TV and defense electronics, but European companies such as France's Thomson and Holland's Philips had also developed world-class enterprises. In Japan, firms such as Sony, Matsushita, Hitachi, Toshiba, and Sharp were showing clear signs of being able to compete against anybody. By the 1990s all of the once-great American TV brands had been acquired by foreign firms: Motorola and its Quasar brand by Matsushita; Magnavox, Philco, and Sylvania by Philips (Holland); RCA and GE by Thomson (France); and Zenith by LG Electronics (South Korea).

Of all RCA's vicissitudes, the most revealing was its pursuit of a would-be blockbuster product called the VideoDisc. This episode carried with it a larger message about the tension in high-tech businesses between the R&D function and commercial success. In RCA's case it helped to kill the firm. Paying far too little attention to changing competitive circumstances, RCA became fixated on the VideoDisc, a technology that would make it possible for TV viewers to watch particular programs whenever they wished. Just as phonographs had reproduced recorded music, a VideoDisc could play back recorded films, concerts, ballets, and other programs, all without commercial interruptions.

If this sounds familiar, it's because the same virtues apply to videotape and DVDs. RCA had pursued a videotape project, but abandoned it when company executives saw the superior Sony Beta system in 1974. RCA's VideoDisc system was not yet ready to market when videocassette recorders (VCRs) appeared in the mid-1970s, but RCA believed that when VideoDisc did become ready it would sell for much less than a VCR. Even so, videotape had an overriding advantage: it could be used to record programs from commercial broadcasts for later viewing at a time convenient for the consumer.

It is useful to keep in mind how all of this looked in prospect. We know now that videotape won decisively, that Japanese companies dominated the sale of VCRs and video cameras, that a vast tape-rental business arose in the 1980s and 1990s and was soon replaced by DVDs, and that domestic consumer-electronics manufacturing collapsed altogether. But such developments in high-tech markets are nearly impossible to forecast accurately, and in the 1960s and 1970s some of these outcomes seemed extremely unlikely. For one thing, it was by no means certain that U.S. copyright law would allow consumers to videotape programs directly from broadcast television. Then, too, RCA accurately regarded VideoDisc as a technology that was less expensive, more elegant, and less easily copied than videotape. Meanwhile, Japanese, European, and American firms were all making expensive bets on their own versions of an uncertain future, as high-tech enterprises must do all the time.

It came down to this: RCA executives bet their company that VideoDisc would emerge triumphant. During the 1970s the firm estimated that by about 1990 VideoDisc would generate annual revenues of $7.5 billion (equivalent to $13.5 billion in 2009). This wishful thinking was based on the assumption that VideoDisc would become the industry standard. That assumption, in turn, derived from RCA's own hubris and its preoccupation with blockbuster products.

Nor was this kind of thinking confined to RCA and the electronics industry. In varying degrees it also appeared at DuPont, Xerox, and other leading-edge technology companies. These firms funded expensive research laboratories, many of whose projects had only tenuous connections to future commercial products.

RCA's own labs had evolved into what people in other parts of the company began to call "the country club." There, it was believed, scientists and engineers were wasting company money on hare-brained experiments, pursuing arcane projects satisfying only to themselves. Some of this was perhaps inevitable, since today's lunatic idea might well turn into tomorrow's breakthrough product. The distinction between good and bad R&D can never be completely clear. But in the case of RCA, other circumstances made the problem worse than it should have been. There was intense mutual dislike between the researchers in New Jersey and the manufacturing managers in Indianapolis. Their physical separation symbolized a real lack of communication, and in the end proved very costly.

Country-club labs in many firms often did what the scientists in charge wanted to do rather than what the company needed them to do. For RCA there was an additional hitch—the tradition of royalties from other electronics firms. In a peculiar sense RCA's labs in effect had their own source of income from these royalties, independent of the company's operating divisions. Ideally the management of technology, like any other function, should be closely related to a firm's markets. In most cases labs should not produce research for sale to all comers unless the company is engaged only in the research business. But RCA's way of thinking had been instilled into its culture long before, beginning with the patent pools of the 1920s. Only later did it turn out to be a serious flaw.

## RCA's Management Report Card

The endgame of the RCA story—the disastrous strategies of inattention to color TV, conglomerate diversification, and expensive gambles on computers and the VideoDisc—represents an outstanding example of sustained failure to get management relationships right. At no time did RCA develop the techniques of decentralized decision making so conspicuous in the government's Controlled Materials Plan under Ferdinand Eberstadt, Procter & Gamble's brand management under Neil McElroy, and General Motors' multidivisional structure under Alfred Sloan.

RCA failed for the same reason that the Ford Motor Company faltered during the 1920s. Both companies paid too little heed to what the customer wanted and lodged too much authority in the hands of one person. David Sarnoff was a far more sophisticated businessman than Henry Ford. But like Ford he began to believe reports of his own infallibility, made too many decisions himself, and stayed too long at the helm. More than anyone else, he created a culture that made something like the computer and VideoDisc disasters not just possible but extremely probable.

One important clue to the shortcomings of his management style is that RCA, like the Ford Motor Company, was not as profitable as it should have been. At Sarnoff's direction, his firm repeatedly sacrificed profits to R&D. By the early 1960s, RCA ranked number 26 on the *Fortune* 500 list of America's largest industrial corporations, right behind Procter & Gamble. But it could hardly have been a more different kind of company. RCA never followed P&G's policies of decentralizing its management structure, finding out what the consumer wanted, and then tying all of its R&D efforts to commercial applications.

It might be argued that Sarnoff's emphasis on R&D sometimes paid off for society as a whole at the expense of RCA, and this issue raises the interesting question of what, ultimately, is the purpose of business. Whatever the answer to that many-sided question, it does not seem reasonable in cases like RCA's to require suicide by the company. Certainly the advent of black-and-white television was accelerated by several years because of RCA's generous research expenditures during the 1930s depression. Similarly, the coming of high-quality color TV would have been delayed for at least a decade without RCA's leadership. Through the years, Sarnoff positioned his company as a kind of national electronics utility whose purpose was to move things forward, not on behalf of RCA's shareholders and employees but rather for the national interest and his own aggrandizement. In this way, too, he resembled Henry Ford, a technological prophet, more than Alfred Sloan, the consummate businessman.

Like Ford, Sarnoff groomed no successors, encouraged no management professionals to develop an independent voice, disdained formal organization, and pontificated on matters he knew little or nothing about. When he summoned the public relations consultant Edward Bernays to help clarify the confused lines of authority within NBC, Bernays began by asking to see the network's organization chart. "My dear Eddie," Sarnoff told him, "this is a company of men, not of charts." Sarnoff's long-time executive assistant Kenneth Bilby, in an excellent biography, gives a vivid account of his boss's daily routine. Sarnoff dismissed visitors and employees at the instant when the point of his meeting with them had been settled. He spurned small talk and cultivated no close relationships with colleagues. He made so many decisions by himself that his schedule became impossibly full.

Sarnoff's style did form a good fit with some parts of the company. Year after year, his unfailing enthusiasm for technology continued to inspire the scientists and engineers at RCA's New Jersey research labs, which were moved from Camden to Princeton and renamed the David Sarnoff Laboratories. As Sarnoff said in 1948, "Princeton is the heart of RCA; the other parts of the company are the organs of the body that function only as the heart functions." But in those other parts that interested him less, his dictatorial approach killed initiatives and did very serious harm. His overall method, as RCA engineer Carl Dreher put it, "required periodic technological breakthroughs, and the time came when none was in sight." When RCA couldn't make its own markets with new products from the R&D labs, it didn't know how to behave as a company.

Sarnoff retired in 1965 at the age of 74. Under subsequent leadership, after RCA had been acquired by its original parent company GE in 1986, all that was left of much value was the NBC television network. The David Sarnoff Laboratories were sold off without a second thought.

## The Perils of High-Tech Markets

The general collapse of the American consumer-electronics industry is not, of course, a story just of RCA and David Sarnoff. In addition, there is the complex issue of national industry life cycles as they have evolved through each of the three industrial revolutions.

For example, machine-based textile manufacturing began in Britain during the late eighteenth century. During the nineteenth century it spread to other industrialized countries, and in the twentieth gradually migrated to lower-wage countries. The pattern in consumer electronics was similar. What happened in the United States with the rise and decline of RCA, General Electric, Westinghouse, and other TV-set manufacturers later began to happen in Japan as well. High domestic wages prompted Sony, Matsushita, Hitachi, and other firms to move some of their manufacturing offshore to Mexico, Malaysia, and China. But the difference between these Japanese companies and RCA is that they adapted and survived as ongoing enterprises. In the United States, General Electric and Westinghouse also survived, although both divested their consumer-electronics divisions.

In addition to national industry life cycles, the fate of RCA and the American consumer-electronics industry was also related to geopolitical forces. Within the United States, defense expenditures associated with World War II and the Cold War changed the nature of R&D inside many high-tech companies. AT&T's renowned Bell Labs had devoted only 2.5 percent of its budget to military projects in 1940, but 85 percent by 1944. The number never returned to a level even close to 2.5 percent. The federal Office of Scientific Research and Development, set up in 1941 to coordinate federal funding of war-related R&D, was reborn in 1950 as the National Science Foundation (NSF). For decades thereafter, NSF shaped the overall direction of R&D in the United States.

The expensive exertions in military R&D by high-tech U.S. companies turned out to be an essential and perhaps decisive factor in winning the Cold War. Then, too, in the case of the computer industry, government outlays for defense-related projects helped give IBM and other firms a commanding lead over foreign competitors, a lead they readily transferred from military to civilian markets. Here the experience of IBM resembled that of Boeing. Both companies' skillful adaptations of military technology facilitated their rise to the top of their industries worldwide.

In numerous other high-tech firms, however, both fundamental research and defense work tended to crowd out commercial R&D. That process likely accelerated the loss of market share to overseas competitors. Although it is hard to make all-purpose generalizations on this subject, the final verdict may be that from the standpoint of their own long-term commercial viability, many American high-tech companies—and certainly RCA—overinvested in defense projects and fundamental research, while underinvesting in R&D that had direct connections to their consumer markets.

One other lesson of RCA's experience is plain. No matter how big the company, how resplendent its heritage, and how talented its

R&D staff, continued success is never assured. In the end, all business comes down to a ceaseless struggle to stay ahead or abreast of the competition. That, in turn, requires constant vigilance toward local, national, and international markets, and unremitting attention to consumers' desires. In markets for high-tech goods and services, trends in consumer preferences are notoriously unpredictable. In the 1970s this uncertainty applied to videotape and VideoDisc. Within a few years, it reappeared with hand-held calculators, fax machines, word-processing software, personal computers, video games, cell phones, and the Internet.

In none of these cases were the size and nature of the market forecast very accurately, even by well-informed experts. One never knows exactly where the next hot item is going to emerge, and expensive R&D bets must be placed routinely, on a continuing basis. But in the meantime, no company can afford to neglect incremental improvements in its existing products, so long as the products are not about to become obsolete. For all of these reasons, high-tech firms are perhaps the hardest of all businesses to manage well.

There is also the matter of changes in external conditions. From 1945 to 1965, in a context of continuous domestic prosperity, immense Cold War defense expenditures, and no effective foreign competition, RCA and many other American firms grew powerful, profitable, and smug. But during the last third of the twentieth century, consumer markets in many industries suddenly became international and much more competitive. At that point American industrial dominance began to erode in the face of European and Japanese economic recovery—a foreseeable development but one that occurred much faster than U.S. business managers had anticipated. As this process matured, the relatively free ride enjoyed by American companies during the first two postwar decades ended abruptly. Foreign competition then inflicted severe and sometimes fatal damage to U.S. companies in the consumer-electronics, machine-tool, rubber-tire, steel, and automobile industries.

For RCA, the tilt toward globalism brought profound consequences. Once consumers became aware of superior alternative products, the company could find no sanctuary in its glorious history or its once-revered brand name. In thousands of stores throughout the United States, millions of customers encountered a choice between a good RCA color TV and a better one made by Sony or Panasonic offered at a lower price. Despite being urged to "buy American," the great majority made the selection almost all consumers inevitably make.

## R&D Done Right: The Chemical Industry

Japanese and European consumer-electronics companies defeated their American competitors during the late twentieth century, but the same thing did not happen in chemicals. From 1945 to the present, no industry, with the possible exception of computers, played a bigger role in U.S. economic growth.

During the period 1945–73, as the American economy was growing at a healthy rate, the chemical industry grew two-and-a-half times as fast. Then, in the decades of slower growth after 1973, U.S. chemical firms, unlike RCA under David Sarnoff, came to understand that they could not afford to keep pouring immense sums into research projects that had little relationship to their commercial markets. DuPont and other leading firms therefore slashed their expenditures on fundamental research. They also reduced their reliance on defense contracts, identified their core competencies, addressed more directly the question of what their customers wanted—and returned to prosperity. They lost some market share to overseas competitors, but on the whole adapted well to new business conditions.

Historically, American firms were not the first movers in chemicals, as they had been in many other industries. During the early years of the twentieth century, the world's top three chemical companies were all German: Bayer, Hoechst, and BASF. Heavily staffed with scientists and engineers, these firms pioneered in dyestuffs, ammonia-based fertilizers, and synthetic drugs such as aspirin. Then, during World War I (1914–18), the products of German firms of all types were barred from the U.S. market. In this newly protected atmosphere, American chemical companies prospered by taking advantage of patented German technology, made available by the federal agency set up to manage the U.S.-based assets of enemy countries. (German firms eventually recovered from the blows they absorbed during both world wars, and in the early twenty-first century were once again among the world leaders in chemicals.)

The American chemical industry's evolution over the 90 years following World War I reflected major military and social events. The industry responded especially well to the need for munitions during World War II and the Cold War, and—in its production of fertilizers, pesticides, and synthetic fibers—to increasing demands for food and clothing during and after the baby boom. It also benefited from the emergence of overseas markets for many kinds of chemical products after the freeing up of international trade. By the twenty-first century, branded products such as Dacron fiber, Lycra elastic fabric, and Tyvek building wrap had become well known throughout the world. All of these products were developed after World War II. The scientific breakthrough that underlay most of them, plus a vast array of others, came to be known as the "polymer revolution" in organic chemistry.

## Polymers and Science

Inorganic chemistry is concerned with elements that form familiar compounds: two atoms of hydrogen plus one of oxygen yield one molecule of water; two of hydrogen, one of sulfur, and four of oxygen form sulfuric acid; and so on. More complex inorganic chemicals are used in the manufacture of optics, superconductors, and silicon-based semiconductors. *Organic* chemicals, on the other hand, contain carbon, most of which has been recycled through once-living organisms. Carbon is unusual in that it can form four symmetric bonds with other elements and therefore serve as the scaffolding for a very diverse range of substances, from DNA to polymer plastics. Carbon's atomic structure lends itself to the creation of endlessly repeating chains of molecules.

A polymer is an organic compound or mixture of compounds, usually of high molecular weight, composed of these repeating structural units. Some polymers occur naturally, but synthetic ones can be designed to have particular combinations of strength and flexibility. They are first produced in a laboratory, and, if commercially promising, scaled up for large-batch or continuous-process manufacturing. Synthetic compounds fit a growing list of applications, and their development by American chemical companies had tremendous importance for the national economy.

During the 1930s, at the dawn of the polymer revolution, petroleum was beginning to replace coal as the industry's chief raw material for organic chemicals. Oil companies therefore joined chemical firms in the pursuit of polymer research. The process to produce synthetic rubber, developed during World War II by Standard Oil of New Jersey (Exxon), led to the transformation of the rubber industry. Exxon and other firms such as Phillips Petroleum and Standard Oil of California (Chevron) set up petrochemical divisions and began to manufacture vast quantities of new synthetic products.

In the laboratories of these companies, and even more so in those of chemical giants such as DuPont, Monsanto, Dow, and 3M, scientists and engineers began to realize that they were practicing something akin to alchemy. Instead of turning base metals into gold, as medieval alchemists had tried to do, they now seemed capable of turning petroleum into almost anything. By the last decades of the twentieth century they were producing substitutes for natural fabrics (nylon, Orlon, polyesters), wood (plastic paneling, Fiberglas), cloth tape (Scotch), glass (Lucite, Plexiglas), and a multitude of other materials—latex paints and varnishes, insulators, adhesives, and synthetic building materials. Especially strong plastics could even substitute for tiles (Formica) and metals (Kevlar, used to make body armor, brake linings, and to strengthen boats, sails, and bicycle tires).

## The Companies

One can see the progress of the chemical industry as a whole by a glimpse at two important companies, Monsanto and DuPont. Monsanto, founded in St. Louis in 1901 to produce the artificial sweetener saccharin, had by 1915 grown to a medium-sized firm that manufactured caffeine and vanillin as well. After the outbreak of World War I it began to make aspirin, of which it eventually became the world's largest bulk producer. Throughout the 1920s and 1930s, Monsanto continued to grow and diversify. During World War II it fulfilled large government contracts, and after 1945 it became a major producer of lawn fertilizers, benefiting from the millions of suburban housing starts that took place during the baby boom. In 1955, Monsanto purchased Lion Oil Company to ensure its supply of petroleum, and then proceeded to achieve world leadership in agricultural chemicals. One of its products, Roundup, became a best-selling weed killer.

During and after the passage of environmental legislation in the 1960s and 1970s, Monsanto, like other chemical firms, was the frequent target of a hostile press. In response, the company adapted its corporate strategy to the imperatives of pollution control and grew especially strong in research and development. Pioneering in biotechnology, Monsanto's scientists developed a line of seeds that produced insect-resistant crops, thereby reducing the need for insecticides. Monsanto also began to offer a line of "Roundup-Ready" seeds that would produce crops resistant to its own weed-killer. Farmers using these seeds could spray Roundup freely on their fields, killing every plant except the cash crop. In effect, Monsanto was trying to have it both ways, selling both insect-resistant and herbicide-resistant seeds. Only the first of these two strategies was unambiguously friendly to the environment, and Monsanto continued to attract criticism. The same was true of the industry as a whole.

The second illustrative chemical company, DuPont, was founded in Delaware in 1802 as a small manufacturer of gunpowder. Over the next two centuries, DuPont supplied munitions for every war fought by the United States. By the 1920s, however, its main business lay not in munitions but in a variety of chemical products such as paints, varnishes, cellophane (the rights to which it purchased from a French company), and rayon (also of French origin).

The most profitable item in DuPont's long history turned out to be nylon, a polymer synthesized in 1934 in its research labs. All kinds of clothing could be made from nylon, either in pure form or blended with natural fibers, and the same was true of carpets. As a replacement for silk, nylon made sheer stockings affordable to millions of women for the first time in history. It also became the chief fiber used in parachutes and for cords in rubber tires. Its exceptional strength also made it ideal for nautical ropes. Nylon became so popular that DuPont not only produced it in vast amounts but also licensed the rights to its manufacture to other firms. By the twenty-first century the company had earned more than $20 billion in profits on this one polymer.

The breakthrough in nylon during the 1930s changed DuPont's corporate culture. As it happened, the discoveries of nylon and of neoprene, DuPont's version of synthetic rubber, had come about through serendipitous events during lab experiments. These occurrences seemed to suggest that if researchers got down to the foundations of chemistry and physics without over-thinking the immediate commercial applications, they might stumble onto a series of spectacular products and make fortune after fortune for DuPont. So, during and after World War II, the company invested unprecedented sums in basic research, looking for useful new polymers but willing to spend lavishly on almost any project that looked promising. For a while this approach appeared to be paying off. DuPont's synthetic fibers—nylon, Orlon, and polyesters—practically transformed the carpet, textile, and apparel industries. By the 1980s more than 70 percent of all fiber used in American manufacturing were synthetic—a dramatic victory over cotton, wool, linen, and silk.

On the other hand, hundreds of research projects on which thousands of DuPont scientists and engineers worked yielded no marketable results whatsoever. And some products that did reach the consumer flopped in a big way. The company lost lots of money on Qiana, an artificial luxury silk that impressed few buyers. It lost even more on a synthetic leather called Corfam, which DuPont believed would transform the world market for shoes and boots. Corfam was durable enough, but it didn't breathe well and was too stiff to be broken in like shoe leather. In the end, retail customers resoundingly rejected both Qiana and Corfam. Meanwhile, the company's fixation on synthetic fibers began to cause frustration during the 1970s, when demand dropped in the wake of changing consumer tastes in clothing, especially the development of "permanent press" 100-percent cotton.

Yet DuPont, like Monsanto, Dow, and other American chemical firms, maintained its leadership in many markets. Having acquired Conoco, a major oil company, DuPont assured itself of plentiful feedstocks for its petrochemicals business. Then, too, like several other major U.S. chemical companies, DuPont restructured itself during the 1970s and 1980s, divesting low-margin commodity chemicals in order to focus on specialty chemicals and other high-tech items. Unlike RCA in electronics, DuPont listened to what its customers were saying, and responded. Its country-club labs went by the board, and it became much better at marketing its products.

## Pharmaceuticals

The pharmaceutical industry underwent even bigger changes than did industrial chemicals. In 1929, only 32 percent of the medicines sold in the United States (by value) were prescription drugs, but 40 years later, in 1969, this percentage had risen to 83. In much of the world, antibiotics had all but wiped out numerous diseases that had plagued human beings for thousands of years. In addition, beginning in the 1950s there had been a series of breakthroughs in psychopharmacology. By the twenty-first century, Prozac, Paxil, Xanax, and similar drugs were being prescribed to millions of people suffering from clinical depression.

The years between World War II and 2009 brought spectacular new arrays of pharmaceuticals. Besides antibiotics and antidepressants, the industry churned out tranquilizers, contraceptives, antihistamines, and many other "antis," including anti-inflammatory, anti-cancer, anti-ulcer, anti-cholesterol, anti-high blood pressure, anti-baldness, anti-menopause, and anti-impotence drugs. Only a few years earlier such products would have seemed figments of the imagination of some frenzied science-fiction writer. But in one of the most remarkable advances in the history of science or business, relentless R&D brought them into existence.

By the early twenty-first century, annual worldwide retail expenditures on pharmaceuticals totaled more than half a trillion dollars. Of this sum, a disproportionate one-third was spent in the United States. Millions of American consumers had become familiar with such brand names as Ortho-Novum (for contraception), Valium (anxiety), Retin-A (skin care), Minoxidil and Propecia (hair loss), Zantac and Prilosec (excess stomach acid), Ritalin (attention deficit disorder), Viagra and Cialis (impotence), Crixivan and Virocept (AIDS), Lipitor and Zocor (high cholesterol), Norvasc and Inspra (high blood pressure), and Estradiol and Evista (estrogen replacement).

American leadership of the pharmaceutical industry had risen in the 1940s and 1950s, then declined in the 1960s and 1970s. It recovered powerfully during the 1980s and 1990s, riding the momentum of a scientific revolution in biotechnology. In the early years of the new century, a little over half of the world's largest drug firms were headquartered in the United States. The most science-based U.S. companies (Pfizer, Merck, Abbott, Eli Lilly), along with their British and European counterparts (GlaxoSmithKline, Sanofi Aventis, Novartis), spent billions of dollars annually on research and development. Almost all of these companies had recently engaged in multiple mergers and acquisitions, swallowing up competitors and sometimes changing their corporate names.

The pharmaceutical industry differs from most others in that companies involved in the race to create new drug compounds have little choice but to spend immense sums on R&D with no guarantee of a return. In this industry, it is a given that only a minuscule number of potential products make it to market—about one in ten thousand compounds, according to some estimates. Those that do can easily cost several hundred million dollars in R&D before a single dose of the new drug is prescribed for a paying patient. In this situation of unavoidably high capital investments, the most ambitious drug companies have grown to giant size.

The tendency toward bigness did not apply to pure biotechnology companies such as Genentech, Biogen Idec, and Genzyme. By the twenty-first century more than 1,300 biotech companies had been created in the United States, and most were relatively small firms with entrepreneurial cultures. Although few made profits during their early years, several were viewed as having great long-term potential—in part because of insights from the huge nonprofit effort called the Human Genome Project (1990–2003). That project, although funded largely by the federal government, willingly shared with private companies its remarkable "map" of human DNA. Many biotech firms were partly owned by large drug firms or venture capitalists, and some were associated with universities.

Because of the odd economics of the pharmaceutical industry, large companies that did develop breakthrough drugs were almost compelled to market them at high prices. They did this in order to recover their enormous R&D expenditures within 20 years, the limit on a new drug's patent protection. Since many of those 20 years were often taken up in testing for toxicity and securing authorization from the Food and Drug Administration, the marketing window was sometimes only five to seven years. After that, any firm could freely manufacture and sell cheap generic versions of the original drug.

A rapid turnover in new drugs became apparent almost as soon as the biotechnology revolution started. For example, only 4 of the 30 best-selling prescription drug items of 1965 were still in the top 30 in 1980, and the same trend continues to this day. Thus, companies with heavy R&D investments find themselves in a perpetual race against the clock.

This situation has led to several new strategies on the part of leading pharmaceutical firms. First, during their brief time as monopolies on the market, patented "miracle" drugs have sometimes been priced at several dollars per pill. Second, "Big Pharma," as the industry has come to be called, spends lavish sums on Capitol Hill, employing one of the largest lobbying networks of any industry in order to protect its interests. In addition, the big firms' incentives to achieve worldwide distribution are stronger than those of other industries, because volume of sales is more important. A fourth new strategy was the onset in 1997 of direct advertising of new prescription drugs to U.S. consumers, through magazine ads and TV commercials.

This last practice broke a long-held taboo and was vehemently opposed by most doctors and managed-healthcare companies. But here, as in so many other cases during the years since 1920, decision making gravitated toward the ultimate consumer. Though the consumer might know little about pharmacology, he or she often did best sense when medical attention was necessary, and naturally had a much stronger incentive than anyone else to try a new treatment. Then, too, thanks to the immense amount of information on the Internet, consumers can do a great deal of medical and pharmaceutical research on their own. They can now easily find out what drugs are in federal testing, and can exert pressure on the Food and Drug Administration to accelerate trials, as many AIDS activists have done. A countervailing trend has been the backlash against the rush to market of drugs such as Vioxx, the anti-inflammatory marketed by Merck. In 2004, when Vioxx was found to increase risks of stroke and heart attack, Merck withdrew it from the market and in 2005 began to defend itself in thousands of lawsuits.

However one might view the recent history of the American pharmaceutical industry from a business perspective, a more important story was that "miracle" drugs brought incalculable benefits to millions of people. For patients who could afford to buy them, or whose insurers would pay for them, these drugs prolonged life or improved its quality in ways difficult to quantify by a monetary index alone. The challenges for the future were how often to prescribe them and how to make them more affordable to more people, both in the United States and throughout the world.

By most estimates, the underlying scientific revolution has not slowed down by much, if at all. In the pharmaceutical industry, as in the related field of genetic engineering, many scientists remain confident that the twenty-first century will bring even greater miracles. Chemical and pharmaceutical firms have responded to the exciting new situation in a variety of ways.

By the twenty-first century, for example, Monsanto had long since divested much of its chemical business, as well as the Lion Oil Company, in order to focus on bioengineered crops. Its patent on the key chemical ingredient of Roundup expired in 2000, and its share of the world herbicide market began to shrink. In response, the company redoubled its emphasis on insect-resistant and herbicide-resistant seeds: for fruits, corn, soybeans and other vegetables, and most important for cottonseed, in which it led the U.S. market by 2006. Overall, Monsanto had retooled its R&D with the aim of finding better ways to grow crops all over the world—including bioengineered "Frankenfoods," as European critics called them. After its corporate reorganizations, Monsanto titled the larger of its two major divisions Seeds and Genomics. The other big division, Agricultural Productivity, continued to make and market herbicides, which the company expected to decline as a profit center. Monsanto no longer regarded itself as a chemical firm at all. "We are an agricultural company," its website announced by 2007.

DuPont undertook a similar reevaluation of its corporate strategy. Betting heavily on its own life sciences reorientation, DuPont divested itself of the Conoco oil subsidiary in 1998, then spent about $20 billion of the sale price on R&D for agricultural biotechnology. Meanwhile, the company began to downsize, divesting in 2002 most of its famous fiber operations—including nylon, Dacron, Lycra, and polyesters—mostly to a new firm called Invista. DuPont kept its brands Kevlar and Tyvek, remained in its traditional paint and finishes business, and increased its R&D in electronics. Like Monsanto, it also moved into genetically modified seeds and other agricultural products. By 2009, more than 40 percent of DuPont's sales were coming from abroad, and it was especially optimistic about emerging markets in Asia.

For both the pharmaceutical and chemicals companies, these drastic reorientations were spurred not only by the trend toward globalization, but also by a scientific premise: that a convergence of research in genetics, information technology, and other fields had created a situation in which prescription drugs, agribusiness, and polymers all shared a common R&D platform. This platform, genomics, offered almost unlimited potential for the engineering of new products ranging across the spectrum of organic chemicals from hydrocarbons to pharmaceuticals to carbohydrates. The new situation posed severe challenges, but unusual opportunities as well. The chemical and pharmaceutical industries' ongoing flexibility in redesigning their R&D and their business models—exactly what RCA under David Sarnoff had failed to do—accounts for their ongoing success in the early twenty-first century.

# CHAPTER FIVE

# Franchising and McDonald's

## Economic and Social Trends after 1973

The onset of widespread franchising in numerous businesses brought another big jump in entrepreneurial opportunity, decentralized decision making, and consumer empowerment—trends exemplified by the dramatic rise of McDonald's Corporation. The McDonald's story unfolded in the midst of profound changes in the economic and social life of the United States, and it is best understood against the background of those shifts. The economic changes began in the 1970s and gathered steam in the 1980s. The social ones started a little earlier. Both had long-term effects that are still being felt in the nation today.

During the 1970s, the 30-year trend of high economic growth that began with World War II began to slow down. In 1973, the Organization of Petroleum Exporting Countries (OPEC), in a move led by Saudi Arabia and Venezuela, quadrupled the price of crude oil. OPEC inflicted a second shock in 1979, and by 1980 a barrel of oil cost about 12 times what it had in 1970, in inflation-adjusted terms.

Oil is such a vital resource that these price rises affected the entire world economy. In many countries, including the United States, the first oil shock started a long period of high inflation, a problem that had begun in a smaller way during the Vietnam War. From 1973 to 1983, the average annual rise in the consumer price index zoomed to 8.2 percent, the highest rate for any ten-year period in American history. (It dropped to 3.8 percent from 1983 to 1993, then to less than 2 percent for the remainder of the century.)

The simultaneous onset of inflation and economic stagnation led to the coining of a new term, *stagflation*. America's industrial self-confidence plummeted, along with its loss of world leadership in steel, heavy machinery, automobiles, tires, machine tools, and other industries. There occurred a general hollowing out of the midwestern "Rust Belt" stretching from western Pennsylvania across Ohio, Indiana, Illinois, and up into Michigan and Wisconsin.

The change was especially conspicuous in automobiles, and in 1980 Japan overtook the United States as the world's leading producer. At the time this struck many Americans as a stunning, almost unbelievable change. Huge imports of oil, consumer electronics, cars, and other goods soon outstripped exports, and the United States drifted into a pattern of large trade deficits. A second type of deficit developed as well, this one in the federal budget. Each year from 1975 until the 1990s, the government spent, on average, about $200 billion more than it took in. The main cause was that the country seemed to be pursuing two, seemingly contradictory, goals at once—stimulating prosperity by cutting taxes while at the same time spending so much on Cold War weaponry that the Soviet Union would be forced to capitulate.

Ultimately, the Soviets could no longer afford to compete, the bankruptcy of their economic system compelling them to give up the long contest. Beginning in 1991, the Soviet Union disintegrated into 15 separate nations. Russia remained a major nuclear power, but the Cold War seemed, at long last, to have ended. Partly because of the reduced need for military expenditures, the American fiscal deficit began to shrink, and in 1998 it became a surplus for the first time in a generation. But the end of the annual deficit could not quickly reduce the immense accumulated national debt, which at the start of the new century exceeded $5 trillion.

Real wages for "production and nonsupervisory workers" (a government term meaning most people employed in factories and offices), which had risen at a steady annual rate of about 2 percent for most of the twentieth century—thereby doubling every 36 years—stopped growing altogether. By the mid-1990s, this very large category of employees was taking home about 10 percent *less* in inflation-adjusted dollars than in 1973. Had the prior trend continued—a trend that had remained intact for more than seven decades—working people would have been earning about 70 percent *more* in the 1990s rather than 10 percent less. The American middle class had begun to shrink, and that trend continued into the twenty-first century.

The total number of hours a full-time American employee worked per year, after having declined drastically from 2,600 in 1913 to 1,600 in 1990, began to turn upward. Toward the end of the century it reached 1,950, the highest number for any industrialized nation. This change reflected a broad societal shift toward shrinking paychecks and life on the run. Largely because of growing opportunities for (and demands on) women, these same societal changes promoted the rise of numerous small service companies and a big increase in franchised businesses. These new companies and franchised outlets supplied a wide range of services once done in the home, such as cooking, housecleaning, and laundry.

Some middle- and lower-income families, squeezed by declining wages and disappearing benefits, found that one job per household no longer sufficed. Frequent "moonlighting" arose, as people began to work at more than one job. From the 1960s to the 1990s, the makeup of households themselves underwent one of the biggest shifts in American history. Lifestyles changed radically, particularly for women:

|  | 1960 | 1995 |
|---|---|---|
| Total households, including single persons living alone | 53 million | 99 million |
| Married couples, as a percentage of all households | 75% | 54% |
| Percentage of couples with children under age 18 | 48% | 26% |
| Percentage of families headed by single mothers | 10% | 24% |
| Percentage of women ages 25-34 not presently married | 11.5% | 41% |

Sources: *U.S. Bureau of the Census* and Andrew Hacker, "The War Over the Family," *New York Review of Books* 44 (Dec. 4, 1997).

These dramatic shifts pointed to rising needs for services provided outside the home, most notably the preparation of food. By the mid-1990s, about 9 million people were working in food service, making it the nation's largest source of jobs. In a change that would have been unthinkable at any previous time in the nation's history, about half of all money spent by consumers on food now went for restaurant or take-out meals.

## Franchising: An Overview

Fast-food franchises became the major suppliers of the food Americans ate outside the home. These restaurants spread so quickly that by the 1980s they not only prepared billions of meals each year but also accounted for 5 of the top 10 brands of all products advertised on network TV during prime time.

Franchising as a business method was not entirely new. It had originated in the middle decades of the nineteenth century, when companies such as McCormick Reaper and Singer Sewing Machine set up franchised outlets to sell their products and show buyers how to use them. These outlets also helped with consumer financing and offered after-sale repair services. Similar reasons prompted the rise of automobile franchises in the early 1900s.

In the years after World War II, a very different kind of franchising sprang up, one organized around service industries rather than cars and other big-ticket items. This "business-format" franchising brought a new, wholly standardized system of retail trade. Using identical formats nationwide, small service firms such as restaurants and dry cleaners could now realize advantages previously available only to big businesses. These included quantity discounts in supplies, access to proven business methods, and—most important—a nationally recognized brand. By the 1960s, franchised outlets had popped up for convenience stores, motels, dry cleaners, and especially for fast-food restaurants.

As American society became increasingly mobile during the postwar decades, franchising grew more rapidly than did any other type of business. College students, travelers, and people moving to new areas benefited from knowing what to expect from branded service operations: McDonald's restaurants, Dunkin' Donuts,

Kinko's copy shops, and 7-Elevens. As a Holiday Inn TV commercial of the 1980s put it, "The best surprise is no surprise." The number of Holiday Inns increased from 162 in 1960 to more than 1,700 in 1980.

By the 1990s, according to the U.S. Census, at least 2,000 different franchising companies were supervising more than half a million retail units. The success rate for these outlets was higher than that for independent businesses, although how much higher remained a matter of controversy. For one thing, it was hard to get accurate information from such diverse operations. For another, the definition of "success" was ambiguous. (It usually meant simple survival over a certain number of years.) A 1990s study by the U.S. House Committee on Small Business put the five-year success rate for all franchised outlets at between 65 and 75 percent, and for those in highly ranked ones at between 90 and 95 percent. By comparison, only 30 to 40 percent of all nonfranchised retail businesses survived for five years.

## The Champion Franchisor

McDonald's, the top performing franchisor of all, claimed a success rate of 98 percent. This company was founded in 1955, and by the 1980s more than 19 out of every 20 American consumers between the ages of 7 and 65 were eating at a McDonald's at least once a year. The McDonald's system had become the nation's largest purchaser of beef and was using nearly 8 percent of its food-potato crop. After McDonald's introduced Chicken McNuggets in 1982, it was the second largest seller of chicken, surpassed only by Kentucky Fried Chicken (KFC). McDonald's share of revenues in the U.S. fast-food market was about equal to the combined share of the three next-largest chains. The clown mascot Ronald McDonald ranked second only to Santa Claus as the "person" most familiar to American children. The Golden Arches became a national icon, then an international one.

All of this, of course, was still true at the close of the first decade of the twenty-first century. By that time, more than 13,000 McDonald's outlets in the United States were taking in a total of about $30 billion annually—$100 for every man, woman, and child in the United States. In 120 nations abroad, 18,000 additional McDonald's had opened, and that number was still growing rapidly. Terms such as *McJobs* and *McMansions* came to symbolize a new standardization of life in the United States. Abroad, McDonald's had become the single greatest symbol of American culture, surpassing even Coca-Cola.

The step-by-step details of how all these changes occurred amount to one of the epic stories in the history of American business—starting with the humble hamburger.

## Early History: The McDonald Brothers

Like almost all businesses, McDonald's had very modest beginnings. During the 1930s, in San Bernardino, California, Dick and Maurice "Mac" McDonald opened their first restaurant, a drive-in with "carhop" waitresses delivering food to customers sitting in automobiles. A few years later, the brothers knocked down the outside walls of their building, installed plate-glass windows, and exposed their kitchen to full public view. This was a radical change in restaurant traditions. In 1948 the brothers took an even bigger step. They closed their little store for three months, then reopened with a new building and a new service concept described by Mac McDonald as "based on speed, lower prices, and . . . big, big volumes." It was still a takeout business only, with no inside seating.

They reduced their menu from 25 items to just nine: hamburgers (the price of which they cut from 30 cents to 15, the equivalent of a drop from $2.80 to $1.40 in 2009), cheeseburgers, potato chips, pie, milk, coffee, and three kinds of soft drinks. Everything customers received from McDonald's now became disposable. The food was to be consumed and the paper cups and wrappers thrown away. Inside the restaurant, there would be no more washing of dishes, glasses, or silverware. McDonald's would cease to be a teenagers' hangout and instead become a family restaurant. Its prices were so cheap and its food of such reliable quality that middle- and low-income parents in San Bernardino could at last feel justified in taking the whole family out to eat.

The McDonald brothers' plan of menu standardization plus high volume meant that staff roles had to be broken down in assembly-line fashion. Like Henry Ford forty years earlier, Dick and Mac now proceeded to define a series of specific jobs: grill man, fry man, counter man, and so on. They let all the carhops go and hired no more female workers because they wanted to discourage young men from hanging out at their restaurant. For the kitchen, they invented high-speed custom equipment to do mundane things such as deposit both ketchup (one tablespoon) and mustard (one teaspoon) onto a bun with just one squeeze of a two-part dispenser. Above all, they built such a continuous customer stream that they could cook the food beforehand and deliver it, still fresh, almost at the moment it was ordered.

Dick and Mac continued to prosper, and their new format began to attract national attention. Beginning in 1952, they started licensing their "Speedy Service System," plus the name McDonald's, for a one-time fee of $1,000 (the equivalent of $8,200 in 2009). Beyond that they provided no operational guidance and charged their licensees no royalties.

## Ray Kroc (1902–1984)

Much as the McDonald brothers' system resembled Henry Ford's assembly line, the Alfred Sloan of the fast-food industry turned out to be Ray Kroc, a 52-year-old salesman based in Chicago. Kroc had nationwide marketing rights to the Multimixer, a machine that could make five milkshakes at once. When Dick and Mac McDonald ordered the unlikely total of ten Multimixers, Kroc went to the West Coast to see for himself how they could possibly sell in such volume out of a single small outlet. At ten o'clock one morning in 1954, he parked his car in front of the brothers' restaurant and watched as long lines began to form far in advance of lunchtime. Kroc was amazed. "That night in my motel room," he later wrote, "visions of McDonald's restaurants dotting crossroads all over the country paraded through my brain."

In his outstanding history of McDonald's, *Behind the Arches* (1995), the journalist John Love draws a vivid portrait of Ray Kroc. A snappy dresser, talented musician, and likeable though sometimes hotheaded young man, he had dropped out of his high school in Chicago. He then combined his daytime sales job with nighttime gigs playing piano in jazz clubs of uneven reputation. (Some were probably bordellos.) During the 1920s he sold real estate in the Florida land boom, then returned to Chicago. Over the next three decades he traveled widely, selling first Lily cups, then Multimixers. In this way he became familiar with soda-fountain and take-out food businesses throughout the country.

By 1954, after so many years on the road, the affable Kroc had become a persuasive salesman of almost anything. On his second visit to San Bernardino, he introduced himself to the McDonald brothers and quickly talked his way into their confidence. At his suggestion, he became their general franchise agent under a contract stipulating that every person he signed up would pay an initial fee of $950, then a continuing royalty of 1.9 percent of gross sales. Of this, 1.4 percent would go to a new company formed by Kroc (which became McDonald's Corporation), the other 0.5 percent straight into the pockets of Dick and Mac. Kroc was to pay all costs of supervising and servicing the franchisees. The brothers would have no expenses at all. This deal was very lopsided in their favor, and it took Kroc six years to work his way out of it.

## Kroc the Crusader

Before the Kroc era, the essence of the fast-food business was simply the selling of franchises. The largest chains, Dairy Queen and Tastee-Freez, sold territorial rights to franchisees who then sublicensed them to store operators. Territorial owners had responsibility for overseeing local stores, but they seldom discharged this task with much energy. Because most of the people who set up new systems envisioned one-time windfalls more than ongoing businesses, the world of franchising tended to attract operators out for a quick score. The big money was in selling the concept, the territory, and often the equipment and supplies—not in running or supervising stores.

Ray Kroc took precisely the opposite approach, and in the short run he made almost no money. He supported his family with his ongoing Multimixer business and through a McDonald's restaurant he himself opened in Des Plaines, Illinois, a suburb of Chicago. As an associate of the McDonald brothers put it, Kroc "thought that if franchisors made their franchisees successful, they [the franchisors] would automatically be successful. His new idea was to provide the franchisees with enough services to be successful." As Kroc later said of his basic idea, "Our slogan for McDonald's operators is 'In business for yourself, but not by yourself.'" Convinced that the McDonald's format was foolproof, he showed prospective franchisees figures from his own Des Plaines store, and even his personal finances. The cornerstone of his system became "sweat equity." Kroc worked brutally long hours and became a personal role model for franchisees.

Meanwhile, he continued to refine the McDonald brothers' original rules. He banned jukeboxes, pay telephones, and vending machines, including coin-operated newspaper boxes and cigarette machines. These items were often found in other restaurants because they brought in more income at little cost to the proprietor. But Kroc wanted no clutter at McDonald's and no hanging out by customers. In the late 1960s, he and his staff converted the restaurants to eat-in as well as take-out establishments. But even then they discouraged loiterers by installing seats made of hard plastic, comfortable only for short periods and designed for rapid turnover of customers.

From the outset Kroc resolved not to sell supplies and kitchen appliances to captive franchisees. He would specify what equipment they should buy, but would not involve McDonald's Corporation directly in its manufacture and sale. For supplies of beef, cheese, condiments, buns, cups, and napkins, he chose contractors who were themselves small entrepreneurs. He mostly stayed away from major companies catering to the restaurant trade, with the sole exception of Coca-Cola. He courted small firms, imbued them with his vision of a great future, and won numerous price concessions. Some of his suppliers had no other customers, and they later developed an important voice within Kroc's system. Many of them formed associations and contributed advice that affected McDonald's policies. But none of them had a written contract, which meant that Kroc could cut them off at any time. He took pride in his "handshake" agreements, and the spirit of this partnership tradition endures at McDonald's to this day.

## Recruiting Franchisees

At first Kroc limited each operator to one store. Later he based the award of additional units on the performance of the franchisee's existing store. If a franchisee fell short of the company's high standards, Kroc's answer to a request for another unit was always no. "When you sell a big franchise territory, you give up the business to the man who owns the area. He replaces your organization, and you don't have control." Kroc's early experience in selling franchises to his golfing buddies around Chicago turned out badly. They had other jobs and tended to regard themselves as silent investors rather than entrepreneurs.

Kroc then started to look for franchisees like Betty and Sandy Agate, a middle-aged Chicago couple who had little money but an exceptional work ethic. One day in 1955, Betty Agate was selling Catholic Bibles door to door, and she walked into the small office in Chicago's Loop that housed Kroc's Multimixer headquarters. June Martino, Kroc's secretary, bluntly asked Agate, "What the hell is a Jew doing selling Catholic Bibles?" Betty replied that she was just trying to make a living. To that, Martino suggested, "Why don't you get a McDonald's instead?" Soon Betty and her husband Sandy were operating a new McDonald's in a Chicago suburb. Before long their annual income was four times that of Kroc himself.

Kroc used the Agates' story to sell other franchisees on McDonald's potential, saying to prospects that Betty and Sandy were getting rich through sweat equity. Eventually Kroc's retellings of their experience spawned more than 200 McDonald's restaurants throughout the country. Nearly all of these stores were managed by owner-operators like Betty and Sandy, who meanwhile had opened additional units themselves.

In the end, Sandy Agate turned out to be too autonomous for his own good. After running his restaurants for a few years, he became convinced that Pepsi-Cola would be a better choice for the local market than Coke, Kroc's standard. So in 1975, when the Agates' 20-year franchise was about to expire, they were told it would not be renewed. For years thereafter, Sandy Agate was known throughout the McDonald's system as the man who crossed Ray Kroc and paid the price.

## June and Lou Martino

The handshake tradition and the fall of the Agates did not mean that Kroc liked to surround himself with yes people. June Martino, who became secretary, treasurer, and a board member of McDonald's Corporation, seldom hesitated to say no. She had worked for Kroc since 1948, seven years before he set up McDonald's, and she had topflight skills in persuading hostile factions to get along with each other. She was forever having to reverse the impulsive Kroc's peremptory firings of almost everybody. By force of will, she held together the hodgepodge of personalities that comprised the original McDonald's team. She became known, Kroc later wrote, as "Vice-President of Equilibrium."

June Martino was also a key recruiter. In the early days, she signed up not only Betty and Sandy Agate but dozens of other franchisees as well. Sometimes prospects would stay at her house while they looked over local stores. She also hired numerous corporate employees. One of them, a college friend of her son, started in the mail room and went on to become a successor of Kroc as head of the company. Another recruit was her husband Lou, who quit his job as a Motorola engineer to open a McDonald's in partnership with June.

Lou Martino was the person most responsible for the quality of McDonald's french fries, which became legendary in the fast-food industry. Kroc and his colleagues, despite continual efforts, had been unable to produce fries of dependably uniform quality. They would buy the best Idaho russets, cut them to precise specifications (9/32 of an inch), then cook them under controlled conditions. But some batches of fries would come out limp, while others would look dark brown on the outside while remaining raw in the middle.

Working at a lab he persuaded Kroc to sponsor, Lou Martino discovered that the chemical makeup of potatoes changes after they're dug out of the ground. Accordingly, McDonald's ordered that before cooking, all potatoes be cured for three weeks, the interval necessary for their high sugar content to convert to starch, and in turn prevent premature browning. Next the researchers found that when dumped cold into the frying vat, different batches of potatoes caused the temperature of the shortening to drop by varying degrees, making it impossible to establish uniform cooking times. Finally, after months of frustrating work, Lou Martino and his team of researchers made their big discovery: regardless of how many degrees the temperature of the shortening fell after the introduction of the cut potatoes, the fries were cooked just right at the moment when the temperature had regained precisely three degrees. Lou and his ecstatic colleagues now created a "potato computer" that buzzed signals to the fry cook. Later McDonald's adapted the same principle for some of its other products.

## The Financial Wizard

One of Ray Kroc's best qualities as a businessman was his recognition of the need for complementary talents. As he once said to some MBA students at a prominent business school, "If a corporation has two executives who think alike, one of them is unnecessary."

Harry Sonneborn, who in the mid-1950s became the third important member of the original team (after Kroc and June Martino), had attended the University of Wisconsin for a couple of years. Meanwhile, he had learned about franchises working at Tastee-Freez. "Harry didn't know or care a damn thing about hamburgers and french fries," said Kroc. "He was a cold, calculating money man, but I needed a guy like that." Only a few months after Kroc hired him, the youthful Sonneborn developed a way for McDonald's to make a little more money immediately and a great deal more over the long term. He did this by putting the firm into the real estate business, first through leasing, then through land ownership. By the 1980s McDonald's was the largest owner of retail real estate in the world. That position, together with a record of financial success unmatched in the industry, derived mostly from Harry Sonneborn's early strategic moves.

Even though McDonald's franchisees themselves had to come up with the money to buy or lease property, McDonald's Corporation itself usually selected the sites. Ray Kroc liked to fly over suburban areas in small planes or helicopters, looking for neighborhoods with "schools, church steeples, and new houses." He thought that families who lived in these new neighborhoods would be natural customers. Then, too, commercial land located near new developments was usually cheap.

Harry Sonneborn now proposed that McDonald's Corporation get into real estate itself by becoming the middle element in what is known as a sandwich lease (no pun here, just a coincidence). The company would take out long-term leases, then sublease the properties to franchisees at a fixed dollar markup. This leasing charge would be in addition to the 1.9-percent-of-gross-sales annual franchise fee, which Kroc later raised to 3 percent. Sonneborn created a subsidiary called Franchise Realty Corporation and gave it the task of locating sites and taking out 20-year leases at fixed-rate annual payments. He then persuaded landowners to put up the leased land as collateral for a building loan. This loan, made to a McDonald's franchisee, would finance the construction of a store.

In the sandwich leases, Franchise Realty's markup to subleasing franchisees was first 20 percent of the original lease fee, then 40 percent. In the early days, this markup brought in between $250 and $500 per store per month ($2,000–$4,000 in 2009 equivalents), and it greatly augmented the cash flow of McDonald's Corporation. Franchisees had to pay all taxes and property insurance costs, which tended to increase with each passing year along with the value of the land. Meanwhile, Franchise Realty's only serious expenses were its fixed-rate lease payments.

As sales at most stores began to grow, Sonneborn had another flash of inspiration. Once a unit's monthly receipts exceeded a certain threshold, its sublease payments to McDonald's would shift from a percentage of the lease fee to a percentage of the unit's gross sales, which came to be set at 8.5 percent. It was this 8.5 percent, in addition to McDonald's 3-percent-of-gross-sales franchise fee, that made the company so extraordinarily profitable over the long run.

In the early 1960s, six or seven years after its founding in 1955, McDonald's Corporation had a reliable income stream but little capital of its own. Sonneborn now moved to alleviate a portion of that problem as well. As part of its deal with new operators, Franchise Realty began to require a "security deposit" of $7,500 ($53,000 in 2009 dollars). Half of the amount was to be returned after 15 years, the other half when the 20-year franchise expired.

As security deposits accumulated, Sonneborn used the money to buy land for new stores. Later on, when the original 20-year leases began to expire, McDonald's often bought existing sites as well. Most of the early purchases turned out to be bargains, because they were made at a moment when suburban land prices stood on the verge of a big jump. Eventually about two-thirds of all restaurants in the McDonald's system sat on land owned by the Corporation. Together with the 8.5 percent subleasing system, the whole arrangement constituted a money-making machine for the company. As Kroc said years later, "Harry alone put in the policy that salvaged this company and made it a big-leaguer. His idea is what really made McDonald's rich."

As McDonald's outlets rapidly multiplied during the period from the late 1960s to the early 1980s, price inflation was running high throughout the country. But McDonald's fixed-rate lease payments to landowners remained flat. Meanwhile, its income from franchised stores surged because of rising overall prices. By itself, inflation pushed nearly all franchisees past the threshold at which they would start paying the 8.5 percent rental. Even a McDonald's hamburger, which had sold for 15 cents in 1967, cost customers 50 cents in the early 1980s. By that time about 90 percent of the profits the company earned from its franchised stores was coming from real estate payments.

Sonneborn's subleasing fee of 8.5 percent on gross sales also aligned the interests of almost everyone involved. It gave McDonald's Corporation a tremendous incentive to maximize systemwide sales through the development of new products, national advertising campaigns, and the enforcement of uniform standards. It slightly diminished the upside profit potential for franchisees, but without in any sense putting a ceiling on it. And still another aspect of the leasing plan practically forced franchisees to keep faith with Kroc's rigorous "QSC" formula (quality, service, cleanliness). As Sonneborn put it, "We connected the lease to the franchise so that any violation of the franchise [that is, any deviation from Kroc's strict operating procedures] could create termination of the lease." This strategy stretched lease law to its limits, but it held up in court against repeated legal challenges.

## The Big Leagues

As late as 1960, five years after setting up McDonald's Corporation, Ray Kroc was still making no money from the company except what his Des Plaines restaurant brought in. Harry Sonneborn as president was being paid $27,500 annually (equivalent to $196,000 in 2009). In lieu of higher salaries, Kroc had given June Martino 10 percent of the company's stock and Sonneborn 20 percent. All three could now visualize McDonald's as a really large chain. But where were they going to get the capital required for national expansion? Almost no fast-food firms were considered sound long-term bets by investment banks and insurance companies, which still regarded franchising as an often shady business. McDonald's was doing well enough, but its balance sheet looked little better than average for the industry.

To remedy this situation, Sonneborn began to tinker with his company's accounting system, as entrepreneurs often do. In particular, he decided to capitalize McDonald's future lease income. That is, he calculated the amount of money that the company would have to invest currently in order to generate the stream of expected future lease payments by franchisees. Then he boldly placed this number on the company's balance sheet as an asset. "It was the greatest accounting gimmick ever devised," Sonneborn said later. "The bankers were bemused and befuddled by it because they had never seen it before, but it surely helped us get some loans." As is always the case under accounting regulations, definitions of what McDonald's had done were recorded in the footnotes of the accountants' reports. But the apparent increase in the company's net worth had the desired effect.

Sonneborn now decided he was ready to approach a major lender and ask for a very large loan. If necessary he would also offer part ownership of McDonald's as an "equity sweetener." After several deals fell through, he finally hit his target with two insurance companies, State Mutual Life and Paul Revere. Each agreed to lend $750,000 (equivalent to about $5.3 million in 2009) in return for 10 percent of McDonald's stock. Sonneborn saw that the deal was a good one, but "Ray was madder than hell." Kroc also objected when other parties took a finder's fee of 2.5%. He caved only when Sonneborn reminded him "that seventy-eight percent of something is a lot better than one hundred percent of nothing, and nothing is what we've got now." This was the real beginning of the company's worldwide empire. Among other things, the new financial credibility permitted Kroc to borrow even more money and eventually to buy out the McDonald brothers for $2.7 million in cash (about $20 million in 2009 equivalent).

In 1965, Sonneborn fulfilled his long-held ambition of taking the company public. Its initial offering was quickly subscribed at the opening share price of $22.50. By the end of the first trading day the price had risen to $30, a week later to $36, and a few weeks after that to $49. Harry Sonneborn and June Martino suddenly found themselves wealthy. Kroc, who had earned no money at all from McDonald's Corporation until 1961, was now in possession of stock worth $32 million, which in 1965 was a big fortune (about $215 million in 2009). McDonald's was listed on the New York Stock Exchange in 1968, and in 1985 it became the first food-service company included among the 30 premium stocks that make up the Dow Jones Industrial Average. By that time, Harry Sonneborn had retired from the company after a dispute with Kroc. Sonneborn's name remains obscure in the annals of American business history, but he was of almost equal importance with Kroc as the architect of McDonald's success.

## Operational Training

In the early days of franchising, as noted earlier, entrepreneurs tried to get rich through one-time sales of their brands and business plans, with little follow-up supervision. Then Kroc engineered a shift by forgoing the quick bonanza in favor of long-term quality, service, and cleanliness: QSC. These he enforced without mercy. He installed a rigorous inspection system developed by his protégé Fred Turner, and soon the initials QSC were famous throughout the industry. Fred Turner later succeeded Kroc as head of the corporation.

When Kroc hired Turner in 1957, his instructions to the new recruit were simple. "Visit the stores" and see what was going on. Turner proceeded to develop a report card on which each store received a grade of A, B, C, D, or F for quality, service, cleanliness, and overall performance. McDonald's came to employ hundreds of "field service consultants" to make surprise visits once every three months. Twice a year all stores underwent "full field" inspections lasting three days.

Turner's first codification of Kroc's QSC system was laid out in a 15-page mimeographed pamphlet that began with an emphatic statement: "Herein outlined is the successful method." By 1985 the instruction manual, known within the company as "the Bible," had grown to 600 pages. It had color photos demonstrating where the pickles, mustard, ketchup, and onions should go on burgers of various sizes. It gave precise instructions about everything: 32 slices of cheese per pound, one-fourth ounce of onions per hamburger, and so on. McDonald's also made instructional films, which evolved into videotapes and DVDs sent out several times a year to each store.

In 1961 Kroc and Fred Turner opened "Hamburger University" in the basement of a McDonald's near Chicago and required all new franchisees to attend its training course. By 1968, the "campus" included two large classrooms in addition to a restaurant. In 1983, after a big expansion in the number of McDonald's outlets, the company opened an expensive new training facility with seven classrooms, 28 faculty members, and a 154-room dormitory. This expanded Hamburger University received accreditation from the American Council on Education for 36 semester-hours of college credit. After the company went international, students who did not speak English were equipped with earphones delivering the teacher's message with simultaneous translation. By 2008, instruction was available in 28 languages. More than 5,000 people were graduating each year, advanced students were taking follow-up courses, and Hamburger U. had accumulated 80,000 alumni.

## Decentralized Decision Making

Fred Turner maintained tight central control of standards, but beyond that, both he and Kroc insisted on decentralization in much the same way that Alfred Sloan, Neil McElroy, and Ferdinand Eberstadt had in other settings. In each case, decentralization increased the flow of information both up and down within the company. As one McDonald's franchisee put it, "I am an independent owner, but the company is only a phone call away. They provide staff services, but operations is the lifeblood of the business and that is what I have control over." By this the franchisee meant decisions about whom to hire and fire, how much to pay employees, and how to price items on the menu.

Most of McDonald's best-known products, such as the Big Mac, Egg McMuffin, and Filet-O-Fish, were first suggested by franchisees. (By contrast, most items Kroc himself developed, such as his own beloved Hula Burger—a melted cheese sandwich topped with a slice of fresh pineapple—went nowhere). In addition, the company's independent suppliers proposed numerous procedural innovations that won quick adoption. Kroc regarded these bottom-up ideas not as challenges to his authority but as evidence of the virtues of franchising done McDonald's style. The whole system, he said, was "the perfect example of capitalism in action."

During the 1960s McDonald's set up regional networks to coordinate dealings with its local stores. By 1990 the company's operations were divided into 35 areas, each overseen by a Regional Operators Advisory Board run jointly by managers from McDonald's Corporation and representatives elected by franchisees from their own number. The boards suggested guidelines for wages, made recommendations about menus, and worked with regional advertising cooperatives.

Franchisees exerted great influence over advertising expenditures through an organization developed during the late 1960s and early 1970s. As Kroc described it, the Operators' National Advertising Fund (OPNAD) "is supported by a voluntary contribution of one percent of gross sales by licensees and company stores that belong to the program . . . . What small businessman wouldn't cheerfully give up one percent of his gross to get our kind of commercials . . . on network television to promote his store? He'd have to be crazy not to."

Here, as in so many other areas, McDonald's worked out a way to benefit from centralized management while still drawing on the expertise of local operators. By the 1980s, a 60-member committee divided between elected franchisees and McDonald's regional ad executives was setting OPNAD's policies. Each franchisee on the committee wielded one vote, each ad manager half a vote, so the franchisees had formal control. The 60 OPNAD members held quarterly meetings to oversee McDonald's national advertising budget, which had already grown to more than $1 billion annually (nearly $3 billion in 2009 equivalent).

## The Importance of Good Franchisees

Kroc had established the McDonald's system in 1955 on the basis of 20-year renewable franchises. So by the mid-1970s, the issue arose of what to do about renewals. Kroc and Fred Turner decided that any store failing to score a consistent average of C or better on the rigorous inspection scorecard should be disqualified automatically. Others might lose as well, on a case by case basis.

In the broad world of franchising, the termination of a franchisee had been rare, because most companies made their money through the licensing of brands and direct sales of equipment and supplies. Kroc and Turner, by contrast, saw the renewal issue as an invaluable tool for disciplining lax operators and improving system performance. They terminated about one of every 14 franchisees who applied for renewal. This seems a small percentage, but it was much larger than comparable figures by other companies, and it had a tremendous ripple effect throughout the McDonald's system. The policy triggered numerous lawsuits by terminated franchisees, but the company won in almost all of this litigation. Because of its unexcelled record in court, McDonald's terms of franchising became the model for the industry. By the twenty-first century, the company was receiving well over 20,000 inquiries per year from prospective franchisees. About one in ten was granted an interview, and one in ten interviewees wound up with a franchise. The waiting period for winning franchisees actually to get a store grew to more than two years.

As a matter of policy, the company had long turned its back on the credentialism that came to characterize certain jobs in big business and other areas such as law, accounting, consulting, and academia. None of the three original corporate employees—Kroc, June Martino, and Harry Sonneborn—had completed a college education, and this pattern was typical of early fast-food entrepreneurs. "Colonel" Harland Sanders of KFC, Dave Thomas of Wendy's, and Kroc himself were all high-school dropouts. As late as the 1980s, after McDonald's had become a very big business, only 14 of its top 26 executives had college degrees. Chairman Fred Turner, who did not, said "For those people who have the ability but who have not been in situations where they could demonstrate it, McDonald's became a place of opportunity with a capital O."

By the 1980s the average McDonald's franchisee was operating 3.1 stores, and some had dozens. As both the corporation and the number of stores grew, managers working in the headquarters at Oak Brook, Illinois, often took higher-paying jobs offered by "master franchisees" who owned many stores. In this kind of job shift, big-business talents gravitated to medium-sized businesses charged with supervising numerous small-business operations.

The emergence of master franchisees became a salient pattern in the growth of both domestic and international franchising, and not just at McDonald's. A single operator could turn a small firm (one franchise grossing $2 million annually) into a medium-sized business (five units each grossing $2 million) or a large one (200 units, which, if each grossed $2 million, comprised a $400 million company). Multi-unit franchising became the dominant mode of growth not only at McDonald's but also at Wendy's and other leading chains. It afforded major entrepreneurial opportunities for successful franchisees, and from the viewpoint of corporate headquarters was by far the most efficient way to expand. Awarding five additional franchises each to 20 proven managers was a lot more practical than betting on 100 untried applicants.

Kroc and Turner reserved many new stores for franchisees with outstanding records. This policy had a snowball effect, and only those snowballs of healthy proportion were permitted to roll down the hill and grow larger. The development of master franchisees, much like the movement of salaried executives out of McDonald's corporate offices into the field, became a way to test and cultivate managerial ability and decentralize the making of big decisions.

## Marketing: Into the Mouths of Babes

Back in 1948, the first purchase at Dick and Mac McDonald's newly designed San Bernardino store had been made by a nine-year-old girl. She bought a bag of 15-cent hamburgers to take home for her family's dinner. "The kids loved coming to the counter," said Art Bender, the original counterman and later Kroc's first franchisee. "They would come with two bits in their fists and order a hamburger and a Coke. They could still see Mama in the car, but they also could feel independent. Pretty soon, it sinks in that this is great for the business; this is important."

The company began to direct much of its television advertising toward children. In the early days of TV, ad rates for Saturday morning shows were only about one-fourth those for prime time. McDonald's franchisees in many cities recognized the bargain and started sponsoring programs for kids. In and around Washington, D.C., franchisees developed a show featuring a costumed clown who soon became identified with McDonald's. When it was decided that he should have a new name, the clown himself, a local actor named Willard Scott, invented Ronald McDonald. When the name and the clown went national, Scott did not get the job, but he later achieved fame as the affable weatherman on NBC's *Today Show*.

By the 1980s, McDonald's was far and away the leader in fast food, but more so with youngsters than adults. It accounted for better than 40 percent of the market for children under the age of seven, ten percentage points above its overall market share. When Ray Kroc became wealthy, one of his favorite philanthropies was the chain of Ronald McDonald Houses, located near hospitals and offering relatives of seriously ill children a pleasant and inexpensive place to stay. The concept was conceived at Kroc's behest by a Philadelphia ad agency.

The children's market was one reason why Kroc's personal fanaticism about cleanliness fit so well with the rest of the company's strategy. Kroc wanted every store to be a place where adults would not feel uncomfortable when their children visited the restrooms. McDonald's giveaways of toys based on Disney characters and its TV ads for kids' "Happy Meals" further reinforced the message that everything at McDonald's would be wholesome and predictable. As Kroc himself put it, "A child who loves our TV commercials and brings her grandparents to a McDonald's gives us two more customers."

In almost every country where McDonald's came to operate, it had the effect of empowering children—or, in another view, exploiting them. The format encouraged children to choose what they wanted and assured them that they would get it quickly. Ronald McDonald began to appear on TV all over the world. In China he became "Uncle McDonald," in Japan, "Donald Maka-donaldo," to accommodate local difficulties in pronouncing the letter "R" and juxtaposing two hard consonants. A group of academic anthropologists studied the company's experiences in East Asia and published their findings in an excellent book called *Golden Arches East* (1997). They discovered that McDonald's not only appealed to children but also became something of a refuge for women in the often male-dominated cultures of East Asia.

## The U.S. Workforce

Another academic study found that the average age of fast-food employees was just over 20, the number of years of education just under 12, and the proportion working part-time 64 percent. The number of employees per store averaged about 40, of whom 64 percent were female, 52 percent students, and 13 percent African

American. These figures were for the industry as a whole, not just McDonald's.

By the 1980s, each McDonald's restaurant, on the average, was employing about 65 workers and five salaried managers. More people in the U.S. workforce were getting their first job at McDonald's than at any other employer, including the Army. By 2008, according to the company, close to 10 million Americans had worked at McDonald's. The employee turnover rate, like that of other fast-food franchises, sometimes reached 200 percent per year. Many employees were either teenagers or senior citizens working part-time, recent immigrants, or high school graduates just entering the workforce.

Until 1966, the company continued the McDonald brothers' policy of hiring no women. Nor did it have a good reputation as a place of management opportunity for minorities. But by the 1980s, 57 percent of McDonald's workers were women, and by the early twenty-first century women comprised about 40 percent of its franchisees, either individually or as part of a husband-wife team. They developed a Women Operators' Network, one of many ancillary organizations within the McDonald's system.

For African Americans the company went to special lengths to help startups, often requiring less than the usual initial investment from prospective owner-operators. In 2008, about 14 percent of McDonald's U.S. franchisees were African Americans—many of them master franchisees, as 320 African Americans operated about 1200 stores. In the same year, about 20 percent of the company's U.S. workforce were African Americans, as were 17 percent of McDonald's corporate officers. Many articles in the print media, especially those targeted primarily to black subscribers, praised McDonald's success at achieving genuine diversity. In *Fortune*'s annual list of the 50 best companies for minorities, McDonald's has consistently ranked at the top or very near it.

## The Negative Side

There are few unmixed blessings in life, and McDonald's, despite its many virtues, is not one of them. Among other issues, its history raises serious questions about labor practices, nutrition, and the exploitation of children.

1. *Labor.* In any food-service business, labor constitutes the largest single expense. About 90 percent of McDonald's franchisees and 60 percent of company-owned stores start off their many part-time employees at the minimum wage. Then, too, as in all fast-food restaurants, an important element of success is a policy of shifting most of the burden of uneven customer flow onto employees. When traffic is low, they're often told to punch out and go home. When it's high, they're asked to stay beyond prescheduled working hours. In temporarily slack periods, they're urged to straighten up the store. As one slogan goes, "If there's time to lean, there's time to clean." Sometimes employees work split shifts based on customer flows at mealtimes throughout the day. They leave work after one "rush," then return on the same day for the next period of heavy customer demand.

In 2007, a business school professor named Jerry Newman published a book called *My Secret Life on the McJob.* Newman had taken a 14-month leave to work at seven fast-food outlets located around the United States, including McDonald's. His highest wage was $6.50 per hour. He found wide variations among different outlets of the same stores. This, of course, is just what one might expect. In McDonald's early years, when Ray Kroc and Fred Turner were working with a few hundred franchises, they could enforce their standards. But rigorous consistency at 13,000 U.S. stores is all but impossible, and the same is true for the 18,000 located outside the country.

During his 14 months on the McJob, Jerry Newman found that many franchisees trained their workers well, but many others didn't. Nor was the food always of uniform quality. In the end, he found himself with greater respect for the workers than he'd expected to have, and less for many of the managers. Everything depended on the attitude of the person in charge of the store, or of the shift.

While this is hardly a surprising conclusion—it applies to workplaces of any kind—it goes against what McDonald's advertising leads the customer to expect. The company's goal is that consumers receive the same quality of food and the same good service in any McDonald's regardless of where it's located or who's in charge. Yet readers of this book likely know from their own experience—as employees and as customers—that all McDonald's are not alike. Sometimes the service is quick, sometimes it isn't. Sometimes the food is hot, sometimes it isn't. Sometimes the restrooms are clean, but often they're dirty. In general, the more urban the store, the lower the grades it earns on Fred Turner's original QSC report card of quality, service, cleanliness, and overall performance. Downtown stores seem noticeably worse than suburban or rural ones, but there are many exceptions.

2. *Nutrition.* When Ray Kroc created the McDonald's system in 1955, most consumers were very poorly informed about nutrition. American schoolchildren routinely learned that "nature's three most perfect foods" were eggs, milk, and liver—all of which are now recognized as heavy in saturated fats. The nutrition labels that today appear by law on nearly all packaged foods simply weren't there. People who wanted to count their calories faced almost impossible barriers. Even so, obesity was not the major national health problem then that it is now. A consumer could go to a McDonald's and get a reasonably healthy meal consisting of a hamburger, an order of french fries, and a Coke, totaling about 500 calories. A slice of cheese for the burger added about 100 more. Normal portions at that time were what children's portions are today, and in some cases less: a Coke was seven ounces compared to today's 12-ounce child's serving.

But as fast-food chains began to multiply, competition grew increasingly fierce. As a result, "portion control" began a wild upward spiral. Burger King's "Whopper," introduced in the mid-1960s, contained 680 calories by itself, 780 with a slice of cheese added. By this time, government-mandated nutrition data had begun to appear on packaged foods in grocery stores. Ironically, however, the more information the government forced the food industry to disclose, the worse the national problem of obesity became. The issue reached near-epidemic proportions even as McDonald's and other chains began to post nutrition data on tray liners and the walls of their stores.

At 7-Eleven convenience stores, a customer could buy "Big Gulp" cups of soft drinks containing 64 ounces—nearly 10 times the size of the Coca-Cola Company's original and longtime standard of six-and-a-half-ounce bottles. A 64-ounce serving of Coke or other sugared drink totals 776 calories, less the space for whatever amount of ice customers choose to add. Even McDonald's and Burger Kings sold 32-ounce cups of soft drinks.

In 2004 the filmmaker Morgan Spurlock released a documentary titled *Super Size Me,* in which he reported the results of eating all of his meals at McDonald's for 30 days. In a nod to fairness, he ordered every item on the menu at least once during the period, and he accepted offers of "Super Size" portions only when specifically asked by the counterperson. On average, Spurlock consumed 5,000–6,000 calories per day. He gained more than 24 pounds during his month-long experiment and claimed the diet made him sluggish and borderline depressed. An expanded version of *Super Size Me* was later released on DVD, and many excerpts from it are available on YouTube. Meanwhile, Spurlock's adventure stimulated many other individual experiments throughout the world, with widely differing results. Some people ate McDonald's salads, drank water, and lost weight. Others shunned large portions and experienced no loss or gain of weight.

By 2009, a customer entering almost any fast-food restaurant confronted a menu offering staggering amounts of calories. At McDonald's it was still possible to order the 600-calorie meals of the Kroc era—or with even fewer calories, now that salads are available. But few customers did; most ordered some combination with double or triple the calories usually consumed at Ray Kroc's original restaurants. An apparently reasonable meal might now consist of a Big Mac (590 calories) or a Quarter Pounder with Cheese (530); a medium order of french fries (450, a large order being 540 and a super-size 610), and a medium-sized Coke or other sugared soft drink (133 calories for small, 194 for medium, 255 for large, 388 for king size). Thus, a Big Mac, a medium order of fries, and a medium-sized Coke would total 1,234 calories. And many customers ordered more than this: two sandwiches, a large serving of fries, a dessert of about 300 calories, and free refills of their drink cups. It was not unusual, therefore, for a person to leave a McDonald's, Burger King, or other fast food restaurant having consumed 2,000–2,500 calories, about a full day's food allotment for an average-sized person. And unfortunately, the great majority of these calories come from fat or refined sugar.

Ray Kroc knew much less than his current successors do about nutrition, and he certainly didn't plan on this kind of outcome. But the executives and franchisees who succeeded him faced a very unpleasant choice: between maximizing good nutrition on the one hand and maximizing competitive success on the other. And like nearly all business managers, they chose the financial bottom line. (An excellent guide to nutrition at about 25 leading chains, including McDonald's, appears at www.fastfood.com.)

3. *Children.* From the start, McDonald's targeted children as customers. They are not the most profitable segment of the customer base, but their loyalty to the company may continue into adulthood, and that was McDonald's aim. Since the moment in 1948 when the nine-year-old girl became the first customer at McDonald's newly designed restaurant, the company has emphasized juvenile loyalty. The list of strategies is apparent to anyone familiar with American popular culture: the mascot Ronald McDonald, the playgrounds built adjacent to (and sometimes inside) restaurants, the special "Happy Meals" available to children, the ceaseless giveaways of toys, the affiliations with Disney and similar companies, and the relentless TV advertising.

In Eric Schlosser's best-selling book *Fast Food Nation: The Dark Side of the All-American Meal* (2001), the author writes: "Most of all, I am concerned about its impact on the nation's children. Fast food is heavily marketed to children and prepared by people who are barely older than children. This is an industry that both feeds and feeds off the young." Schlosser's book is the most effective attack on the food industry since Upton Sinclair's famous novel *The Jungle* (1906), which exposed the horrors of meatpacking in Chicago. *Fast Food Nation* is not aimed specifically at McDonald's, though it contains plenty of information about the company. Rather, it's a broad indictment of American culture in general, with fast food as the author's chief exhibit. The exploitation of children is a theme throughout its pages, and the Disney company comes in for savage treatment as well.

In the end, Schlosser accurately concludes that the success of fast food is the result of overt choices: by adults because of its time-saving convenience and inexpensive prices; by children seduced by its advertising and the quick delivery and engineered tastiness of its products; and by parents who give to their children the power to make decisions about where and what to eat. Here, as in so many other ways, decision making since 1920 has continued to move steadily downward in hierarchical organizations—including the family.

In an even broader sense, as the economist Joseph Schumpeter wrote in 1942, the coming of free-market capitalism not only enabled masses of people to achieve major material gains, but also freed them "to make a mess of their own lives." Even though prevailing social and economic trends powerfully shaped the range of choices, each person now had "all the individualist rope he needed in order to hang himself."

## Internationalization

By the 1980s, the American market was beginning to choke on the proliferation of fast-food outlets, and if McDonald's wished to keep growing, the logical next step was expansion abroad. The same was true for other chains. In the 1980s, about 400 American firms established nearly 40,000 stores outside the United States, an increase of more than 70 percent in foreign outlets during this one decade. By 2005, more than half of the restaurants in the McDonald's system were located outside the United States, and a new store was opening somewhere every three hours, a much faster rate than in the home country.

Following the pattern established by IBM and other pioneering multinationals, McDonald's tried to tailor its operations to local cultures. In Japan it offered teriyaki burgers, in India a hamburger with no beef. In Germany customers could get McRibs with beer, in Norway McLaks (grilled salmon), in Uruguay McHuevos (hamburgers topped with poached eggs). In Saudi Arabia McDonald's had separate seating sections for men and women, and each store closed four times a day for prayers.

Although it had little chance of doing so in foreign nations, McDonald's tried to downplay its American origins. Its Canadian operation, started in 1968, was run by a Canadian. Its large Japanese system began in 1971 as a 50-50 joint venture between McDonald's on the one hand and the young entrepreneur Den Fujita and the Daiichiya Baking Company on the other. Soon Den Fujita bought out the interest of Daiichiya Baking, ran the McDonald's operation himself, and became almost as famous in Japan as Ray Kroc was in America. By 1983, the gross sales of McDonald's Japan had surpassed those of the largest indigenous Japanese fast-food chain, Sushi Company, which operated more than 2,000 stores.

Eventually McDonald's reached into so many different countries that *The Economist* magazine began to measure relative costs of living by comparing the prices of Big Macs throughout the world. In 2007, for example, the average was $3.41 in the United States, $5.20 in Switzerland (the highest number), and $1.43 in China (the lowest). *The Economist* also drew conclusions from these figures about the degree to which local currencies were overvalued or undervalued by the standard of the American dollar. For both cost of living and relative currency values, the magazine's annual "Big Mac Index" proved remarkably reliable. Meanwhile, despite all its efforts, McDonald's remained a quintessential American symbol, the number-one emblem of U.S. consumer culture.

## Past and Future

In the early twenty-first century, the top 50 franchised restaurant systems oversaw well over 100,000 outlets within the United States. Of these, about three-fourths were owned by local franchisees, one-fourth by the franchisor. The differences among companies were extremely wide: 85 percent of the 13,000 McDonald's outlets were owned by franchisees, 15 percent directly by McDonald's Corporation. By contrast, 100 percent of the 21,000 Subway stores were owned by franchisees. Subways, which typically occupied very small retail spaces, averaged only about 20 percent of McDonald's $2 million sales per store.

A business academic named Jeffrey Bradach wrote that the growth of franchising represented "the mass production of organization itself." This was a real milestone in the evolution of American business. And, like many other milestones, it was almost completely unforeseen. In earlier times, practically nobody had predicted the sudden appearance of retail innovations such as department stores, mail-order houses, nonfranchised chain stores, supermarkets, or shopping malls. Yet in retrospect, it is clear that each of these formats filled a new societal need as the purchasing power of Americans and their geographical patterns of residence changed.

As noted earlier, McDonald's tremendous growth made it harder and harder for the company to keep all of its franchisees in line. The larger the system grew, the more difficult it became to enforce the Quality, Service, and Cleanliness formula developed by Ray Kroc and Fred Turner. Yet McDonald's continued to record by far the highest sales-per-store figures in the industry; and it was strong testament to Ray Kroc's original vision that his company remained the leader in fast food two generations after its founding.

Kroc's style of franchising represented another benchmark in the persistent effort by American managers to balance centralization with decentralization in the face of changing external conditions. Franchising at McDonald's and other companies proved to be an extraordinarily flexible way to place decision making at the spot where the best information was available to resolve particular problems. Then, too, very useful information came from the networks of McDonald's suppliers, which sprang up everywhere, often sponsored by the central corporation but always kept independent of it. In each of these arrangements, the management talent and financial clout of big business complemented the local knowledge, personal drive, and sweat equity typical of small startup firms.

At the beginning, in the 1950s, the McDonald's system had been put together by entrepreneurial visionaries with little schooling but lots of energy and common sense. The special contribution of Ray Kroc, June Martino, and Harry Sonneborn was their ingenious combination of methods for aligning the incentives of every participant so as to make the whole of the McDonald's system exceed the sum of its parts.

As Kroc liked to put it, "Franchising has become an updated version of the American Dream"—because it offered rewards commensurate with individual effort. But he also said, "None of us is as good as all of us." Kroc and his colleagues perfected an organizational formula used successfully by thousands of McDonald's franchisees in more than a hundred countries. And despite the serious flaws that arose mostly after Kroc's own era, few companies in any industry have ever matched that kind of achievement.

**FIND YOUR WAR JOB**
**In Industry – Agriculture – Business**

*Top: In the early 1940s the U.S. Office of War Information distributed posters such as this one urging women to "find your war job."* Corbis and Minnesota Historical Society.

*Bottom: Individual companies reinforced the idea of women's contributions to the war effort, as in this poster from Westinghouse. Corbis.*

*Top: The investment banker and War Production Board vice-chairman Ferdinand Eberstadt, whose ingenious Controlled Materials Plan thrust industrial mobilization forward during World War II.* Corbis/Bettmann-UPI.

*Above: The hard-driving Eberstadt, by now back on Wall Street, testifying in 1954 before the Senate Banking Committee.* Corbis/Bettmann-UPI.

*Opposite top: Like Ford Motor Co. and nearly all other big businesses, Boeing had modest beginnings. Here is its first home in Seattle, under military guard during World War I.* Used with the permission of The Boeing Company.

*Opposite bottom: Boeing employees stitching fabric onto the wingframe of a biplane for the U.S. Army, 1922.* Used with the permission of The Boeing Company.

Top: Boeing's B-17 bomber, the famous Flying Fortress of World War II. Used with the permission of The Boeing Company.

Right: David Sarnoff of RCA and Guglielmo Marconi, inventor of wireless radiotelegraphy, at the RCA transmitting center on Long Island, New York, 1933. Corbis/Bettmann-UPI.

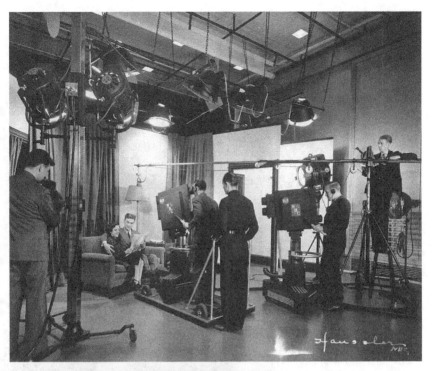

Top: Experimental broadcasting by RCA's subsidiary NBC in 1936, the earliest days of television. Courtesy of Baker Library, Harvard Business School.

Left: Watching an early model TV set, late 1930s. Corbis/Schenectady Museum, Hall of Electrical History Foundation.

*Top: David Sarnoff at the 1939 New York World's Fair, broadcasting announcements about the progress of television.* Corbis/Bettmann-UPI.

*Right:Sarnoff after the triumph of color TV in the 1960s: the business dandy at the height of his fame.* Courtesy of Baker Library, Harvard Business School.

*Above: Ray Kroc's first McDonald's restaurant in Des Plaines, Illinois, built in 1955 and now a museum.* Corbis/Bettmann.

*Left: Ray Kroc in 1963, age 61. McDonald's Corporation had opened 315 restaurants in 37 states, but had not yet gone public.* Bettmann/Corbis.

*Above: A proud Kroc in the late 1960s, when McDonald's became an eat-in as well as a takeout restaurant.* Corbis/Bettmann.

# PROLOGUE TO PART II

In the first five chapters of this book, we've examined the history of American business by analyzing social and economic trends since 1920. Part I proceeded chronologically, based on the history of each industry covered—period by period, decade by decade, and year by year. We've paid special attention to a few companies of tremendous importance: Ford, General Motors, Procter & Gamble, RCA, Boeing, and McDonald's. We've also looked at industrial mobilization for World War II, which, like each company history, illustrates the major themes of the book:

1. *The relentlessness of change.*
2. *The growing empowerment of consumers and entrepreneurs.*
3. *The tension between centralized and decentralized decision making and the general triumph of decentralization.*
4. *The ongoing tension between the dark side of business and the government's catch-up role as regulator.*

As noted in the introduction to the book, none of these themes have progressed without interruption. Although there are important exceptions to all of them, they've shown remarkable persistence. The same four themes will appear in the final three chapters. The major difference is that these chapters are organized primarily by topic rather than chronology. They treat the whole history of their subjects since 1920 rather than just a single decade or period: one chapter on women and minorities, one on the financial system, and one on information technology.

None of these chapters can be comprehensive. Many books much longer than this one have been written about each of the topics. There are many excellent works, for example, not only about the general histories of women and of minorities, but specifically about women in business, African Americans in business, and so on. Because this book is so brief, it can't cover these subjects with the same depth as specialized studies. So what follows in the next chapter—the first of the final three—is an *overview* composed of sections about the business experience of women, African Americans, and Hispanics. Women make up just over half the population, and their influence in business has grown dramatically since the 1970s. For most of the nation's history, African Americans were the largest minority group. And Hispanics, who have immigrated in significant numbers not only from Mexico but also from two dozen other countries, now make up the largest minority group, comprising by 2009 about 15 percent of the nation's population and still rising. The number of minorities examined here could be much larger, of course: Asians, Jews, Muslims, and so on. But the length of this book is no match for America's great diversity.

How can we thoroughly unravel the many roles of women in business? Obviously, we can't. Nor can we do justice to the full range of business adventures encountered by African Americans and Hispanics. But we can provide a brief historical analysis of the business experience of these three groups.

The chapter on finance also shows a pattern very much in flux, particularly in recent years. Before the 1940s, each side of the financial sector's balance scale of risk and reward made frequent and wild moves, up and down, much like the mood swings of a manic depressive. But from the 1940s until the 1980s, the regulatory controls imposed in the wake of the Great Depression prevailed. Those controls brought both the risks and rewards under tighter control through an intricate system based on financial transparency and administered by business and government, acting together in responsible concert. Then, during the 1980s, business began to chip away at the regulations, removing strictures piece by piece. It did this with the assent of government, which sometimes acted wisely but more often foolishly or not at all. The result was a wave of financial innovations carried out under a relaxed regulatory regime. The innovations brought very high rewards—especially to financiers themselves—but also very high risks to smaller investors and the national economy. By the twenty-first century, the financial system had begun to spin seriously out of control for the first time in 70 years. Its gyrations endangered not only the financial sector but the "real" economy as well. Once again the government faced the challenging prospect of playing catch-up—this time a more difficult task because of the newly globalized nature of finance.

The final chapter of this book takes up the fabulous story of information technology: "IT," as it has come to be called. Here one sees how IT became "it"—perhaps the most exciting development in the history of business, and one that shot forward with unprecedented speed. The Internet, though now pervasive in the lives of billions of people around the world, is still very young, having exploded only in the late 1990s. The stories of IBM, Hewlett-Packard, Intel, and Microsoft—companies that pioneered the IT revolution—already seem a bit old hat, which is an odd circumstance from a historical point of view. The final chapter considers not only these firms but also the hundreds of startups epitomized by the terms "venture capital" and "Silicon Valley," as well as major second-generation companies such as Amazon.com, eBay, and Google.

# CHAPTER SIX

# The Empowerment of Women and Minorities

## Overview

Whatever the faults of McDonald's Corporation, its story is as good a model for the progress of women and minorities as that of any other large firm. In 2009, about 41 percent of its owner-operators were women or minorities. Ralph Alvarez, a Cuban American, was its president and chief operating officer, the number-two post in the company. About 24 percent of its corporate officers were women and 25 percent were minorities, mostly African Americans. As we have seen, this progress required a sustained effort to recruit minority franchisees, as well as a radical change from the company's original policy of hiring no women to work at its restaurants.

Capitalism works best under purely meritocratic conditions, and money should know no color or gender. But any economic system reflects the underlying values of the broader society in which it operates, and in many ways both American business and the workforce have always been divided along lines of gender, race, and ethnicity. These divisions affected the ways in which people thought about business and also influenced the strategies followed by different kinds of companies. Business as a whole neither took the lead in promoting diversity nor lagged behind most of the rest of society.

Until the late twentieth century, nearly all of the important characters in the story of major American companies were white men. Women and minorities joined the narrative in large numbers during World War II, but for the most part as unnamed masses of wartime factory workers. Certainly women and minorities have always labored productively both inside the household and outside the home for pay. But until recently, their entrepreneurial potential was severely shackled, at least in the national economy of mass-marketed goods and services. Most of their successes came in industries catering primarily to specialized markets: women producing for and selling to other women, African Americans to other African Americans, Hispanics to other Hispanics, and Asians to other Asians. There were thousands of successful entrepreneurs among women and minorities, but nearly all of them operated under a relatively low ceiling above which they could not rise no matter how capable they were.

Big changes did come over time, however, and the outlook today is drastically different from that in 1920, or even 1970. Women and minorities now can at least compete for leadership positions in the nation's top companies, but nothing in this dramatic rise has come easily. Breaking through centuries of repression took heroic measures of fighting and striving.

## Women in Business

Today more than 70 percent of all retail purchases (by value) are made by women, and since 1920 women's power as consumers has grown faster than has that of men. So, too, has women's power as employees and executives. Yet women still do not stand on an equal economic footing with men. More often than not, important business decisions were made for and about both women and minorities rather than by them.

Since 1920, the percentage of women in the potential out-of-home workforce who have paying jobs has approximately tripled. So women entered the labor market and the business world in a major way, but relatively late in the 230-odd years of U.S. history since 1776. During the nineteenth century and most of the twentieth, women's jobs were concentrated in a few areas: teaching, nursing, library work, domestic service, and products and services oriented toward other women, such as dressmaking, millinery, and hair and beauty salons. Numerous women were already working in corporate offices, as well. As early as 1920, women comprised half of the nation's clerical workforce, as compared to only 2.5 percent in 1870. This shift derived in part from the invention of the modern-keyboard typewriter (1872) and the telephone (1876); and also from expansions in the office staffs of large firms. By 1920 more than 90 percent of stenographers and typists were female, as well as half of all bookkeepers. Many men who had been bookkeepers moved into the better-paying profession of accounting, which they dominated for the rest of the century.

The number of female managers, officials, and proprietors rose slowly, from 4.5 percent of the total in 1900 to 11 percent in 1940 to about 40 percent today. Under the emergency of World War II, millions of women temporarily filled "male" positions in workshops and factories, where they earned better pay than ever before, though less than men performing the same work. During the postwar housing boom, women began to establish a strong presence in fields such as residential real estate, and by 1977 they comprised 44 percent of all real estate brokers nationwide.

Then, in the closing decades of the twentieth century, women achieved spectacular gains in prestigious professions long dominated by men. Today women make up far higher percentages of all lawyers, university professors, physicians, dentists, pharmacists, and certified public accountants than they have at any other time in the nation's history. This very quick progress in the professions owed much to changes in federal law, and the same held true for management jobs within companies. Women and minorities benefited especially from legislation passed during the 1960s: the 1963 Equal Pay Act for women, and the 1964 Civil Rights Act and other laws spearheaded by African Americans. The Equal Pay Act was deeply flawed, since it exempted executive, professional, administrative, and teaching positions. Title VII of the Civil Rights Act banned job discrimination based not only on race, color, national origin, and religion, but also on sex. Congressional opponents of this bill had inserted the word *sex* into its provisions, thinking that by doing so they would kill any possibility of passage; but they proved too clever for their own aims. The bill passed, and the women's movement skillfully adapted the new law to its own relentless quest for equal opportunity. In 1972 Congress amended the Equal Pay Act of 1963 to remove the exemptions for executive and other positions, and in the same year it passed the landmark Equal Employment Opportunity Act, which benefited women and especially minorities.

## Entrepreneurship

Throughout the nation's history, there have been many more female entrepreneurs than is commonly believed, and the long tradition of women's businesses catering to other women continues today. Some entrepreneurs whose names became especially well-known built thriving enterprises in cosmetics and hair care: Elizabeth Arden, Helena Rubenstein, Madame C. J. Walker, Estée Lauder, and Mary Kay Ash. The last three women eventually took their places among some of the greatest of all American entrepreneurs.

Madame Celeste J. Walker (1867–1919) was a daughter of former slaves. During the late nineteenth century and early twentieth, she built up a hair-care and hot-comb business that earned her a personal fortune of several million dollars, part of which she spent on an elegant mansion overlooking the Hudson River in New York. Bereft of formal education, Walker proved to be an exceptionally shrewd business manager. By the time of her death, some 25,000 agents were marketing her line of products, primarily to African Americans.

Estée Lauder, who was born in 1908 to immigrants living in Queens, New York, got her start by mixing skin creams in her kitchen and selling them to a beauty parlor. When the parlor's owner set up a salon in Manhattan's Upper East Side, Lauder and her husband/business partner found entrance into a more promising market. Besides supplying the new salon, the tireless Lauder gave demonstrations at resort hotels and at private social gatherings in New York City and Palm Beach, Florida. Determined to move her client base upscale, she began to target elite department stores such as Saks Fifth Avenue, I. Magnin, and Neiman Marcus. Some of her main competitors—Max Factor, Helena Rubenstein, and Revlon—often sold through drugstores, but not Lauder. By 2009, the company's annual revenues exceeded $7 billion and had nearly a 50 percent share of the cosmetics market in U.S. department stores. Lauder herself, who died in 2004 at the age of 97, had a reputation as one of the most energetic, ruthless, and resourceful executives in American business—the only woman listed in *Time*'s top 20 businesspeople of the twentieth century.

Mary Kay Ash started her company in 1963 at the age of 45. After having invested her life savings of $5,000 (the equivalent of about $35,000 in 2009) in her inventory for her budding business, she began to teach hundreds of other women how to sell cosmetics door to door. She imbued these agents with a cheerleading spirit and a reluctance to take any customer's "no" for an answer. She gave her sales agents a 50 percent commission, and her business prospered almost at once. By the time of her death in 2001, Mary Kay Cosmetics had annual sales of more than $2 billion and employed 800,000 representatives (most of whom worked part-time) in 37 countries. By 2009, 35,000 full-time Independent Sales Directors worked for the company, 14,000 of them in the United States. Many Sales Directors earned six-figure incomes. "We offer them the opportunity to have it all," Ash once said of her policy of encouraging women to combine their careers with a full family life. She liked to wear a bumblebee lapel pin, and to say that bumblebees flew quite well even though the laws of physics seemed to suggest that they could never get off the ground.

Only in the closing decades of the twentieth century did it become possible for large numbers of women to seek the kind of entrepreneurial independence pioneered by Walker, Lauder, and Ash. As late as 1972, less than 5 percent of all U.S. companies were owned by women. Just one in seven women-owned firms had paid employees, and the aggregate receipts of these firms were a minuscule 0.3 percent of the national total for all companies.

Then came dramatic progress. Only ten years later, in 1982, women-owned businesses comprised one-fourth of all companies and generated about 10 percent of total receipts. By 1992 these numbers had risen to more than one-third of all firms, generating nearly 20 percent of total receipts. Minority women had made especially large gains. Between 1987 and 1996, the number of firms owned by Hispanic women rose by about 200 percent, by Asian women 150 percent, and by African American women 135 percent. By the early twenty-first century, businesses owned by women accounted for about one-fourth of all U.S. sales, and women were starting more than 40 percent of all new firms.

American opinion toward the issue of women in the out-of-home workforce flipped between the 1970s and the end of the century. In a poll taken in 1977, a sample of adults were asked, "Do you agree or disagree that it is much better for everyone involved if the man is the achiever outside the home and the woman takes care of the home and the family?" In response, 66 percent said they agreed. The same question asked in 1996 elicited only 38 percent agreement.

By then, about 65 percent of mothers with preschoolers were working outside the home, a figure five times what it had been in 1950. (That percentage is still rising, though only slightly.) For married women with school-age children, more than three-fourths had paying jobs or were looking for work, and many remained responsible for taking care of children after returning home (the "double day," as many women called it). By the twenty-first century, about 30 percent of children aged five and under were being taken to daycare centers, up from a scant 6 percent in 1965. The number of these centers increased markedly beginning in the 1990s, as did the number of companies offering onsite child care. In addition, some 25 percent of employed mothers, and more than 60 percent of mothers in poor families, were receiving help from relatives in caring for preschool children during working hours.

## Highly Compensated Women

Opportunities for women in top management were slow in coming. As late as 1970, a time in which women made up 75 percent of all American clerical workers, they accounted for less than 4 percent of managers and administrators earning more than $15,000 per year (the equivalent of $82,000 in 2009).

It was symptomatic of the problem that for three generations most elite business schools admitted only men. Harvard, for example, took no women into its regular MBA program until 1963, and even its class of 1973 was less than 5 percent female. By 1983 this figure had plateaued at about 26 percent—still a minority but a big gain nonetheless. For the class of 2010, the number had grown to 36 percent. Nationwide, women MBA students grew from 4 percent of the total in 1960 to about 35 percent in 2009, as compared to 52 percent for women medical students in 2009 and 56 percent for law students. But numbers alone could not tell the whole story. In a survey done 15 years after graduation, members of the Harvard MBA class of 1983 were asked, "How has being a woman affected your career?" In response, more than half said negatively and less than a fourth said positively.

In 2009, highly compensated female executives were earning only about 70 percent as much as their male counterparts, a gap ten percentage points lower than for working women in general. Part of the reason why higher-ranking women suffered a greater gender-based discrepancy was that in large corporations women tended to gravitate or be relegated to positions in staff departments known as the "three R's": public relations, industrial relations, and human resources. A smaller percentage of women were assigned to "line" jobs such as division presidents or vice-presidents, and general managers of sales or production departments. In contrast to staff jobs, these positions included profit-and-loss responsibilities and carried higher salaries. In the eyes of many women, the issue of compensation, considered by itself, was not a simple one. As the renowned economist Claudia Goldin put it in 2006, "Is equality of income what we really want? Do we want everyone to have an equal chance to work 80 hours [per week] in their prime reproductive years? Yes, but we don't expect them to take that chance equally often."

In *Fortune* 500 companies, 15 percent of all corporate directors were women in 2009, up from 11 percent a decade earlier, and from virtually zero in 1960. There were 13 women CEOs, up from three in 2000 and none in 1960. Viewed from one perspective, this was significant progress. Still, only a small percentage of women had broken through the "glass ceiling" and attained top management positions in big American businesses. (The term "glass ceiling" was coined in 1986 by two writers in the *Wall Street Journal*, Carol Hymowitz and Timothy Schellhardt.) The proportion was even lower in other countries. Whereas 15 percent of the directors of large U.S. companies were women, the corresponding figure in Britain was about half that. According to one survey, women held about 40 percent of management positions at all ranks in American firms, but only 20 to 30 percent in European ones and, by most estimates, far less in Asian companies.

The ultimate pattern of women's roles in American management was hard to predict. For one thing, there remained a perception that many women wished to follow an uninterrupted career path while others opted for what the writer Felice Schwartz called the "mommy track," a phrase that in itself angered some women. Then, too, there was a wide variance according to industry. Among firms of significant size, about 30 percent of nonprofits were headed by women, as compared to only 3 percent for semiconductor firms.

In some industries, a significant number of male executives still seemed threatened by the idea of having a female boss. Many women believed that this attitude had to be met head-on, with forthright assertions of authority. Darla Moore, president of Rainwater, Inc., a financial firm that wielded power as an institutional investor, commented in 1998 that she and other high-ranking women tended to be "outliers, mavericks, misfits"—and that this was a good thing. She advised other women who aspired to power to ignore such counsel as: "You should be a nice girl," and "You ought to fit in." Moore derided this kind of guidance as leading to "a colossal waste of time." Carleton Fiorina, who headed Hewlett-Packard from 2000 to 2005, said shortly having been fired by HP's board that her critics had spoken of her "as either a bimbo—too soft, or a bitch—too hard." Like many other high-profile CEOs of both sexes, Fiorina had taken some very bold steps. She oversaw HP's acquisition of

Compaq, a leading manufacturer of personal computers, and at one point laid off 36,000 employees.

Overall, it is clear that during the period since 1920, and especially since 1980, women have made immense progress in business. Not only are more women participating at all levels but their influence has changed some fundamental aspects of business culture. Family-friendly policies such as flex time, liberal leave for new parents, and onsite daycare facilities have emerged from women's insistence that companies take a more realistic attitude toward human needs. In addition to women's direct accomplishments in business, the policy changes they have effected were, in and of themselves, major contributions to the larger society. But there is still a long way to go before women reach parity with white men.

## African Americans

The civil rights revolution began with World War II, when large numbers of African Americans served in the armed forces. During the conflict black service people were often restricted to segregated units, but their major role in both military action abroad and industrial mobilization at home constituted a milestone in their long quest for equal opportunity. President Harry Truman's executive order to integrate the military, which he issued in 1948, signaled the beginning of the end of legal segregation in the United States. Over the next two decades, a combination of judicial decisions and federal legislation struck down barriers in education, public accommodations, and employment. Although much remained to be done, more progress had been made during the last part of the twentieth century and the first decade of the twenty-first than in any other period since the end of legal slavery in 1865.

As businesspeople, African Americans had a long history of entrepreneurship, beginning well before the Civil War. Historically, most black enterprises, like most firms owned by women, had been small, undercapitalized, and in constant danger of insolvency. Then the early twentieth century ushered in what some writers have called a "golden age" of black business, as greater numbers of African Americans started companies and a few became millionaires. Between 1900 and 1930 the number of black-owned enterprises increased by 700 percent. Like many women-owned businesses selling to other women, most black-owned firms targeted African American consumers. The same was true of other ethnic minorities, whose enterprises often served the needs and tastes of their own groups.

During the early decades of the twentieth century, blacks had achieved notable success in banks and insurance companies that catered to the African American community, and, as the story of Madame C. J. Walker attests, in the hair-care and beauty-aids business. A survey done in 1944 concluded that six types of black-owned firms predominated at the time: beauty parlors, barber shops, restaurants, grocery stores, shoe-repair shops, and funeral homes.

The question of whether black entrepreneurs should focus on black customers was, and still remains, a controversial issue that cuts across the political spectrum. From the formation of Booker T. Washington's "conservative" National Negro Business League in 1900 to the emergence of the "radical" Nation of Islam 30 years later, such a policy seemed to be a viable formula for self-help. The African American intellectual W. E. B. DuBois, who disagreed with Booker T. Washington on many strategies for black progress, once argued that "Ten million people who join in intelligent self-help can never be long ignored or mistreated." Business was particularly important for advancement because "No race that has anything to contribute to the markets of the world is long in any degree ostracized." Nevertheless, DuBois and other business advocates also acknowledged that for black entrepreneurs to cater only to members of their own race put them at a disadvantage, by targeting a less affluent segment of the population and therefore limiting possibilities for business growth.

Management positions in predominantly white firms did not begin to open up for African Americans, even those with college degrees, until the 1970s. The number of African Americans graduating from college approximately doubled between 1970 and 2000, and a higher percentage of graduates entered business than had previously been the case. Because of the big increase in college graduates, the black middle class grew much larger after 1970.

At the same time, an economic irony began to appear. Middle-class black consumers became more integrated into the white-dominated mainstream of American business, and therefore less likely to spend their money at traditionally black-owned enterprises. This trend had the unintended consequence of diminishing the relative economic and social status of thousands of local black business leaders. At the start of the twenty-first century, African Americans owned nearly half a million firms. Yet on a per-capita basis, blacks were less than a third as likely to own a business as were whites. The receipts of black-owned firms made up about 1 percent of the national total, even though African Americans comprised about 13 percent of the population.

Still, there had been substantial progress in particular sectors. During the twentieth century as a whole, the most important black-owned firms were in the insurance industry. The North Carolina Mutual Life Insurance Company, founded in 1898, attracted first-rate talent and by 1920 employed 1,100 people. A second major firm, Atlanta Life Insurance, was established in 1905 by Alonzo Herndon, a former slave who had made his seed money in the barber-shop business. Other big companies included Supreme Life Insurance (Chicago, 1921), United Mutual Life Insurance (New York, 1933), and Golden State Mutual (Los Angeles, important especially in the 1960s because of its innovations in group sales). By 1960, 46 black-owned insurance companies were in operation, and in 1971 North Carolina Mutual had more than $1 billion of insurance in force (about $5.5 billion in 2009 equivalent). By the 1990s, after a series of mergers, 19 black-owned companies had in force $23 billion of insurance.

During the closing decades of the twentieth century, black incomes had risen very significantly as a percentage of white incomes. Gains in accumulated wealth, however, came more slowly. In 1984, black households had a median net worth only one-twelfth that of white households, and 25 years later this figure had not changed much. Yet by that time several thousand African

Americans had become extraordinarily wealthy through careers in business, entertainment, and professional sports—a situation unprecedented in American history. There were a few middle-class examples as well. In Queens, one of the five boroughs of New York, median black household income exceeded that of white households.

## Entrepreneurs

Black-owned enterprises have succeeded in a wide variety of industries. As reported in the magazine *Black Enterprise,* the largest number of wealthy African American businesspeople today are owners of automobile dealerships or fast-food franchises. Historically, in addition to life-insurance companies, one of the best-known firms owned by blacks was Motown Records, founded in the 1960s by Berry Gordy, scion of a prominent Detroit family. With sales of $61 million (equivalent to about $225 million in 2009), Motown was America's largest black-owned nonfinancial firm in 1977 and number two in 1985, when its sales reached $149 million ($300 million in 2009 dollars). In 1988 the company was sold to MCA Records, and black America suffered a symbolic loss.

Another large firm was Johnson Publishing, which puts out *Jet* and *Ebony* magazines and has a stake in radio, real estate, insurance, and beauty products. From the 1970s until the present time, this company has ranked either number one or number two among nonfinancial firms owned by African Americans. The brainchild of John Johnson (1918–2005), one of the leading black entrepreneurs of his generation, Johnson Publishing had sales of $50 million in 1977, $361 million in 1997, and $472 million in 2007.

A third prominent entrepreneur was Reginald Lewis, founder of the TLC Group, a conglomerate that in 1987 engineered a $985 million leveraged buyout of Beatrice International Foods, a company doing most of its business overseas. Lewis thereby created the largest black-owned business in American history; his published autobiography was entitled *Why Should White Guys Have All the Fun?* In 1993 he died of a brain tumor at the age of 50, and his wife, Loida Nicolas Lewis, then ran the firm for several years, gradually selling off all of its disparate parts by 1999.

The first black-owned cable TV system, Black Entertainment Television (BET), was founded in 1980 by Robert L. Johnson. By 1990 it offered 24-hour programming to 27 million households through 2,200 cable systems in the United States, Puerto Rico, and the Virgin Islands. By 2009 BET was reaching 85 million households. Robert Johnson sold his company to the media conglomerate Viacom in 2000, and in 2001 he became America's first black billionaire. Among many other business interests, he became principal owner in 2002 of the National Basketball Association's Charlotte Bobcats.

One of the most influential black entrepreneurs in American history is Oprah Winfrey, the actor, TV talk-show host, publisher, and philanthropist. In addition to her work before the camera, Winfrey founded the Harpo Production Company to create films and television programs, and sponsored Oprah's Book Club, whose listed titles were almost guaranteed best-seller status. In 2000, *Time* listed Winfrey, who was then 46 years old, as among the 100 most important people of the twentieth century. In 2003 she became the first African American woman billionaire. Winfrey's male counterpart in several similar roles was Bill Cosby, the entertainer and philanthropist. Cosby was co-owner of the Philadelphia Coca-Cola Bottling Company, which during the 1990s was the third largest black-owned business after TLC Beatrice and the John Johnson publishing group.

In many cities, enterprises of all types owned by African Americans and other minorities benefited from "set-aside" programs begun in 1967 by the U.S. Small Business Administration. These programs specified that a certain percentage of government contracts must be awarded to minority-owned companies. By the 1980s, set-aside contracts were exceeding $2 billion annually. A Supreme Court decision of 1989 cut back on set-aside requirements for projects funded by state and local governments, but the mandates remained a useful promotional device in federal contracts, where they accounted for almost $4 billion in funding by 1990.

Federal loans and grants made to businesses owned by African Americans and other minorities grew from $200 million in 1969 to $7 billion in 1991 ($1.2 billion to $11.5 billion in 2009 equivalents). These firms sold only $83 million in goods and services to the government in 1969, but $17 billion by 1991 (about $500 million to $28 billion in 2009 dollars). Set-asides began to plateau during the 1990s, amid litigation and other controversies. These battles were often less about minority status than about the definition of "small business," especially when small firms performed subcontracted work for big companies. Opponents argued that the real benefactors of set-asides often turned out to be very large firms. Meanwhile, there was little question that set-asides had benefited black enterprises—in effect, by providing vital seed money.

## Highly Compensated African Americans

Only in the late twentieth century did predominantly white corporate America begin to give blacks the chance to compete for high-level positions in large firms. One milestone was the appointment in 1957 of the former baseball star Jackie Robinson as vice-president of the food-service company Chock Full O'Nuts. This event is usually regarded as the first occasion of an African American's acceptance into the ranks of top management in a large and predominantly white firm. Yet even during the 1960s and 1970s, when blacks began to be hired as executives in greater numbers, they were, like white women, often placed in staff departments: human resources, community relations, and public affairs, rather than in front-line positions in production and marketing.

In 1987, Clifton R. Wharton, Jr., became the first African American CEO of a *Fortune* 500 company, TIAA-CREF. In 1995, Noel Hord was named CEO of the Nine West shoe manufacturing company. By 2007, there were six African American CEOs in the *Fortune* 500, but three of them had lost the top spot by February 2008. This was not because of their race but because of poor performance by their firms or industries, in which many whites were fired as well: finance (Stanley O'Neal of Merrill Lynch), entertainment (Richard Parsons of Time Warner), and retailing (Aylwin

Lewis of Sears, where he had become CEO after Sears' acquisition of Kmart, of which he had also been CEO).

As with white women, examples of African American CEOs of large companies remained rare, and African Americans' ascent up the hierarchical ladder in big companies was not a particularly rapid one. Although reliable research on this subject remains sparse, one obvious explanation is that blacks did not gain significant access to the most elite colleges and universities until very late in the game.

Historically, even the few blacks who did attend the nation's best schools often found the going rough after graduation. H. Naylor Fitzhugh, for example, who earned degrees at both Harvard College (class of 1931) and Harvard Business School (1933), was turned away by one prospective employer after another when he entered the job market. Fitzhugh then went into the printing industry, becoming an independent salesman in Washington, D.C. In addition to his own work, he established the New Negro Alliance, through which he persuaded firms operating in mostly African American neighborhoods to hire local residents. In another initiative, he began what became a 30-year relationship with Howard University, where he was instrumental in establishing a marketing department and organizing the school's Small Business Center. In 1965, some 32 years after receiving his Harvard MBA, Fitzhugh was finally hired by a leading firm, PepsiCo. There he developed an innovative marketing campaign directed specifically at African Americans, who constituted a significant block of potential consumers. By the time of his death in 1992, Fitzhugh had served as a mentor to scores of other African Americans making their way in the business world.

African Americans' access to the best colleges and universities increased markedly from 1980 to 2009. While these new opportunities helped some black students a great deal, by no means did graduation from a prestigious institution assure them of equal treatment in major firms. African Americans' sometimes slow progress up the corporate ladder was analyzed in *Breaking Through,* an important study by David A. Thomas and John J. Gabarro published in 1999. The authors found that because of deep-seated and often subtle racism, African American and other minority recruits in large firms usually had to pay a "tax" in the form of additional time spent proving themselves in entry-level positions as compared to the time spent by white recruits. Once the "tax" was paid—and it frequently had to be paid not only at the entry level but for positions at the next couple of tiers as well—minority executives ascended the corporate ladder at higher levels as rapidly as did others. In the meantime, however, precious and unrecoverable time had been lost in their careers.

Outside the culture of big business, African Americans were sometimes less likely to be hindered by the reluctance of supervisors to recommend timely advancement. Blacks were particularly drawn to careers in meritocratic fields such as music and professional sports, where comparative ability was unmistakably identifiable. Large numbers of African Americans also succeeded in reaching the very highest ranks of the U.S. military—the one large organization that had devoted several decades to systematic efforts toward the achievement of racial equality, and in this particular arena a model for the rest of society.

By 2009, the conspicuous progress of African Americans in achieving very high posts in both the military services and government (Colin Powell, Condoleezza Rice, Barack Obama) was not matched by the recognition of blacks in big business. Large corporations still needed to figure out how better to welcome into the high reaches of management not only African Americans but other minorities and women of all races.

## Hispanics

From its origins, the United States has been, as the cliché puts it, "a nation of immigrants." Today most immigrants are regarded as nonwhites—that is, "minorities," and the percentage of people who identify themselves as minorities is higher than at any other time in the nation's history. In 1982 self-identified minorities made up 21 percent of the nation's population. By 2008 the number had leaped to 33 percent: Hispanics about 15 percent, African Americans 13 percent, Asians and Pacific Islanders 5 percent. The total percentage of minorities is predicted to exceed 50 percent of the total population by the year 2042.

Today the largest group of immigrants by far is Hispanics. In Texas, California, and New Mexico, nonwhites (mostly nonwhite Hispanics and African Americans) outnumber whites. In Hawaii the nonwhite population, mostly Pacific Islanders and Asian Americans, comprises 77 percent of the total. But there is a statistical problem in citing all of these percentages, as there is when one discusses the business experience of women and African Americans. It is the fallacy of bundling together all members of a group and considering them as aggregates rather than individuals.

When many native-born white Americans speak of Hispanics, for example, they seem to have in mind nonwhite Mexicans, and—for some whites—undocumented workers who have crossed the Rio Grande in the dead of night. But such stereotypes can only cloud intelligent discussion of the issues. In the first place, "Hispanic" and "Latino" are not racial categories but ethnic ones. Then, too, although the majority of recent immigrants have indeed come from Mexico, there are at least 25 other Hispanic or Latino countries in Central America, South America, and the Caribbean. Recent arrivals to the United States have emigrated from each of those countries, and from some in large numbers. Many have almost nothing in common with immigrants from other Latino countries except that their first language is not English but Spanish or Portuguese.

What does all of this have to do with business? At least three major elements:

First, as with earlier waves from Europe, most recent Hispanic immigrants are young, single, hard-working people who contribute to the nation's economy disproportionately to their numbers.

Second, and again as with all earlier waves of immigrants, there are generational differences. The children of immigrants almost always do better economically than their parents did, and this kind of progress tends to continue with subsequent generations. It is not precisely the same as "assimilation," because the United States has grown so diverse that the prospect of assimilation to some stereotypical ideal has become the biggest of all myths. By

the twenty-first century the country had long since become a federation of ethnic groups as much as a federation of states. And
despite some of the horrors of the nation's history—most notably,
of course, race-based slavery—it accomplished this feat better than
did any other large nation with the possible exception of Brazil.

Third, as with women and African Americans, in discussing
the business experience of Hispanics it is necessary to aggregate
the available data. In so doing, however, one must remember the
limitations and fallacies inherent in this kind of grouping. So, as in
our earlier look at women and African Americans, it's appropriate
to discuss both the aggregate data and individual cases of business
achievement.

## Aggregates

Since the 1980s, the share of minority-owned firms in the United
States has increased faster than the minority share of the population, even though the latter figure has grown from 21 percent to 34
percent. This is an enormous change in the ethnic makeup of so
large a country during so brief a time.

Minority-owned firms have grown at an especially fast rate
in very recent years. A study by the Small Business Administration, for example, showed that during the brief period 1997 to
2002, the number of black-owned firms increased by 45 percent,
and Hispanic-owned firms by 31 percent. Even these numbers,
however, are a bit deceptive taken by themselves. For one thing,
"firms" is a very imprecise denominator. Only about 2 percent of
all U.S. firms are publicly traded corporations, but these companies generate about 61 percent of total business receipts. Then,
too, even among smaller firms, those with employees generate
very many times the revenues of nonemployer sole proprietorships: in 2002, this ratio was 36 times for white-owned firms,
34 for black-owned, and 29 for Hispanic-owned. In the case of
nonpublicly traded companies, the average white-owned business
took in $1 for every 56 cents received by a Hispanic-owned firm,
and 43 cents by a black-owned firm.

Overall, this somewhat confusing array of statistics paints the
following picture: Big progress has been made in Hispanic-owned

businesses, as in African American–owned businesses, especially in recent years. Still, the differences between minority firms as compared to white-owned firms remains significant. It seems likely that blacks and Hispanics, like nearly all other categories of consumers, have gravitated toward purchasing at low-cost mass retailers, just as they earlier gravitated toward buying fast food at McDonald's and other franchises. Wherever their outlets are located, the mass retailers, most notably Wal★Mart but also Costco, Target, and Home Depot, drastically undersell local firms and attract huge customer bases. That these stores themselves employ large numbers of minority workers, most of whom receive some further discounts and therefore patronize the stores even more regularly, clouds the statistical portrait of minority businesses, at least on the retail side.

Put another way, it is not hard to imagine how different the portrait would look in the absence of giant retailers. It would likely resemble black enterprise in the days before the arrival of supermarkets and other low-cost mass retailers. In such a situation, African Americans might give more of their patronage to black-owned neighborhood stores, Hispanics would support Hispanic-owned shops, and so on. The ownership of businesses, therefore, is not a wholly reliable index for the economic progress of any group: it is merely one piece of the puzzle.

Another piece is labor markets. Many Hispanic workers, especially recently arrived immigrants, work in low-wage jobs. Thousands of businesses of all kinds—from big farms to small factories to meat-processing companies to janitorial and lawn-care companies—benefit from the advantage of paying wages that are low by U.S. standards but quite high by Latin American standards. Most of these businesses, but by no means all of them, are owned by whites. As noted above, the number of minority-owned firms has multiplied rapidly in recent years.

So the situation is far from simple. In many ways it resembles the historical pattern between about 1880 and 1910, when waves of immigrants from central and eastern Europe poured into the United States at the rate of almost a million per year. Just as recent immigrants are concentrated in the Southwest (California, Arizona, New Mexico, Texas), those of a century ago tended to congregate in large northeastern cities. For a time, Manhattan's Lower East Side was tightly packed with new arrivals from Europe and was the most densely populated large neighborhood in the world. Greeks, Italians, and Russian Jews like the young David Sarnoff were beginning new lives in what was—as it is today for Hispanics—a land of genuine economic opportunity. And the bitter opposition from many sources to what was then called the "new immigration" had much in common with similar controversies today.

## Highly Compensated Hispanics

Like women and African Americans, Hispanics began during the 1980s to receive, at last, the opportunity to compete for some of the best jobs the business system had to offer. By 2008, seven Hispanics headed *Fortune* 500 companies, about the same number as African American CEOs and about one-third the number of women.

The most conspicuous pioneer was Roberto Goizueta of Cuba, who led the Coca-Cola company from 1980 until his death in 1997 at age 65. Goizueta had been born into a wealthy family in Havana, educated in a Jesuit high school in Cuba, then had earned a degree in chemical engineering at Yale. After the triumph of Cuba's communist revolution in 1959, he and his family defected to the United States—in possession of $40 and 100 shares of Coca-Cola stock that his family had purchased while Goizueta was working for the company in Cuba. After his defection, Coca-Cola assigned him first to the Bahamas, then to its Atlanta headquarters, where he rose rapidly within the organization. He was made president in 1979, at the age of 48, then CEO in 1980. Coca-Cola was already one of the best-known brands in the world, and during Goizueta's tenure the company became more profitable than ever and, through several major acquisitions, much larger. As he himself became a billionaire, Goizueta—like many other immigrant businessmen (Andrew Carnegie perhaps the best example)—established a philanthropic enterprise. The Goizueta Foundation's stated mission was "to assist organizations that empower individuals and families through educational opportunities." In 1994, Emory University in Atlanta named its business school for Goizueta, and in 1999 his estate pledged $20 million to the university.

Another prominent CEO of Cuban birth was Carlos Gutiérrez, whose family fled the country in 1960, when he was six. They settled first in Miami and then in Mexico, where Gutiérrez attended a branch campus of the Monterrey Institute of Technology. In 1975, he took a sales and management-trainee job with the cereal giant Kellogg, where he began a steady rise up the ranks of the corporation. In 1990 he became vice-president for product development, with offices at Kellogg's headquarters in Battle Creek, Michigan. In 1999, the company's board of directors elected him president and Chief Executive Officer. Gutiérrez served for five years in the top spot before departing for Washington, D.C., in 2004 to become the secretary of commerce.

Also in 2004, Advanced Micro Devices (AMD, a *Fortune* 500 company, founded in 1969 and headquartered in Silicon Valley) named Hector Ruiz chairman and CEO. Ruiz was born in Piedras Negras, Mexico. He earned B.S. and M.S. degrees in electrical engineering from the University of Texas at Austin, followed by a Ph.D. at Rice. In 2005, *Electronic Business Magazine* named Ruiz its "CEO of the Year," partly for his leadership of AMD's "50 x 15" initiative, which seeks to bring inexpensive Internet service to 50 percent of the world's people by 2015.

In 2008, still other Hispanic CEO's of *Fortune* 500 firms were:

Alain J. P. Belda of Alcoa, the aluminum giant. Born in Morocco, Belda emigrated to Brazil, where he was educated at Universidade MacKenzie in São Paulo. He joined Alcoa Aluminio, Alcoa's Brazilian subsidiary, in 1969, working as a financial planner. He became president of Alcoa Aluminio in 1974 and served in that post for 15 years, during the last four years of which he oversaw all of Alcoa's Latin American operations. He was appointed executive vice-president of the parent company in 1994, president and Chief Operating Officer in 1995, and Chief Executive Officer in 2001.

William D. Perez of Wm. Wrigley & Company, the nation's largest chewing gum company. Perez was born in Akron, Ohio, but raised in Colombia. He worked for many years at the S. C. Johnson firm of Racine, Wisconsin ("Johnson's Wax"), serving as CEO from 1996 to 2004. He then briefly held the CEO's position at Nike before moving to Wrigley in 2006. He was the first non-family member ever to head the closely-held chewing-gum firm, which is based in Chicago and had annual sales of about $4 billion. In 2008, Wrigley was acquired by the candy giant Mars for $23 billion, with the understanding that Perez would remain as Wrigley's CEO.

Fernando Aguirre (born in Mexico, educated at Southern Illinois University) of Chiquita Brands. Before coming to Chiquita as CEO in 2004 at the age of 46, Aguirre had worked for Procter & Gamble for 23 years, spending much time in Brazil, Mexico, and Canada.

Paul J. Diaz of Kindred Healthcare, Inc., based in Louisville, Kentucky. Kindred operates a chain of hospitals, nursing homes, and related enterprises. Diaz, a lawyer and financial specialist, was also CEO of Kindred Pharmacy Services.

The increasing appearance of Latin Americans at the helm of U.S. companies is not just a result of the economic and professional progress of American Hispanics but a consequence of globalization. In 2008, for the first time in history, the companies in Standard & Poor's index of 500 American firms received half their earnings from outside the United States. In 2002 this fraction had been only one-third, and far less than that a short time earlier. The rising global trade in goods and services has brought more globally oriented professional executives. Thus, by 2008, the CEOs of 16 of the largest 100 companies headquartered in the United States were foreign born. These firms included PepsiCo (Indra K. Nooyi of India, a woman); Chevron (David J. O'Reilly of Ireland); Dow Chemical (Andrew N. Liveris of Australia); Citigroup, the world's largest bank (Vikram S. Pandit of India); Coca-Cola (E. Neville Isdell of Northern Ireland); and Altria Group, the parent of Philip Morris companies (Louis C. Camilleri, born in Egypt of Maltese parents, educated in Switzerland). Orit Gadeish, an Israeli woman, chaired the large Boston-based consulting firm Bain & Company from 1993 to at least 2008.

For the American economy, globalization was not an unmixed blessing. Consumers benefited from inexpensive imports, but many of these same consumers were hurt in their roles as producers. The migration of manufacturing abroad hollowed out the industrial base, especially in the Midwest. High-paying factory jobs disappeared and the middle class shrank. The entire issue, symbolized by the North American Free Trade Agreement (NAFTA) and the gargantuan trade deficit with China (embodied for many people by the irresistible power of Wal★Mart), became an acrimonious political football. The issue grew hotter as the early twenty-first century progressed, dividing the country along lines of region and class.

The central issue of this chapter has not been globalization, but rather the changes in the status and power of women, African Americans, and Hispanics. On the whole, the evidence is unambiguous: very slow gains for all three groups until the 1970s, followed by tremendous progress from the late 1970s to the present. That progress is a significant element in the pattern of relentless change and growing empowerment of consumers and entrepreneurs so conspicuous during the years since 1920.

# CHAPTER SEVEN

# The Financial System

## The Background

As Ray Kroc often said, it was Harry Sonneborn's financial innovations that took McDonald's Corporation into the big leagues. First came his sandwich real-estate leasing to increase the company's cash flow; then came his gimmick of enhancing the company's balance sheet by capitalizing future lease payments.

Innovations of this kind have been common since the nation's beginning. During the 1790s, Secretary of the Treasury Alexander Hamilton put the country on a sound financial footing through ingenious measures designed to strengthen its credit abroad and increase its money supply at home. Like Sonneborn, Hamilton made big bets on future growth and rooted his policies in those bets. Although Hamilton's rival Thomas Jefferson opposed these measures at the time, Jefferson's $15 million Louisiana Purchase ten years later would not have been possible without the credit system set up by Hamilton. Dutch and British bankers purchased U.S. government bonds and paid the necessary cash to Napoleon in exchange for the Louisiana Territory, an acquisition that doubled the size of the United States.

In this book, we have seen many comparable innovations. In the public sector the vast expenditures for World War II were financed in every conceivable way. And in the private sector, Alfred Sloan's turnaround of General Motors was helped a great deal by General Motors Acceptance Corporation, set up by the company's financial staff to provide credit to GM's dealers and retail customers. More broadly, at GM's corporate headquarters the staff made astute use of financial ratios such as inventory turnover, net profit on sales, and return on investment. These kinds of ratios are crucial to business operations. They provide quick photographs of a firm's present condition, and year-to-year trends in the numbers turn the photographs into movies. Ratios become even more useful when managers compare numbers for their own firms with those recorded by other companies in similar industries.

Unlike Alfred Sloan, Henry Ford disdained the use of mathematical ratios as management tools. Ford detested all aspects of "financeering," and his misgivings typified the bewilderment and suspicion of numerous other Americans. Ford's confusion was based mainly on his own ignorance, but during many periods of American history, widespread suspicion of the financial sector has turned out to be justified—and seldom more than during the years from the 1980s to the present. Commentators of all political stripes have spoken of this recent period as a "New Gilded Age" comparable to the late nineteenth century. That period, like the more recent one, was marked by extraordinary innovations on Wall Street but also by abuses that enriched insiders at the expense of small shareholders and consumers. Neither the innovations nor the abuses can be understood without a look at the general role of finance in business.

## The Functions of Finance

All firms, of whatever size, share some basic and often urgent financial problems: how to meet the payroll, how to get and maintain working credit for other day-to-day operations, and how to raise the occasional large sums necessary to develop new products and build new facilities. These problems are relentless, and companies need a constant inflow of reliable financial information in order to manage them.

Investors have similar requirements. Owner-investors, individual shareholders, and financial institutions such as banks, insurance companies, and pension funds must have trustworthy information. Otherwise, they can't make intelligent decisions about where and how much to invest, or what form their investments might take—whether stock ("equity"), long-term bonds, or short-term loans.

The basic function of financial systems is to channel funds from investors (savers) to companies (users); then, later, to distribute appropriate amounts of the companies' earnings back to the investors. The system transfers capital across time, as in the issuance and repayment of a 10-year corporate bond; and also across space, as funds move from one region or country to another.

Each transfer may require intermediate steps. A vital one is the pooling of large amounts of money from household savers by banks, insurance companies, and mutual funds (which are investment pools containing many different stocks or bonds or both). Companies can then draw on these accumulated pools of money by borrowing from them or by selling their own stocks and bonds to them. After that, as firms market their products or services to consumers, portions of their earnings move back to investors. This transfer process includes dividends on stocks and interest payments on bonds and loans.

Over the period since 1920, one of the most important trends in American business was a colossal increase in the amounts of money handled by the financial system. Both investments and earnings grew by very large multiples, and the system for channeling funds back and forth between savers and users became much more efficient.

## A Deluge of Data

This increased efficiency derived in large part from a steady growth in the amount of information available to managers inside companies and to investors outside. On the inside, the development of ratio analysis and other tools brought a new abundance of data on nearly all aspects of the company. On the outside, a second force emerged when regulatory agencies began to insist on standardized accounting procedures and the public disclosure of hitherto privileged information. (As always, the government had to play catch-up, as innovations and frequent scandals outran existing laws against fraudulent behavior.) Still a third force was the rapid progress of information technology itself—from the pen and ledger, to computers and spreadsheets, and finally to online transactions by vast numbers of individual and institutional "day-traders" trying to outwit the market. The new volumes of data made possible a higher degree of sophistication at all levels.

Over several decades, players from both the public and private sectors developed the new financial tools and pushed for their standardization. During the first half of the twentieth century, the Federal Trade Commission, the Federal Reserve System, the Securities and Exchange Commission, and other public agencies acted in concert with an assortment of private bodies. These included the American Institute of Certified Public Accountants, the Financial Accounting Standards Board, the New York Stock Exchange, and the National Association of Securities Dealers (NASD, which later set up the NASDAQ exchange). Well-coordinated public and private efforts built an effective infrastructure that helped make American capital markets the world's largest and most advanced.

In snowball fashion, the availability of more information attracted additional investors, and the pools of money available to businesses grew larger year by year. Growth was interrupted by the Great Depression of the 1930s, but it was also very much bolstered by new regulations that came directly out of the government's catch-up response to that catastrophe.

Meanwhile, the depth and scope of the capital markets steadily increased. One early marker was a greater public acceptance of common stocks as suitable investments, which began in the 1920s and took a big leap forward 60 years later, during the 1980s. A second milestone was the growing need to finance permanently high government expenditures, which started in the 1930s and surged with the coming of World War II, the Cold War, and the welfare state.

The passage in 1974 of the landmark Employee Retirement Income Security Act (ERISA) had powerful effects on securities markets. ERISA compelled all companies with retirement plans to put aside, in a trust fund separate from the assets of the company, money to meet payments owed to current and future retirees. This new legislation promoted the growth, over time, of huge capital pools that by law had to be invested both productively and prudently. The stock market turned out to be the preferred destination for most of these funds because stocks usually brought higher returns than did bonds, fixed-income securities, or bank deposits.

The largest of all pension funds, the California Public Employees Retirement System (CALPERS), made immense investments in equities. Eventually it began to wield power (as a stockholder) to influence the policies of corporations in which it held major blocks of shares. Beginning in the 1980s, the increasing strength of CALPERS and other institutional investors such as mutual funds signified another shift downward in decision making, in this case from managers to shareholders. The change was not a radical one, but it did force many American companies to adopt more stringent financial discipline.

The emergence of mutual funds in the 1960s and their very rapid proliferation during the 1990s deepened and broadened the capital markets still more. The retirement plans of many corporations gave individual employee-participants the opportunity to choose one or more mutual funds in which they could invest their retirement savings. Whether they invested through a retirement plan or by direct purchase, even people with modest incomes could diversify their holdings through the vehicle of mutual funds. In doing so they faced less risk than they would by purchasing shares of a single company's stock. The wide array of different funds provided investors at all income levels with a myriad of choices. Those who felt comfortable tolerating more risk in the hope of higher returns could select an aggressive mutual fund over a conservative one.

In the twenty-first century, sitting at home in front of our monitors, you and I have more information and more tools at hand than most of the lords of money had in 1920, or even 1980. Like portion control at fast food outlets, this new freedom gives us enough individualist rope to hang ourselves and lose our money. But it also represents another example of growing entrepreneurial opportunities and decentralized decision making. The whole system depends crucially on the financial transparency written into law beginning in the 1930s. Unfortunately, that transparency started to get murky during the closing years of the twentieth century and can no longer be taken for granted.

## Wall Street and the Stock Market

Investments in stocks and bonds can bring big returns, but playing the market can also be like casino gambling. The opportunities for corruption by insiders have always been substantial, which is why Henry Ford and many other Americans grew so distrustful of Wall Street. Then, too, very little of the daily buying and selling of stocks actually provided funds to the companies whose shares were being traded. Instead, most of that activity comprised a "secondary market" that merely shifted ownership of the shares from one person or institution to another.

Firms usually financed their operations through two other routes: retained earnings, which were far and away the most important source of funds for large companies; and borrowing via bank loans, corporate bonds, and other financial instruments. The issuance of stock did provide some direct financing for companies, particularly in the case of "initial public offerings," or the first sale of stock by a company to the public. During the Internet craze of the 1990s, the general public began to watch the movement of "IPO" share prices much as they watched box-office revenues from blockbuster movies.

For the period since 1920 as a whole, equity investors' real returns from dividends plus share-price appreciation ("real" meaning adjusted for inflation) averaged roughly 7 percent annually. (For the late 1980s and all of the 1990s they averaged a lot more than that.) As against this 7 percent, annual returns from government and high-grade commercial bonds, which have always been regarded as safer investments, averaged only 2 percent. So over the long term, the market nicely rewarded most investors in stocks.

The market also provided continuous quotations of share prices, which by the end of the twentieth century appeared in newspapers and online reports for nearly 10,000 companies in the

United States. (In 2006 the *New York Times* and most other papers stopped printing daily quotations since they were so easily available online.) These continually updated share prices were, and still are, important for three different reasons.

First, the selling price of a stock registers the market's beliefs about the present and future performance of the company. Sometimes these beliefs are borne out by events, sometimes not. Second, share prices as aggregated in such indexes as the Dow Jones Industrial Average, the Standard & Poor's 500, and the NASDAQ composite, offer a window on the state of the national economy. The Dow Jones, which was established in 1884 for railroads and updated in 1897 for industrial firms, comprises 30 stocks considered among the most solid of the 3,000 or so listed on the New York Stock Exchange. The other two indices include far more companies than the 30 averaged for the Dow Jones: for Standard & Poor's, 500, as its name implies, and for the NASDAQ composite over 3,000. All of these indices are dynamic, meaning that as some companies drop off the list, better-performing companies take their place.

A third reason for the importance of share prices is that as securities markets grew more "democratized" they became major repositories of the national wealth. At the start of the twentieth century, only about half a million Americans owned stocks. By 1929, after the greatest bull market in history up to that time, this figure had increased twenty-fold, to about 10 million. By the early years of the twenty-first century, after the even bigger bull market of the 1990s, stocks were owned by more than 100 million Americans, mostly through investments in mutual funds and retirement funds. By that time about 9,000 mutual funds were doing business in the United States, some 6,000 having been started during the 1990s alone.

Although share prices and market indexes are good yardsticks, their movement often exaggerates underlying business trends. In September 1929, for instance, the Dow Jones Industrial Average climbed to 381, but by July 1932 it had dropped by almost 90 percent, to 41. It crept upward over the next four decades, dipping during occasional recessions but maintaining its gradual climb, reaching almost 800 in 1980. Then, toward the end of the 1980s, it began ascending to heights that by prior standards seemed phenomenal, surpassing 11,000 in 1999. It topped 14,000 in 2007, then began to decline. Its pattern during the first decade of the twenty-first century resembled that of earlier periods rather than the skyrocketing record of the 1990s.

For many individual companies, the ups and downs of the stock market were even more dramatic. During the 1920s the share prices for RCA and other electronics firms gyrated wildly. Toward the close of the century the same thing happened for startup Internet firms. Despite these extreme examples, share prices remain one of many useful signals about the condition of the national economy. Others include well-known macroeconomic indicators: interest rates; the rates of inflation, unemployment, business investment, and consumer spending; the federal deficit; and the value of the dollar versus foreign currencies.

The volume of trades on the New York Stock Exchange, which had averaged fewer than 3 million shares per day before the 1960s, shot up to almost 160 million shares per day by 1990, then to 1.6 *billion* in 2007. Meanwhile Americans shifted enormous sums out of low-risk savings accounts, certificates of deposit, and bonds, and into the shares of publicly held companies. By the early twenty-first century, more than one-fourth of all U.S. household wealth was invested in stocks, as compared with only one-tenth during the 1980s.

In the closing decades of the twentieth century, "private equity funds" (a euphemism first used by corporate raiders making hostile takeovers during the 1980s) began to take a conspicuous role in American finance. In contrast to the corporate raiders, private equity funds headed by venture capitalists put up cash in return for a portion of the stock (or stock options) of numerous firms in biotechnology, computer software, and other high-tech industries. Many of these companies were startups, and most were young firms in need of capital for product development: the list includes Microsoft, Federal Express, Apple Computer, Cisco Systems, and Genentech. If a firm became successful enough, its initial public offering could yield millions of dollars for both the venture capitalists and the entrepreneurs who had founded the company. Through this route many entrepreneurs made very substantial fortunes at a young age—some in their twenties or thirties.

Abundant venture capital became a key ingredient for the surge in high-tech industries that fueled American economic growth during the 1990s. Much more money was available for startups in the United States than elsewhere, for a variety of reasons: a favorable tax climate, lenient bankruptcy laws, and a decidedly entrepreneurial culture. By the mid-1990s about as much venture capital was being invested in Massachusetts as in Great Britain; more was available in California than in all of continental Europe. Then, too, about 37 percent of American venture-capital investments during the late 1990s went toward startup companies, as compared to only 12 percent in Europe. In succeeding years, that 37 percent began to decline, although the United States remained a fertile field for venture capital. Europe began to catch up as a site for private-equity investments, including not only venture capital, but also hostile takeovers of existing firms.

The pattern of investments in high-tech stocks brought very significant changes to the nature of the stock market. During most of the twentieth century, a company that ranked high in sales and employment was likely to have a correspondingly high "market capitalization" (total value of its stock). These relationships seemed to connect Wall Street and its paper assets with the "real" economy of fixed assets, and with the manufacture of steel, automobiles, and other tangible goods. Such products were emblematic of the Second Industrial Revolution, which was based on machine mass-production and cheap transportation.

During the information-based Third Industrial Revolution, the market capitalizations of some high-tech companies came to have much less correlation with either their sales, fixed assets, or number of employees. For example, America's two largest firms at the very end of the twentieth century, General Motors and Ford, had combined annual sales of $306 billion, 940,000 employees, and market capitalization of $134 billion. By contrast, the two leading software companies at that time, Microsoft and Oracle, had combined sales of $22 billion and 63,000 employees—about $1/14$

the sales and employment of the two auto giants. Nevertheless, Microsoft and Oracle had a combined market capitalization of $462 billion, nearly 3.5 times that of the car companies; and, measured as a multiple of their sales and employment figures, 49-fold (3.5 times 14). The "market cap" of Microsoft alone was $418 billion, reflecting that company's tight hold on the standards for computer operating systems and its readiness to profit from the expansion of the Internet. What these new financial relationships implied for the future was not very clear, but they signaled a sharp break with the past and caused a good deal of rethinking by both securities analysts and the buying public.

Several government officials, including Chairman Alan Greenspan of the Federal Reserve System, warned that share prices for stocks of high-tech companies had become dangerously overvalued. When, in December 1996, Greenspan spoke of "irrational exuberance" by investors, he was understating the case. Not only did the Internet bubble burst in 2000–01, triggering huge individual losses and a national economic recession; but even more dangerous bubbles in housing, real estate, and credit began to develop under the nose of the Federal Reserve itself. Those bubbles burst in 2007 and 2008.

By that time, whatever happened on Wall Street rippled throughout the world because business had become so globalized. During the years after World War II, the United States had led a prolonged and very successful movement for freer trade worldwide. Tariff barriers dropped, cross-border trade increased, and the global economy became much more integrated. For the American economy, the sum of imports and exports rose from less than 9 percent of GNP in 1960 to more than 30 percent by 2009, a tremendous change.

Meanwhile, money and other forms of capital began to move rapidly from one country to another, as the opportunity for high returns appeared now here, now there, but forever in motion. There was also a big increase in the establishment of factories and sales offices in other countries. Multinational corporations based in the United States, Europe, and Japan led the globalization movement, in both production and marketing. Companies tended to build manufacturing facilities wherever the cost of production or of marketing was most favorable. For production, this usually meant the place where sufficiently skilled labor was least expensive. For marketing, it often meant the place with the best combination of low internal trade barriers and large numbers of potential customers.

Besides purchasing unprecedented amounts of imported goods, the United States served as host for numerous incoming transplant factories. But "outsourcing" by U.S. companies far surpassed the infusion of manufacturing plants built in America by foreign-owned firms. To repeat a pair of statistics mentioned in the introduction of this book—statistics that denote a profound set of social changes as well as economic ones—60 percent of the nation's labor force had worked on farms or in mines and factories in 1920; by 2009, that 60 percent had dropped to 13 percent. Excluding agriculture, the drop went from 35 percent to 11 percent—which meant, among other things, a huge relative loss in the nation's manufacturing capacity.

One of the many results of the shift to a service economy was that the miracle of America's industrial mobilization during the 1940s could not remotely be duplicated today. During the war with Iraq that began in 2003, production requirements were minuscule by the standards of World War II, or even those of the war in Vietnam, when American heavy industry still possessed tremendous production capacities. This fact was unfortunately borne out by shortages of reliable vehicles and body armor for U.S. troops fighting in Iraq.

## The Rising Importance of Finance

As the new money pools began to grow larger during the 1980s, they came to represent an important new source of capital that mutual funds and other institutions might invest in businesses of various kinds. Traditionally, investment banks—firms such as Goldman Sachs, Lehman Brothers, and Morgan Stanley—had restricted their underwriting of corporate debt instruments to "investment grade" bonds issued on behalf of safe, well-established companies. Wealthy individuals as well as insurance companies and other financial institutions were the usual purchasers of these bonds. Because the bonds involved little risk to the buyer, they carried relatively low rates of interest.

But with the growth of mutual funds, pension funds, and similar money pools, the sum of available capital began to exceed the total amount that could be invested under the old pattern of small risk and small return. In this new context, innovative financiers began to look outward and to imagine a different pattern altogether: widespread issuance not only of low-risk investment grade bonds, but also of high-risk and high-yield bonds. Because of the higher risk, the new instruments came to be called "junk" bonds.

Michael Milken of the investment bank Drexel Burnham Lambert pioneered the issuance of junk bonds and their sale to mutual funds and other institutional investors such as insurance companies and savings and loan associations. During the 1980s, Milken arranged high-yield developmental financing for such intrepid entrepreneurs as Ted Turner of Turner Broadcasting and William McGowan of MCI Communications, which was the first serious challenger of the long-distance telephone monopoly then held by AT&T. In most cases the deals benefited all concerned parties. But for savings and loan institutions, investment in junk bonds—along with some extremely unwise government deregulation—brought a financial debacle that cost the federal government and state governments about $200 billion in bailouts (over $300 billion in 2009 dollars).

The availability of junk bonds also made possible the hostile takeover movement that became widespread during the 1980s. The control of giant companies such as RJR Nabisco could change hands overnight through "leveraged buyouts" financed with junk bonds. The "leverage" here referred to a new practice of using the acquired firm's own assets as partial collateral for the issuance of junk bonds that were sold to raise the sum needed to buy a controlling interest. Like venture capital, it was another form of private equity, but often with a narrower purpose: not so much the promotion of innovative industries, but a source of lavish profits for "corporate raiders."

As is often the case with novel methods of finance, the pioneers found themselves operating in gray areas of the law, and sometimes they crossed the line into clear illegality. Several financiers, including Milken himself, were prosecuted under the federal securities laws and sentenced to jail terms. Milken's firm, Drexel Burnham Lambert, was forced into bankruptcy and went out of business. In the meantime, however, the advent of new capital pools and high-yield bonds had made major funding available to a far broader spectrum of American business.

Some writers on American finance have suggested that these developments effected a "democratization" of opportunities and rewards once reserved for the privileged few. Others assert that "democratization" cannot be the appropriate word. Their argument is that a disproportionate share of the vast profits from financial manipulations went to a select handful of financiers, thereby accelerating a national trend toward a greater inequality in the distribution of wealth and income.

Still another innovation in securities trading was the rise of "hedge funds"—somewhat misnamed because their "hedges" did not act as quite the safeguards against loss that the name implies. These organizations, whose activities were often shrouded in deep secrecy, dealt mostly in "derivatives": futures, options, swaps, forwards, and other instruments derived from conventional securities or commodities. Many hedge funds made tremendous amounts of money through large-scale trading based on complex mathematical models. These models were designed to continuously rebalance the risks to the fund—risks that originated from changes in the world economy.

Hedge funds came to manage immense amounts of money, most of it invested by mutual funds, pension funds, and wealthy individual investors—all seeking the large returns many hedge funds delivered. The managers of hedge funds accepted no investments from "retail" customers with low net worth. Yet the hedge funds grew very rapidly, and many of them attracted as employees and advisors some of the brightest people in the country, including university professors and Nobel Prize winners. Sometimes, however, hedge funds failed. The crash of the giant firm Long Term

Capital Management in 1998 was so serious that it threatened the health of the nation's financial system and triggered another government bailout, this one organized by the Federal Reserve. Even so, hedge funds continued to grow rapidly because they usually earned high returns.

However one interprets the meaning of these developments from the 1960s to the present, four facts stand out. First, tens of millions of Americans were taking part in the financial system as investors—a much higher percentage than at any other time in the nation's history. Second, the pools of available capital were now far deeper and came from more diverse sources. Third, the system had become less regulated and much more opaque, contravening the transparency that had supported the capital market's integrity since the 1930s. And fourth, a few thousand speculators and investment bankers had become rich—very, very rich.

In about 2004, individual hedge fund managers began to receive annual compensation packages exceeding $1 billion. In 2007, one manager "earned" $3.7 billion, and two others garnered nearly $3 billion. A significant part of this money came from a percentage of the hedge funds' growth in total value, although the managers seldom risked significant amounts of their own money in the funds. But because the Internal Revenue Code favors capital gains over "ordinary income," the new billionaires paid only 15 percent tax on these huge sums rather than what otherwise would have been 35 percent, the usual rate for high earners. Thus, a person compensated at $3 billion for running a hedge fund saved $600 million *annually* by paying at a tax rate about half that paid by the clerical staff of the same firm.

Overall, the financial sector of the American economy had accounted for 8 percent of all U.S. corporate profits in 1950. But that figure grew to 20 percent in 1990, and then to 34 percent in 2003—an almost unbelievably high figure given the size of the American economy.

Where did all the new money for financial-sector profits come from? Mainly, from a boom in lending: to businesses, governments, consumers, homeowners, and college students. In the space of a single generation, from 1981 to 2007, consumer debt as a proportion of disposable income grew by 27 percent, and home-mortgage debt by 44 percent. By 2009, total credit card debt in the United States was approximately $1 trillion (in 1981 it had been $50 billion, or about $130 billion in 2009 dollars). Mortgage debt was about $11 trillion in 2008. And the two forms of debt were now related, since many people had taken out home-equity loans to help pay off their credit-card balances. About half of all credit-card holders made only the minimum required monthly payment, thereby vastly increasing their total interest payments and perpetuating their debts for an indefinite future. And when the housing bubble burst in 2007, the alternative of equity loans diminished as the market value of homes began rapidly to decline throughout the country.

The source of the housing crisis represents a major exception to the general trend since 1920 of decentralization in decision making by businesses. Before the savings and loan debacle of the 1980s, local "S&Ls" had been pillars of many communities and the chief source of home mortgage financing. Lending officers knew their local communities well—much like the decentralized draft boards and rationing agencies of World War II. The money the S&Ls lent came almost entirely from local savings deposits, for they knew who could meet monthly mortgage payments and who could not. After the S&L catastrophe of the 1980s, however, about one-half of the existing 3,200 S&Ls perished, and many experts believe that this episode contributed to the mortgage crisis that exploded in 2007.

Whereas local S&Ls had carefully determined applicants' ability to meet their home-loan payments, national mortgage brokers often did little local scrutiny. (The very name of the leading lender, Countrywide Financial, symbolized this crucial difference.) In part because the new lenders were financed not by local savers but by international pools of money, they felt no responsibility to local communities. Without compunction, they set out to make as many loans as possible. They urged unsuspecting borrowers—who were often low-income purchasers of their first homes—to accept types of loans that would yield the highest and quickest compensation to the brokers themselves. Often these were "variable interest" loans with rates that could increase by up to 100 percent after a year or two. The national brokers also loaded the new-style mortgages with fees and penalties piled on top of subprime interest rates, which themselves reached as high as 12 percent.

After closing their deals with home buyers, the brokers sold thousands of individual mortgages to large banks and other institutions, which promptly "bundled" them into new securities. National rating agencies, paying far too little attention to the actual underlying values, then gave the securities investment-grade appraisals, which made them attractive to buyers of all kinds. In combination, these practices put the (very high) risk of default almost entirely on the final holders of the securities, and ultimately on the national economy.

The disconnect between any local knowledge of borrowers' creditworthiness, on the one hand, and the ultimate holders of the now-securitized bundles of mortgages, on the other, had become almost complete. This was the exact opposite of the rationing and conscription practices of World War II. Those systems had worked so well because of intimate knowledge of local communities and a patriotic determination to be fair to everyone.

The new situation, by contrast, was designed to make enormous amounts of money for the new-model mortgage brokers — regardless of the consequences to borrowers, to the purchasers of securitized mortgages, or to the national economy. Fundamentally, it was a huge scam, almost entirely unregulated because of splintered responsibilities among sometimes feuding agencies: the Federal Reserve System, the Office of the Comptroller of the Currency, the Federal Deposit Insurance Corporation, the Office of Thrift Supervision, and state banking regulators. Again, financial innovations had raced far ahead of any effective government effort to play catch-up.

Not everyone was fooled, of course. Edward Gramlich, a member of the Board of Governors of the Federal Reserve System who had studied the nature of poverty, warned as early as 2001 that the freewheeling new housing brokers should be brought under regulatory control. In the same year, the U.S. Treasury officer Sheila Bair urged subprime lenders to adopt a code of "best practices." Both Gramlich and Bair were rebuffed. So were others who warned, year after year, that the housing bubble—the constantly rising prices of homes, both old and new—would inevitably burst. In 2004, the Federal Reserve Bank of New York actually issued a report stating that "no bubble exists." Edward Gramlich nevertheless continued to make his dire warnings. "Why," he asked in 2007, "are the most risky loan products sold to the least sophisticated borrowers? The question answers itself." Chairman Alan Greenspan of the Federal Reserve System believed that housing prices might go down, but that declines would occur in only a few locales.

Unfortunately, Greenspan was wrong. In 2006 the national housing bubble began to quaver, and in 2007 it burst. Home prices plummeted by 5 percent, 10 percent, 20 percent, and sometimes even more in different regions of the country. Yet many distressed homeowners could find no buyers, even at reduced prices, to relieve them of their financial burden. By 2008, foreclosures and late payments had leapt to their highest rates since 1979, a year that preceded a long and deep recession. After the housing bubble burst in 2007, hundreds of thousands of people lost their homes outright. They endured the indignity of foreclosure and eviction, with no compensation whatever. Many other homeowners found themselves in a situation of "upside-down" mortgages, in which they owed more than their homes were now worth. And people who had taken out home-equity loans to pay off the balances on their credit cards discovered that their homes could no longer serve as collateral.

Credit-card balances themselves had been greatly inflated—not only by reckless consumer spending, but also by a series of measures designed by banks to pump up their profits from card operations. These included annual charges for use of the cards, very high interest rates (18 percent was common), excessive fees for late or skipped payments, and—most shameful of all—the practice of "universal default." Through this mechanism, if a credit-card holder was even one day late in making a payment, the applicable interest rate could be increased, often by a large amount, not only on the affected card but also on all other cards used by the same consumer.

Taken together, these credit-card practices—along with the relentless pushing of more and more offers onto the public (in 2008 the average college senior possessed four credit cards)—enticed millions of people into a debt trap they stood almost no chance of escaping. Many consumers had little idea of how they had fallen into this situation. Credit-card contracts were often nearly impossible to decipher, even by professional accountants. The card-issuing banks were careful *never* to state on monthly invoices such basic information as how long it would take the cardholder to pay the full balance by remitting only the required minimum; or what the total amount of interest payments would be under different schedules of repayment. Because of the nature of compound interest, information of this kind would be little short of astounding if disclosed to most credit-card holders.

Much of the nation's consumer-credit system—as exemplified by subprime mortgages and credit-card ruses—had come to resemble sharecropping arrangements between landlords and powerless tenants. And the situation worsened in 2005, when Congress passed much tougher personal bankruptcy laws. In 2006, because of this legislation, bankruptcy filings dropped by two-thirds, even as more and more Americans desperately needed some form of protection from creditors whom they could not possibly repay.

## The Social Fallout

These developments, in combination with the decline of the manufacturing sector and the outsourcing of millions of well-paying U.S. jobs, signaled a sea change in American society. And that change fueled vigorous national debates over at least three broad topics: diverging wealth and incomes among segments of the American people; the globalization of business; and the future of the nation's democracy.

After 50 years of broad consensus on middle-class values that had begun during the Great Depression, a cultural shift began during the 1980s and continued into the twenty-first century. By 2008, when the median household income was $62,000, surveys found that about 50 percent of the American people believed that the country was divided economically between "haves" and "have nots"; 34 percent identified themselves as have nots. Both of these percentages had approximately doubled just since the 1980s.

Within companies, institutional loyalty by both managers and employees shrank almost to the point of disappearance. Job-hopping, which had long been regarded as a sign of employee incompetence, now became the norm in corporate hierarchies from top to bottom. Rates of compensation between top managers and ordinary employees diverged enormously. Mass layoffs became commonplace. Cynicism grew on all sides, along with a resolve to "look out for number one"—that is, oneself. Wall Street drifted into a series of practices that seemed to grow more questionable year by year. So did the behavior of many consumers, who spent as if there were no tomorrow. Although it's too early for mature historical judgment of these recent events, it's hard to imagine that in the future they will be regarded with admiration.

The growing separation of the nation's financial sector from its "real" economy of goods and services accelerated during the 1980s, which became known as the "Greed Decade." It was the first time in the nation's history that a financial innovator such as Michael Milken could receive $550 million (the equivalent of $1.2 billion in 2009) as a single year's "earnings" from a company he did not own. Milken's employer, the investment banking house Drexel Burnham Lambert, sponsored what its own traders called an annual "Predators' Ball." At this event, the displays of wealth (lavish food, drink, entertainment) reached heights that would have surprised even Thorstein Veblen, the economist who coined the term "conspicuous consumption." The popular movie *Wall Street* (1987) depicted rapacious financiers blithely breaking up companies after pocketing one-time gains in the sale of their securities. The best-selling novel by Tom Wolfe, *The Bonfire of the Vanities* (1987), portrayed a financial community deranged with pointless avarice.

In real life, a few speculators such as Ivan Boesky, who made hundreds of millions of dollars in illegal stock manipulations, were indicted and sentenced to jail terms. Boesky was a graduate of the Detroit College of Law, now the Michigan State University College of Law. Michael Milken himself (University of California, Berkeley, then Wharton School of Finance, University of Pennsylvania), was prosecuted by federal authorities on more than 90 counts, and he pled guilty to several felonies. He was sentenced to ten years' imprisonment, of which he served almost two years before being paroled. The Houston energy-trading giant Enron, regarded as one of the most innovative and profitable of all American companies, was revealed to have cooked its books so thoroughly that even its own lawyers and accountants could hardly unravel what had happened. In 2001, Enron's share price dropped from over $90 to a few cents. Its president Jeffrey Skilling (Southern Methodist University, Harvard Business School) and Chief Financial Officer Andrew Fastow (Tufts University, Kellogg School of Management, Northwestern University) were sentenced to long prison terms—six years for Fastow, who cooperated with prosecutors; 24 for Skilling, who did not. Enron's chief executive officer, Kenneth Lay (University of Missouri, then Ph.D. in economics, University of Houston), who was prosecuted at the same time as Skilling, died of a heart attack in 2006, during the period between his conviction and sentencing, which likely would have been for 20 to 30 years. Enron's auditor, the big international accounting firm Arthur Andersen, went into bankruptcy and then disappeared altogether. The list of other high-ranking executives prosecuted during this period would be a long one. The most prominent cases were those of Dennis Kozlowski (Seton Hall University) of the conglomerate Tyco International, whose sentence in 2005 was 8 to 24 years in prison; and Bernie Ebbers (Mississippi College) of the telecommunications giant WorldCom, sentenced in 2006 to 25 years.

Contrary to many expectations, these scandals did not have a broad effect in reforming the behavior of top executives, particularly with regard to excessive compensation. Statistics disclosed by law to the Securities and Exchange Commission during the 1990s and then widely reported in the press revealed that CEOs of large U.S. companies were being paid, on average, about 400 times as much as the lowest-paid workers in their own firms. That number was far higher than corresponding ratios in Europe and

Japan, and ten times the multiple in the United States itself as recently as 1975, when it had been about 40.

During the Great Depression, Procter & Gamble's CEO Red Deupree had cut his own salary and stopped his annual bonus because of the financial distress of P&G's employees and customers. Other CEOs, including Thomas J. Watson of IBM, also took big voluntary cuts. Even during boom periods such as World War II and the 1960s, most top managers showed a sense of stewardship and moderation about their pay. But from the 1980s onward into the twenty-first century, American executives seemed to become obsessed with exorbitant pay packages—much like professional athletes, the difference being that most athletes were paid strictly according to performance.

A large part of the steep rise in executive pay derived from compensation through the cashing in of stock options, which were liberally granted by boards of directors. Some of the rise was also related to plausible new theories about rewarding executives for superior achievements by the firms they headed. In most cases, however, executive compensation went up regardless of how well a company performed. A study done by the *New York Times* found that for 383 large firms in which the same CEO remained in office from 1993 to 1997, the average price of company shares doubled but CEO compensation quadrupled—from under $2.8 million annually to more than $10 million (equivalent to $13.5 million in 2009). Compensation consultants, behaving like agents for athletes or show-business personalities, drafted stock-option and other "incentive" plans that ensured executives' good fortune no matter what happened to their firms. Often it was difficult even for company lawyers and accountants to calculate the total compensation of top executives; their contracts were deliberately obfuscated with confusing contingencies and near-incomprehensible footnotes. Worst of all, the steep upside of stock options (often with exercise prices that declined as circumstances changed, an indefensible practice), encouraged high-ranking managers to engage in ever-riskier strategies for their companies—and by extension for the national economy.

The magazine *Business Week,* a mainstream organ of corporate America and hardly a bastion of radical reform, began during the 1990s to argue vehemently that CEO compensation had spun out of control. In 1999, the magazine noted that "the link between pay and any objective standard of performance has been all but severed." An apogee of sorts was reached in 2007, when five top Wall Street firms, after having lost a total of $74 billion because of the crisis in subprime home mortgages and other foolish investments, proceeded to pay $38 billion in bonuses to their employees. Most of this bonanza went to top executives. The five firms were Lehman Brothers, Morgan Stanley, Goldman Sachs (which had a good year relative to the others), Merrill Lynch (which because of adverse publicity reduced some of its bonuses) and Bear Stearns (which canceled some of its bonuses). At the same time, to offset their losses, several of these banks sold multibillion-dollar ownership shares in their firms to oil-rich governments or companies in the Middle East. In effect, top executives were selling off parts of their firms so that they could pay themselves billions of dollars in bonuses.

## A Problem of Business, or of Government?

In these many examples, which go far toward explaining the sharp rise in the financial sector's share of overall corporate profits, the core problem is not mainly one that can be solved by business. The world that companies live in is too competitive for self-policing, all the more so in an era of globalization. Instead, it is a problem for government. Just as the rules of professional sports must be set by the leagues and enforced by impartial umpires and referees, so the rules of business must be set and enforced by government.

But from the 1980s onward, the growing popular feeling that taxes were too high and that the government was the problem and not part of the solution starved the referees and umpires, making them less efficient in enforcing the rules. This starving of (and contempt toward) the Securities and Exchange Commission, the Commodity Futures Trading Commission, the Department of Justice, and the Internal Revenue Service meant that government was abdicating its role. The SEC began to outsource some of its regulatory functions to bond-rating agencies such as Moody's and Standard & Poor's. Although these agencies had high historical reputations, they soon drifted into conflicts of interest in dealing with their clients—including investment banks marketing subprime home mortgages. These were new kinds of securities with which the rating agencies had no experience because there was no historical record of their performance. But if the agencies did not give "investment grade" ratings to the banks' bundles of securitized mortgages, they risked losing this very profitable business—the banks themselves were paying fees for the work done by the agencies. In such a situation, no party was looking out solely for the interest of the investor. Moody's itself became a publicly traded corporation in 1998, and over the next decade its share price multiplied sixfold and its profits ninefold. Essentially, the rating agencies' profits skyrocketed at the expense of their integrity as neutral judges of the value of bonds. The agencies' vital role in promoting corporate transparency was now severely compromised.

In any era of history, most companies have wished to disclose as little as possible about their internal affairs. This is not because the companies are evil, but because of other considerations: trade secrets, competitive pressures, and the old tradition of family ownership—disclosure of the firm's condition amounting to an unseemly parading of the family's finances. For these reasons, whenever the transparency mandated by a regulatory system can be avoided, it is avoided.

The remarkable financial innovations of recent decades have compounded this inherent characteristic of business. If you, as a financial executive, are managing a hedge fund and dealing in derivatives, you're operating in a world that you want to keep as opaque as possible—never revealing the kinds of data that are routinely submitted to the SEC by publicly traded companies. If you take a company private (buy all its common stock), you no longer have to make the reports to the SEC that a publicly traded company must. Private equity—whether the takeover is internal or external, friendly or hostile—means opacity; that is one of its greatest attractions.

So too with restating corporate earnings that had been earlier inflated so as to raise a firm's stock price: opacity. Bundling thousands of home mortgages (many of them subprime loans) and selling them with minimal disclosure: opacity. Marketing immense sums of unregulated securities that few purchasers can possibly understand ("structured investment vehicles," "collateralized debt obligations," "credit default swaps"): opacity. Offering student loans that carry easy ways out for the lender: opacity. Writing incomprehensible credit-card contracts, then imposing high fees and raising interest rates through universal default: opacity. Backdating stock options or not expensing them on a firm's income statement: opacity, and perhaps outright theft.

All of these devices contributed to the vast increase in the financial sector's profitability. Systematic evasions of the requirements for transparency on which the structure of capital-market regulation had been based for 60 years led to a new and mostly unregulated "shadow banking system." And because of the nearly universal business preference for opacity over transparency, movement of vast sums from the regulated system to the unregulated became inevitable.

During the summer and fall of 2008, this movement of vast sums into the shadow banking system culminated in a potentially catastrophic financial crisis. Three of the five major investment banks failed: Bear Stearns, which was bailed out by the federal government and purchased by JPMorgan Chase for $10 per share, down from $170 in 2007; Merrill Lynch, which was acquired by Bank of America under a similar public/private bailout; and Lehman Brothers, a 158-year-old firm which filed for bankruptcy when the government refused its pleas for help.

Meanwhile, the international insurance giant AIG (American International Group), whose obligations totaled several trillion dollars, tottered on the brink of collapse because it held so many assets of extremely shaky underlying worth: securitized home mortgages, credit default swaps, and other novel financial instruments of whose actual value nobody could be certain. This situation plagued numerous other financial institutions besides AIG.

To meet this situation—the most serious threat to the American economy in 75 years, since the wave of bank failures that ushered in the Great Depression—the U.S. Treasury and the Federal Reserve devised an emergency bailout. The cost to the taxpayers? Initial estimates ranged from $700 billion to $800 billion, but the actual eventual cost would depend on how banks, other businesses, and consumers reacted.

Without revision and better enforcement of the regulations, there would continue to be less transparency in the capital markets. Without transparency, there would be no *credibility*—and, sooner or later, no *credit*. Both of these words, after all, derive from the Latin *credo*, which means "I believe." The catch-up required to bring the situation under government control would likely be as difficult as any in American history. If consumers and investors ceased to believe in the honesty of the system, then credit would dry up and the whole economy would begin to drift into long-term stagnation.

## Widening Gaps in Wealth and Income

Between 1962 and 1990, the net worth of the poorest 20 percent of Americans shrank, while that of the top 20 percent increased by almost 90 percent. These numbers, like the emergence of the shadow banking system, signified an emphatic reversal of prior trends. In 1949 the richest 1 percent of Americans had owned 27 percent of the nation's wealth, but by 1995 they owned nearly 40 percent. In the latter year the average net worth of the richest 1 percent of households was almost $8 million, while that of the bottom 40 percent averaged less than $1,000. By 2008 about 30 percent of all Americans under the age of 35 had a negative net worth.

All reliable studies confirmed these trends and pointed to changes not only within the United States but also to big differences between the U.S. and other advanced industrialized countries. In the twenty-first century, a United Nations study found the following contrasts in income distribution:

**Income Multiples of the Richest Ten Percent of the People as Compared to the Poorest Ten Percent**

Japan 4.5

Germany 6.9

France 9.1

United States 15.9

The U.S. figure resembled those of socially stratified middle- or lower-income countries such as Turkey (16.8), Nepal (15.8), and Uganda (14.9).

One of the most preferred indices of income distribution is the Gini Coefficient, which ranges from zero to 1.0 and is named for its inventor, the Italian mathematician Corrado Gini. A Gini Coefficient of zero means that every person in a country has exactly the same income. A coefficient of 1.0 means that one person has all the income in the country. Therefore, the lower the coefficient, the more equal the distribution of income. Today, the lowest coefficients—which are in the middle .20s—are found in Japan, Scandinavia, and European countries such as Germany and Holland. By the early twenty-first century, the U.S. coefficient had climbed to the upper .40s. This figure, the nation's largest since calculations began in the 1960s, is closer to those for developing countries in Africa and South America than for highly industrialized nations, and its rise occurred almost entirely after 1979.

Between 1979 and 2008, after-tax incomes for the highest-paid 1 percent of Americans increased *thirty times* as much as for the bottom 20 percent. Of all net income gains during this period, 80 percent of the total dollar amounts went to the top 1 percent. Given the nation's traditions, these numbers border on the incredible. By 2008, inequality of income was the widest it had been since 1928, the year before the stock market crash began the Great Depression. Even on Wall Street, real unease had begun to grow. As the fund manager William Gross put it in 2008, "We are clearly in a period of excess, and we have to swing back to the middle or the center cannot hold."

There were many reasons for the extraordinary shifts in income distribution. One was the declining power of labor unions, another the increasing wage premium accruing to highly educated people. Still a third was the changing technology of work in the information-based Third Industrial Revolution. These shifts increased the spread between entry-level hourly laborers such as those working in McDonald's, and highly skilled "knowledge workers" such as software engineers.

But public policies played a strong role as well. Laws passed by Congress in 1981 increased the gap by flattening the graduated income tax. The top marginal rate was reduced from 70 percent to 50 percent, then to only 28 percent for the period 1988–90. It was raised to 40 percent during the 1990s, and toward the end of the decade federal surpluses began to appear. Then, in 2003, Congress again reduced the marginal tax rate, to 35 percent, along with other tax cuts for the wealthy and also for corporations.

Because these numbers apply to different dollar amounts for the maximum marginal rates, they are not precisely comparable. But the main point is very clear: at the behest of the administrations of Presidents Ronald Reagan and George W. Bush, Congress awarded deep tax cuts to the wealthiest Americans while sharply increasing military expenditures. In both cases the federal budget deficit immediately began to rise and the income gaps between rich and poor Americans grew larger. Whether or not wide variance of income distribution was (and is) a serious problem depends on the observer's ideology. In general, the more conservative the observer, the less serious the problem seems to be; the more progressive the observer, the more serious.

Should government be an instrument for the redistribution of wealth and income? Most conservatives would answer no, most progressives yes. About 80 percent of professional economists, who as a group are not particularly progressive, answered yes in a poll published in 2006. The larger truth, which most people don't think about very much, is that government usually redistributes wealth and income no matter what policies it follows. The real questions are "by how much?" and "in what direction?" Sometimes the redistribution is substantial and the direction obvious, as in sharply graduated income-tax systems on the one hand or big tax cuts for the wealthy on the other. Sometimes it's more subtle, as in the degree of regulatory enforcement, the aggressiveness with which the government pursues tax cheats (who have become more numerous since the 1980s), and the extent to which it grants waivers and other concessions to public or private interest groups.

In many cases, the stakes are extremely high, and all the major participants know it. During the brief period between 2000 and 2005, the number of registered lobbyists in Washington more than doubled, from 16,000 to 35,000. The number of elected legislators is 535 in the House and Senate combined. And, of course, Washington lobbyists spend vast amounts of time with agencies in the executive branch as well as the legislative. They also try to influence Supreme Court decisions through *amicus curiae* briefs. Nationally, the number of lobbyists in 2009 was about 265,000.

Nobody wants the United States to become a place where enterprising people can't become wealthy no matter how hard they work. And almost nobody really wants to pay taxes. On the other hand, by 2009 federal deficits had accumulated to such an extent that the national debt exceeded $10 trillion—a whopping 70 percent increase since 2001—and it was still growing at about $1.5 billion per day, the annual equivalent of $1,825 for every person in the country.

In 2006 the overall national savings rate (public and private) turned negative for the first time since World War II, and remained so for the next several years. This was a startling development, unique among advanced industrialized countries. More than half of all federal IOU's were held abroad, notably by the central banks of China and Japan. And about 20 percent of federal tax payments were going to satisfy interest on this huge and growing debt. So the federal government, like most other levels of government, and like most individual American consumers, was living far beyond it means. At some point this national binge, like all binges, would have to end. The questions were when, how, and at what cost to long-term prosperity.

# CHAPTER EIGHT

# Information Technology

## IT as "It"

Globalization as we know it would be impossible without modern information technology (IT) and the decentralization of decision making. Wal★Mart and other giant retailers could not manage their empires as they do—with instant feedback of daily sales from all stores for every item on the shelves. No major company could adjust its "lean inventories" for sales or production without IT algorithms that program variables such as raw-material prices, seasonal demands for products or services, and business-cycle forecasts. In financial markets, it would take hours or days rather than seconds to calculate the value of derivatives and other complex instruments.

None of the companies analyzed so far—Ford, GM, Procter & Gamble, Boeing, McDonald's—nor thousands of other important firms all over the world—could compete in their industries without the use of modern IT. Firms based on computers, software, and the Internet wouldn't even exist. We would never have heard of Microsoft, Intel, Hewlett-Packard, Dell, Apple, Cisco, Sun Microsystems, Oracle, EMC, Yahoo!, Amazon.com, eBay, or Google. And, of course, there would be no such thing as e-mail.

Just as large companies in all industries have a Chief Executive Officer (CEO), a Chief Operating Officer (COO), and a Chief Financial Officer (CFO), they now also have a Chief Information Officer (CIO). This person is responsible for every aspect of communication, often including "intranets" that link each of the company's units—labs, factories, offices, stores—across the globe. In some firms the title is Chief Technology Officer or Vice President of Information Systems, but in nearly every case, these executives rank high in the company's hierarchy and report directly to the CEO.

From the 1980s to the present, Information Technology has been "It." Historically, a few other industries have been as important as IT, and one or two have arisen as quickly; but no other has ever grown so important so fast or has continued to change so relentlessly. And no other has so facilitated the empowerment of consumers and the decentralization of decision making.

## Computers

The first modern electronic computer used in business was the Univac, which was about the size of a small truck but could perform only a minute number of functions that even the tiniest computers can today. Univac was introduced in 1950 by Remington Rand, at that time a leading high-tech firm. But it was another company, IBM, that rapidly emerged as the dominant player in electronic information technology. Under IBM's leadership, IT became the most dynamic industry of the late twentieth century.

From the time of its founding in the 1880s, through a series of mergers and name changes, the company that became IBM had been the leader in punch-card machines used for sorting and filing information. In 1924, CEO Thomas J. Watson changed the name yet again, to International Business Machines, even though the company was not yet very international. During the 1930s, IBM prospered from sales to the federal government, which needed data processing for the new Social Security system and other public projects. An even bigger expansion resulted from defense contracts it landed during World War II. All the while, IBM maintained its focus on selling to the private sector, where it had a well-earned reputation for superb service to customers.

During the 1950s IBM achieved supremacy in electronic computers by leveraging its skills in marketing and customer relations, even though it sometimes lagged in technology. Then it broke through on that front as well. In the 1960s, after conducting the most expensive privately financed R&D effort in history, IBM introduced its revolutionary System/360 series. Just as a full circle has 360 degrees, the new computers would serve all purposes, from scientific to defense to business uses. System/360's spectacular triumph in the marketplace made IBM so strong that for three decades the company's name was almost synonymous with the information technology industry around the globe.

At first, computers had not been designed to communicate with one another, and only one or two visionaries had even dreamed of anything like the Internet. With System/360, however, IBM took the first crucial steps. It achieved "compatibility" by devising a common operating system for all its computers, of whatever size or purpose. Pressure from federal antitrust authorities then forced IBM to allow its customers to accept "plug compatible" accessories made by other companies for use with IBM computers. In this way, IBM's immense R&D expenditures indirectly supported its competitors in the development and sales of IBM-compatible machines as well as their own peripherals and other products. The result, from the 1960s onward, was a burst of creative energy by scores of hardware and software firms. In the early years, the major companies included Control Data, which made peripherals and supercomputers; Amdahl, with its core memories and disk drives; Memorex, a manufacturer of tape drives and other items; and Electronic Data Systems, a service firm whose success made a billionaire of its founder, former IBM salesman H. Ross Perot. That the name of none of these firms is a household word today symbolizes the unprecedented dynamism of IT.

After System/360, the next evolutionary step was the development during the 1960s and 1970s of "mini-computers" (typically weighing about 200 pounds) by Digital Equipment and other companies. Then, most important, came the personal computer (PC) in the 1970s and 1980s. The first primitive PC appeared in 1974, marketed by a tiny calculator company in Albuquerque, New Mexico. This machine, called the Altair, lacked even a keyboard and a monitor. It was of interest primarily to electronics hobbyists.

One such hobbyist was Bill Gates, a 19-year-old Harvard undergraduate who quickly became enthralled with the new machine's potential. Gates and his friend Paul Allen wrote a version of the existing BASIC programming language for the Altair and set up the company that later became Microsoft. Convinced that he would have to act quickly, Gates dropped out of Harvard and moved with Allen to Albuquerque, where they marketed their company's programming language to the firm making the Altair. Gates and Allen worked furiously to build Microsoft into a viable business, eventually moving it to their hometown of Seattle. The firm that manufactured the Altair failed to prosper, but Microsoft was now positioned to exploit a fabulous opportunity foolishly handed to it by IBM, as we shall soon see.

Meanwhile, in 1977, a small California company led by the young entrepreneurs Steve Jobs and Steve Wozniak introduced the Apple II personal computer. This was a modern, user-friendly, and relatively expensive machine that came with a keyboard and external disk drive, and could easily be connected to a monitor and other peripherals. By 1981 the Apple II had been purchased by more than 120,000 customers, most of them business firms using early forms of spreadsheet software.

Because of its technological sophistication and ease of use, the Apple II inspired fierce brand loyalty among its original buyers, many of whom stuck with the company through its later ups and downs. Apple Computer might have become the dominant player in PCs over the long term, but Apple disdained the office market. It refused to license its operating system and thereby foreclosed the compatibility of its machines and software with those of other companies, a quality so appealing to many purchasers of computers.

With the introduction of IBM's own PC in 1981, overall sales proceeded to take off. IBM shot into the lead, as the industry shipped 800,000 PCs in 1981, 2.5 million in 1982, and more than 6 million in 1985. Most machines were still sold to business customers, who were attracted by the power of IBM's brand, its unmatched reputation for customer service, and its "open architecture," which could accommodate other firms' software products. IBM's PC was not appreciably superior to units offered by other companies and was distinctly inferior to the more expensive Macintosh, made by Apple. But the mere fact that such a prestigious firm as IBM had entered the personal computer sweepstakes gave a big boost to the machine as a legitimate product in both the business and consumer markets. By today's standards all PCs of this era were oversized, clumsy to operate, and maddeningly slow.

IBM earned a lot of money from PC sales during the early 1980s, but in doing so it planted the seeds of its fall as undisputed ruler of the industry. Determined to cash in on the PC boom quickly, IBM made two momentous decisions. It chose to outsource both the disk operating system and the microprocessor—the intricate chip that forms the principal "brain" of all personal computers. IBM's outsourcing contracts delivered bonanzas to a pair of young firms that soon took their places among the most successful companies in the history of business.

One was Microsoft, founded in 1975 and by the 1980s one of the world's leading software firms. The other was Intel, founded in 1968 and by the 1980s the world's chief provider of high-end microprocessors. Because of IBM's prior move to open architecture, Microsoft and Intel could supply software and microprocessors not only to IBM but also to the makers of IBM "clones"— PCs produced by dozens of other companies, including foreign ones. Many of these firms offered their PCs on quicker delivery schedules and for much lower prices than those of IBM. As a company, IBM now seemed to have become relatively inflexible, burdened by layers of corporate bureaucracy. Not only did it begin to falter in PC deliveries, it also failed to grasp the emerging importance of software as opposed to hardware.

From 1981 onward, by supplying IBM and other manufacturers as the PC market skyrocketed, Intel and Microsoft grew very fast and earned enormous profits. Their CEOs became international celebrities. In 1997, *Time* selected Andrew Grove of Intel as its "Person of the Year." By that time, Bill Gates had become the wealthiest and best-known businessman on Earth. His company, Microsoft, had grown so powerful through its stranglehold on the standards for operating systems that it began to encounter serious challenges from antitrust authorities, much as had happened earlier to IBM.

At the start of the twenty-first century, the worldwide IT industry was divided approximately into 80 percent industrial sales—that is, business-to-business marketing, much of it workstations, PCs, software, and services—and 20 percent sales directly to consumers, mostly of PCs, related software, and video games. Americans had purchased more than twice as many personal computers, per capita, as had Europeans or Japanese, and U.S.-based companies led in most other aspects of information technology. IBM was still the world's largest computer firm, and one of the best. After a decade of decline, beginning in the 1980s, it had recovered some of its old luster by transforming itself into a services company with an emphasis on consulting and electronic commerce. It had not, however, regained its former position of unchallenged primacy in the IT industry.

## The Changing Role of Government

During and just after World War II, the U.S. government underwrote most R&D expenditures in electronics, including computers. A second pillar of public support came from huge federal purchases of equipment from IBM and other firms. In addition, the government designed and paid for the complex interconnections that evolved into the Internet. Most of these efforts were made as part of the Cold War struggle to stay ahead of the Soviet Union. Thus, the IT industry owes more—far, far more—than either its current business titans or its billions of consumers realize, to early investments by the U.S. government.

Once the computer industry began to mature in the 1960s and 1970s, and once software became as important as hardware, business gradually began to replace government in the leadership role. Government remained a big presence, but it was no longer the key participant. After IBM's slippage in the 1980s, there was no single chief player, although Microsoft became far and away the leader in software. The most significant cluster of information-technology companies was located in and around "Silicon Valley," a small region of California south of San Francisco that included the cities of Palo Alto, Santa Clara, and San Jose. IBM in New York and New Jersey, and other firms clustered around Boston, Minneapolis, and Austin, Texas, were major players as well.

No European company mounted a serious challenge to the American firms' supremacy in either industrial or consumer markets. During the 1980s, however, there came a very serious threat from Japan. For a time it appeared that powerful firms such as Fujitsu, NEC, Hitachi, and Toshiba might do to American IT companies what Sony and Matsushita had done to RCA and the American consumer-electronics industry. But by the early 1990s this threat had apparently passed, because of relentless progress in the United States.

At that time more than 6,000 high-tech firms were operating in Silicon Valley alone. Most were relatively small, many were start-ups, and almost all were characterized by a porous, informal, and decentralized corporate culture. Even the largest and best-known of the Valley's high-tech companies—Sun Microsystems, Intel, Hewlett-Packard, Apple, Oracle, Cisco—tended to do business in very nontraditional ways. These big companies often lived up to their own informal slogans: "Kick Butt and Have Fun" (Sun); "Only the Paranoid Survive" (Intel); and "The HP Way," a cooperative approach to innovation pioneered by Hewlett-Packard, the oldest Silicon Valley firm.

## How the Valley Developed

During the 1930s, William Hewlett and David Packard had been students of Frederick Terman (1900–82), a professor of engineering at Stanford. Terman, who eventually became known as the "father of Silicon Valley," in 1938 lent Hewlett and Packard $538 (the equivalent to $8,100 in 2009) to set up an enterprise in Packard's garage in Palo Alto. The new firm, Hewlett-Packard, grew steadily and rose to national prominence when it entered the computer business in the 1960s.

For the rest of the century HP pioneered in the development of one electronics device after another: some it sold to businesses, others directly to consumers. The company came to employ more than 100,000 people but retained its ability to reinvent itself and move quickly into the next generation of high-tech equipment. HP became successively the world leader in hand-held calculators, electronic medical instruments, and ink-jet and laser printers. It was especially good at devising custom electronics devices for particular industries. "The HP Way" of systematic innovation was widely copied. Numerous HP alumni went on to form their own firms, such as Steve Wozniak, cofounder of Apple Computer, and Thomas Perkins, cofounder of Kleiner Perkins, the venture-capital giant.

During the early 1950s, Professor (and by then Dean) Frederick Terman persuaded Stanford University officials to set aside 1,000 acres of property adjoining the campus and invite high-tech firms to move in as tenants: thus was born Stanford Industrial Park, later called Stanford Research Park. Over the next 30 years more than a thousand companies spun out of Stanford, and several dozen located their operations in the Park. William Shockley, who had won the Nobel Prize as co-inventor of the transistor, moved Shockley Semiconductor Laboratories into the Park in 1955.

Two years later, eight of Shockley's best employees seceded and set up their own firm, Fairchild Semiconductor. The embittered Shockley (and others as well) began to refer to the defectors as the "Traitorous Eight." But secession and job-hopping soon came to be seen as a conventional way of doing business in Silicon Valley, and the Traitorous Eight became simply the "Fairchild Eight." Fairchild itself began to spin off companies (the most important being Intel), and these firms in turn spawned still newer ones.

In the larger American economy as well, job-hopping was becoming much more common than in Europe or Japan, where both law and custom valued business stability more than innovation. In Japan, most recruits to major firms assumed that they had signed on for their entire careers, an assumption shared by their employers. And in several European countries, the law required as much as six months' notice before an important person could leave an established firm. These laws and customs have changed recently but still do not approach the American model of constant turbulence and entrepreneurial turnover.

Even so, in almost all industrialized countries, including the United States, employees of high-tech companies can be compelled to sign "non-compete" contracts in which they pledge to forgo work on competitive products for a specified period after their departure. Courts in some American states enforced these contracts more stringently than did their counterparts in others. California's notably lax approach was one reason why entrepreneurs found Silicon Valley such a hospitable environment.

But the most important reason for the secession of employees and the creation of new companies in Silicon Valley was neither law nor custom. Instead, it was the extraordinary speed at which electronics technology was hurtling forward—relentlessness was becoming even more relentless. In 1959, one of the Fairchild Eight, Robert Noyce, invented the integrated circuit. This device combined in one small silicon chip numerous functions that earlier had required many discrete transistors and components wired together on a circuit board. The integrated circuit was invented simultaneously at Texas Instruments. It became for the Third Industrial Revolution what the steam engine had been for the First, and electricity and the internal-combustion engine for the Second.

In 1968, Robert Noyce and another member of the Fairchild Eight, Gordon Moore, cofounded Intel. Moore's name soon became famous because of his prediction that the number of transistors that could be put onto a microchip would double every year. (In 1975 he extended the period to 18 months.) Geometric progressions of this sort usually drop off after a short time, but "Moore's Law" held firm into the twenty-first century, reflecting the highest sustained rate of efficiency gains in the history of any industry. In 1960, transistors cost about $1 apiece. This was the equivalent of nearly $6 at the end of the century, but by that time 10 million transistors could be produced for less than $1, and the almost unimaginable total of one quadrillion transistors were being turned out each month. By 2009 the number had grown so large as to be virtually incalculable.

In practical terms, the operation of Moore's Law meant that the cost of any task a microchip could perform was declining so fast that a myriad of applications arose that earlier would have been uneconomical. In the twenty-first century, for example, new cars contain dozens of chips that do everything from monitoring engine operations and scanning radio frequencies to switching off interior lights at precise intervals after passengers leave the car. Computers could have performed these operations as early as the 1950s, but a car accommodating the necessary equipment would have had to be as big as an average-sized house.

Still another of the Fairchild Eight was Eugene Kleiner, who made his mark primarily as a venture capitalist. Kleiner Perkins, the firm he cofounded in 1972 with the HP alumnus Thomas Perkins, became a model for similar companies. Together, these venture-capital firms took very prominent roles in the spinoff-start-up-shakeup process that became the essence of doing business in Silicon Valley.

In 1985, a California photographer named Carolyn Caddes put together a book of images and text she titled *Portraits of Success: Impressions of Silicon Valley Pioneers*. She reunited the Fairchild Eight and arrayed them in the same pose they had taken for a similar portrait 26 years earlier. At the end of the 1985 session, it struck her that "in spite of graying hair, a few bald spots, and several paunches, these eight men looked like a group of overgrown boys." They still dressed as they wished, worked odd hours, and in general came across as adolescents determined to have fun. The gee-whiz, geeky quality retained by the aging Fairchild Eight was also evident in the personalities of Bill Gates and other leaders of the industry. It inspired the writer Robert X. Cringely to title his 1992 book *Accidental Empires: How the Boys of Silicon Valley Make Their Millions, Battle Foreign Competition, and Still Can't Get a Date*.

## Organizational Innovation

In 1997, the magazine *The Economist* did a careful article on Silicon Valley's success, and it remains as good as any short analysis yet published. Many factors *The Economist* identified as central to the region's culture resonate with the themes of this book. They include the market's creative destruction of old products by new ones, the release of economic energy through entrepreneurial opportunity, and the balancing of centralized and decentralized management within organizations. The author of the survey argued that over the long run Silicon Valley's "most important contribution may well be organizational, not technological." He went on to enumerate the essential components of this new kind of business success: relentless change, a high propensity to take risks, patience with temporary failure, tolerance of job-hopping, rigorous meritocracy, cooperation across firms, and flexible organizational structures.

Several analysts of Silicon Valley have commented on its similarity to other industry clusters. When the New York Stock Exchange was in its youth, numerous investment banks and brokerage houses sprang up on Wall Street, the address of the Exchange. Other industries evolved through the same kind of pattern: automobiles around Detroit, motion pictures in southern California, amusement parks in central Florida, and so on. Wherever these industry clusters arise, it becomes easier for denizens to share ideas, make deals, and accelerate the progress of firms within the cluster—versus their competitors located elsewhere.

Of course, many clusters ultimately fail. In the nineteenth century the British cotton textile industry grew up around Manchester and prospered for several decades. In the twentieth century it lost its lead to overseas competitors who were quicker to modernize, and eventually it collapsed. Something similar happened to Detroit and the American automobile industry.

One threat to Silicon Valley's continued dominance was a penchant by entrepreneurs to create new firms for the primary purpose of selling them to big companies inside or outside the Valley, such as Cisco and Microsoft. Then there is the Internet, which makes thousands of innovations immediately available throughout the world, thereby reducing some of the need for physical clustering. A final threat lay in what *The Economist* accurately identified as the remarkable insensitivity of "Silicon Valley's nerds" to the problems of government and the broader needs of society. Their lack of concern for subjects other than money and the next "cool idea" might itself represent a threat from within. But not even the harshest critics could deny the powerful role of Valley firms in the rise of information technology.

# The Internet

Like the computer hardware industry, the Internet was a child of the Cold War. It began life in the 1960s within the Defense Department's Advanced Research Project Agency (ARPA), which set up a series of computer networks for cooperative R&D. The most important visionary was ARPA'S J. C. R. Licklider, a computer scientist whose 1962 series of memos discussing a "Galactic Network" foreshadowed most of what we now know as the Internet. The Defense Department endeavored through its ARPANET to facilitate "internetworking" among scientists at universities and government agencies across the nation. Planners decentralized the Internet (as it came to be called) through backup routes involving satellite communications, telephone wires, and other links.

The Internet grew more complex as it expanded from four host computers in the late 1960s to 2,000 by the mid-1980s. For several years, the heaviest users remained scientists and engineers working on advanced R&D projects. But without anyone's having planned it that way, many of those widely dispersed users in universities and research firms began to enter the system in order to "chat" (exchange ideas) and to organize "bulletin boards."

During the 1980s the National Science Foundation (NSF), the government agency most directly concerned with funding R&D of all kinds, took over administration of the Internet. NSF forbade any commercial use of the system, formalizing what had long been an implicit policy. But the Internet's business potential became so attractive to so many users that the NSF prohibition lasted for only a few years. The first providers of commercial services began to use the system in 1989, and a year later the rules were changed. For all practical purposes the Internet was privatized in 1990, and officially so in 1995 when NSF withdrew in favor of privately owned "backbones." By that time the number of linked networks had mushroomed from about 25 in the early 1980s to 44,000 in 1995.

Over the next several years, growth on all fronts proceeded so fast that statistics about "cyberspace" and the Internet became obsolete almost as soon as they were calculated. The Internet Council, a short-lived organization formed in 1995 and funded by telecommunications firms and Silicon Valley businesses, distributed information such as the following:

In 1993, about 90,000 Americans had regular access to the net. Seven years later, at the close of the century, that number had grown by a factor of one thousand, to 90 million. The *Internet Industry Almanac* estimated that in 2000, 327 million people around the globe used the net. By 2009, according to *Internet World Stats*, the number had grown to about 1.5 billion.

The big stimulus to this mushroom growth was the World Wide Web, so named by the English physicist Tim Berners-Lee, one of its developers. No single language dominates the many billions of pages now available on the Web, but in 2008 English was by far the most common, followed by Chinese. About 37 percent of users worldwide were based in Asia, 27 percent in Europe, 19 percent in North America, and 9 percent in Latin America.

The *Internet* and the *Web* are not, of course, synonymous terms. The Internet is the "network of networks," and the Web is the immense assemblage of documents and other content available online. During the late 1980s and early 1990s, Berners-Lee and a team of scientists working at a physics research lab in Switzerland had envisioned "a pool of human knowledge" that would be stored on the Internet. It would be made accessible through a system of "hypertext markup language" (html) that could adapt to different data formats on various types of computers. Such a system, through a "hypertext transfer protocol" (http), would also manage the movement of data between Web servers (information storage centers) and Web browsers. Berners-Lee did not call it a "web" for nothing, because in a web one can go not just up or down, as in a hierarchical file directory, but in any direction. A web user can link anything to anything else, even on someone else's site. That was the fundamental breakthrough.

A rudimentary version of this system proved immediately popular not only at the Swiss lab but also at similar sites in the United States. One of these was a federally sponsored center at the University of Illinois set up for the further development of supercomputers. When the boom in interconnected PC-based workstations made that mission less urgent, the center shifted its attention to networking technology. A team that included the undergraduate student Marc Andreessen quickly developed an enhanced Web browser ("Mosaic") that could run on most PCs and accommodate color images as well as text. In late 1993 the federal government released Mosaic over the Internet to the general public, free of charge. Within a few months, more than a million copies of the browser had been downloaded. In 1994 the 22-year-old Andreessen and other members of the team left Illinois to go into private business, and soon they were distributing a much improved version of Mosaic, which they called "Netscape Navigator." Their company quickly became one of the hottest properties in American business, and in 1999 it merged with America Online, at that time the leading service provider and later the firm that purchased Time Warner.

The availability of the World Wide Web (for which Tim Berners-Lee and his colleagues charged no fees whatsoever)—plus commercial ventures such as Mosaic, Netscape Navigator, Internet Explorer (owned by Microsoft), Firefox, Safari, and other browsers—made the Internet accessible to masses of ordinary citizens. All over the world, hundreds of millions of people began to use the Internet not only to obtain information but also to contribute new data to the system. They did this through their own blogs, individual or commercial websites, and enterprises such as Wikipedia, the now-gigantic nonprofit encyclopedia.

As the twenty-first century began, it remained difficult for even the best-informed analysts to predict the degree to which cyberspace might replace stores, banks, and other commercial establishments as the preferred place to do business. Most of the profits rung up by Internet businesses during the 1990s had gone either to purveyors of pornography or to America Online and other service providers. Still, thousands of entrepreneurs saw unlimited possibilities in various forms of online commerce. The race was on, and during the late 1990s a "dot.com" craze took off, attracting huge amounts of money. By 1998 Yahoo!, a Web-based company with 637 employees, had about the same market capitalization as did the aerospace giant Boeing, which then employed 230,000 people. The stocks of numerous other Internet companies sold at astronomical prices even though the firms themselves lost large sums year after year.

In September 1999 Jack Welch, CEO of General Electric, was quoted in *Fortune* as saying that electronic commerce "is clearly the biggest revolution in business in our lifetimes." Welch, the most respected professional manager of his generation, asserted that it would affect every aspect of business: "It will change relationships with employees. We will never again have discussions where knowledge is hidden in somebody's pocket. . . . It will change relationships with customers. Customers will see everything. Nothing will be hidden in paperwork. . . . It will change relationships with suppliers. Within 18 months, all our suppliers will supply us over the Internet or they won't do business with us."

Overall, the proliferation of Internet-related commerce was the most significant development in American business at the close of the twentieth century. Thousands of entrepreneurs rushed to establish a presence in what they hoped would be the most rewarding marketplace of the twenty-first century. The investment balloon puffed up wildly until 2000, when it began a rapid deflation that killed off numerous startups. But this was only a temporary interruption. Most of the visionaries, from J. C. R. Licklider in the 1960s to Tim Berners-Lee in the 1980s, had been right. So had Jack Welch. The Internet is now accessible almost anywhere, through PCs, mobile phones, and cellular devices of many other kinds.

The immense potential of the Internet can be captured in one set of statistics that has only partly to do with business: in 1998, about 620 billion e-mail messages were sent worldwide. In 2000 almost 1 trillion were sent in the United States alone, much of it unwanted advertising, or "spam." (During the same year, the U.S. Postal Service delivered about 100 billion pieces of mail, and much of this, too, was "junk mail.") By 2009, annual e-mail messages in the United States had grown to more than 3 trillion, an average of ten thousand for every person in the country. And the number was still growing by about 300 billion per year—one thousand additional messages for every person, year after year.

The Internet and the Web have already had as powerful a cultural impact as the automobile and television had in earlier generations. And, like those landmark innovations, its influence will continue, likely forever. It will be seen and heard in numerous forms—from blogs and the downloading of music, to web-cams, podcasts, Wikipedia, YouTube, Facebook, MySpace, and numerous other innovations still to come. It represents the most remarkable outpouring of information, and decentralization of access to that information, in world history.

## Companies and Personalities

Information technology also embodies one of the greatest arrays of entrepreneurial opportunities ever: startups or existing companies devoted to hardware, software, portals, and other enterprises of almost every type. Engineers and entrepreneurs have flocked to Silicon Valley and other centers of the industry from all over the United States and from overseas. Numerous companies have been founded by immigrants—in particular by people from India and Taiwan—Sabeer Bhatia of Hotmail and Jerry Yang of Yahoo! being among the best known. The histories of three other companies also illustrate particularly well IT's release of entrepreneurial energy by people of diverse backgrounds:

1. *Amazon.com.* In 1994, a 30-year-old financial analyst named Jeff Bezos was working at the D. E. Shaw hedge fund, researching potential Internet-related investments. It suddenly occurred to him that the best single candidate for e-commerce might be—of all things—books. No other industry seemed so ripe for radical change. Book publishing had long been notoriously hidebound, trapped by the unpredictability of sales for the 80,000 or so new titles brought out each year. Because of the uncertain demand for most new books—many selling in the hundreds, most no more than a few thousand, some in the tens of thousands, and a tiny number in the millions—retail distributors were almost forced to charge large markups for all books in order to cover their losses for poor-selling ones. Production runs ("printings") were nearly

impossible to plan with much accuracy, except for novels by Danielle Steele, Tom Clancy, and a few other "brand" authors. The management of inventories was antiquated.

Jeff Bezos was not a book person, but a computer whiz turned financial analyst. Born in Albuquerque, he had grown up in Houston and Miami. At age five he had been given the last name of his mother's second husband, Miguel Bezos, an immigrant from Cuba and an Exxon engineer. After finishing high school in Miami, Jeff Bezos had gone to Princeton, where he graduated Phi Beta Kappa with majors in computer science and electrical engineering. He had a modest, engaging manner, which concealed an exceedingly analytical and creative mind. Even as a baby and a small boy he had been a confirmed tinkerer—trying to take his crib apart with a screwdriver, wiring his room with an electric alarm that went off whenever anyone entered.

In 1994, sensing the apparently limitless possibilities, Bezos presented his idea of online bookselling to his employer. When the hedge fund refused to invest, Bezos left his well-paying job and drove across the country to Seattle, a center of Internet action. After a few fits and starts, he founded Amazon.com. The original name was Cadabra.com, which Bezos abandoned because it sounds too much like "cadaver." Amazon, one of the world's great rivers, better expressed the grandeur of his vision.

At that time Bezos was only one of several thousand bright young entrepreneurs with visions of online magic. Amazon.com began selling books in 1995 with deep discounts, an unmatched ease of ordering (the "shopping cart" and "one-click" systems), and customer reviews posted alongside each book on the Amazon website. In 1997 Amazon issued its initial public stock offering, and the price took off. By 1999 Jeff Bezos's net worth was more than $10 billion; at the age of 35, he ranked number 19 among the world's richest people. *Time* named him its "Person of the Year" for 1999. All of this, however, was just Act I in the drama of Amazon.com, and of Internet commerce generally.

Act II began the very next year. In 2000, the dot.com bubble burst and numerous personal fortunes—most of them chimerical in the first place—suddenly vanished. Hundreds of dot.com startups disappeared. But those with sound business models, wise management, and ample financing survived. In this new business climate, as companies hemorrhaged money and entrepreneurs searched for reliable income streams, long-term financing turned out to be indispensable.

Amazon, for example, had started with an $8 million investment from venture capitalists. It had then taken in $62 million from its 1997 IPO, had received $326 million in 1998 through an issue of high-yield corporate bonds, $1.25 billion in 1999 in convertible bonds, and $681 million more in convertibles in 2000. But Amazon remained consistently in the red until 2002, more than seven years after its founding. By that time Bezos's personal net worth had declined by $8.6 billion because of a steep fall in the company's share price. Unlike most other dot.com entrepreneurs, he had anticipated this kind of industry shakeout, partly because of his background in finance. But he had expected Amazon to turn a profit in its fourth or fifth year of operation, certainly not so late as its seventh. Undeterred by setbacks, Bezos relentlessly continued to build his company. Amazon became famous for growth through acquisitions of small Internet-based firms and a willingness to divest all units that didn't fit its evolving strategy.

Here is a sample of its acquisitions, most of them purchased with shares of Amazon stock and minimal outlays of cash: in 1998 it bought the Internet Movie Database. In 1999, Alexa Internet, Exchange.com, and Accept.com. In 2003, CD Now, an online music retailer. In 2004, Joyo.com, a Chinese portal for e-commerce. In 2005, BookSurge (print-on-demand), Mobipocket.com (eBook software), CreateSpace (on-demand DVDs). In 2006, Shopbop (online retailing of clothing and accessories). In 2007, dpreview.com (digital photography review) and Brilliance Audio (the biggest U.S. independent publisher of audio books). During these same years, Amazon steadily added to its array of services through internal initiatives such as MP3 downloading. All of these moves were calculated to grow the business by making online shopping not only much broader in product lines, but also very much simpler and easier for the customer.

Eventually, Amazon worked out cooperative arrangements with a long list of retailers and manufacturers: Target, Sears, Marks & Spencer, The Gap, Lands End, Nordstrom, Lacoste, Timex, and many others. The range of products available through

Amazon became vast: not just books, DVDs, and MP3 downloads, but also clothing, sporting goods, toys, watches, tools, auto parts, jewelry, and just about anything else that could easily be shipped to customers. By the early twenty-first century Amazon was operating throughout Europe and Asia as well as North America, filling more than 50 million orders per month. Its revenues for 2007 reached $15 billion and its profits almost $480 million. In 2008 it employed 17,000 people—55 percent of them in North America, 45 percent in other countries. Most of these numbers, however, would soon be obsolete, for the company's most striking aspect remained sheer growth: of sales, profits, number of employees, and items available for purchase. By 2009 Amazon's stock price had gone up again, and with it Jeff Bezos's personal fortune.

2. *eBay.* This famous online auction site was founded by Pierre Omidyar, an Iranian-American born in France. Omidyar grew up in Washington, D.C., and attended St. Andrew's Episcopal School in Bethesda, Maryland. Next he enrolled at Tufts University, from which he graduated in 1988 with a degree in computer science. He then went to work for a subsidiary of Apple Computer. In 1991, at age 24, he started his first online company, Ink Development, which he later converted to eShop. At age 28, he established Auction Web, a site from which people could buy and sell all sorts of items free of charge. This service grew so fast that Omidyar was forced to levy small fees just to cover his own costs. Thus, in 1995, eBay was born.

"Trust between strangers," as Omidyar put it, became the foundation of the company's success. Anyone could participate, and by 2008 eBay had 220 million customers and 300,000 regular sellers located around the world—all, in both categories, registered with the company. Some sellers, of course, operated on a larger scale than did others. About 20 percent of the sellers accounted for 80 percent of the sales, and for them eBay amounted to an online storefront.

Pierre Omidyar remained chairman of the company throughout these years, but in 1996 he turned over day-to-day operations to Jeffrey Skoll and in 1998 to Margaret "Meg" Whitman. Whitman remained president and CEO for the next ten years, during which she became—like Omidyar and Skoll—a billionaire, as well as one of the most prominent women in American business.

The nature of eBay's operations has always made it an extremely unusual company. Its slogans are "Shop victoriously!" and "Whatever it is, you can get it on eBay." The first sale in 1995 was of a broken laser pointer, for which the winning bidder paid $14.83. When Omidyar asked this buyer if he understood that the item was broken, the response was "I'm a collector of broken laser pointers." So in one sense eBay serves as a giant online yard sale, a worldwide flea market of used merchandise, some of it junk. But, as with the laser pointer, one person's junk is another's collectible. One person's useless stuff meets another's real need. In the history of business, no better example can be found of the extreme, almost total, decentralization of marketing. Buyers and sellers can find each other in all niches and microniches, no matter how small. The genius of eBay—like that of other online enterprises such as dating services, Facebook, MySpace, and blogging—is the bringing together of large numbers of people who otherwise would have no convenient way of connecting.

eBay was financed in much the same way as was Amazon: first through venture capital (about $6 million in 1997 and 1998), then through the IPO of its stock ($72.5 million in 1998, followed by a whopping $1.3 billion follow-on issue in 1999). The company's revenues come from fees it charges to sellers. By 2008 these fees ranged from 20 cents to $80 per listing, depending on the value of the item offered, and up to 5.25 percent of the final sale price. Not every sale on eBay is an auction. Under a fixed-price "Buy It Now" provision, a purchaser can win the sale immediately and stop the auction.

Over the years, most of eBay's several billion sales have been of routine goods or collectibles. Occasionally, however, the bizarre transaction occurs, in the tradition of the broken laser pointer. In 2004, an old and half-eaten grilled-cheese sandwich bearing what appeared to be an image of the Virgin Mary sold for $28,000. Also in 2004, the original hillside HOLLYWOOD sign brought $450,400, after spirited bidding. In 2005, the wife of a British radio disk jockey, having listened to her husband flirt on the air with a famous model, offered his Lotus sports car for 50 pence on a Buy It Now basis. The car sold within five minutes. Also in 2005, a Volkswagen owned by Joseph Cardinal Ratzinger before he became Pope Benedict XVI brought more than $277,000.

Most buyers and sellers on eBay have to be aware that they are risking their money on sight-unseen transactions with unknowable partners. The possibilities for fraud are almost endless, on both sides. Often the condition of many posted items has been deceptively described—forgeries of old coins and other antique items being especially common. For expensive goods, collusive "shill bidding" has sometimes driven prices artificially higher. The time limit for auctions has been manipulated by "sniping"—the practice of entering bids at the last second, sometimes through software designed for the purpose. In addition, many sellers have posted items that cannot be legally sold. Sometimes they've done so sincerely (in 1999 a man offered one of his kidneys), sometimes in jest (individuals, towns, and on one occasion the nation of New Zealand). Then, too, methods of payment have been corrupted in almost every way imaginable. eBay, therefore, has had to augment trust between strangers with a long series of corrective mechanisms.

For this task, Meg Whitman proved to be the ideal CEO. An economics graduate of Princeton with an MBA from Harvard Business School, she began her career at Procter & Gamble, where she learned invaluable lessons about brand management. She further honed her marketing expertise at the Bain consulting firm, at the Walt Disney Company, as president and CEO of Floral Transport Delivery (FTD, the world's leader in its field), and finally as a high-ranking manager at Hasbro, the toymaking giant. When an executive placement ("headhunting") firm put her in touch with Pierre Omidyar in 1998, eBay had only 19 employees and yearly revenues of about $4 million. Ten years later, when Whitman stepped down as CEO, eBay's revenues had grown to $7.7 billion for 2007 and the company employed 14,000 people. In 2004 and 2005, *Time* listed her as one of the world's 100 most important people. In 2005, *Fortune* named her the most powerful woman in

American business. And in every year from 2000 through 2007, *Business Week* ranked her as among the nation's 25 most powerful executives.

Working the long hours of most CEOs, Whitman, along with her neurosurgeon husband, managed at the same time to raise their two sons. Reflecting in a 2007 interview on her experience at eBay, she said that founder Pierre Omidyar "taught me about communities on the Web. But what I brought to the table was that I knew what we were going to need if the company continued to grow. My job was to uncover what was going well. I think sometimes when a senior executive comes into a company, the instinctive thing to do is to find out what's wrong and fix it. That doesn't actually work very well. People are very proud of what they've created, and it just feels like you are second guessing them all the time. You are much more successful coming in and finding out what's going right and nurturing that. Along the way, you'll find out what's going wrong and fix that."

In 1998, the number of things that required fixing made up a long list. Since such huge numbers of people bought and sold on eBay, fraud could never be eliminated entirely. But over the years, the company developed a feedback system in which buyers and sellers rated one another, and this proved to be a major check on deceptive practices. Sellers received grades ranging from one to five, and eBay averaged and posted these grades as part of every listing of an item for sale. This system was itself vulnerable to abuse, since grades were aggregated irrespective of the value of items sold. A seller could get high grades for 50 cheap sales and a low grade for one very expensive sale, and thereby receive a high overall grade. eBay adjusted its system accordingly. It also offered a section for comments, allowing buyers and sellers to post remarks of up to 80 characters—the equivalent of about three lines in a newspaper column. Overall, the system has worked reasonably well.

To combat the danger of fraud in payment (false credit card numbers, claims of non-delivery, bouncing checks, and so on), the company began to use PayPal, an online clearing house founded in 1998 for electronic commerce. By February of 2000, PayPal was handling 200,000 eBay auctions daily, and by April of the same year one million. In 2002, Meg Whitman decided to buy PayPal, for which eBay paid $1.5 billion. By 2008 PayPal was managing about 165 million individual accounts throughout the world, for eBay and outside clients as well. It had defeated several major competitors such as Citicorp's c2it, which ceased operations in 2003, and Yahoo!'s PayDirect, which closed in 2004.

In much the same pattern as Amazon.com, eBay's rapid growth occurred primarily through acquisitions—dozens of them. eBay purchased online auction companies in many countries, starting with Germany's Alando in 1999. It bought PayPal in 2002. In 2004 it acquired a 25 percent interest in *craigslist,* the online classified advertiser. In 2005, it spent $2.6 billion to acquire Skype, a European firm whose software enables subscribers to make long-distance phone calls over the Internet. Also in 2005, eBay acquired Shopping.com, a comparison shopping firm serving customers in the U.K. and France as well as the United States: the price was $635 million. In 2005 and 2006, eBay bought several European classified ad companies similar to *craigslist.* In 2007 it paid $307 million for StubHub, a rapidly growing online seller of tickets for plays, concerts, and professional sporting events. StubHub charges 25 percent of the selling price on every ticket sold. Its main competitor is the much older Ticketmaster.

In 2006, eBay launched eBay Express, a site devoted to selling new merchandise—not at auction but for fixed prices. This step put it into direct competition with other online retailers with more experience in this kind of commerce, including Amazon. Still, the compelling impulse for eBay, Amazon, and most other companies in any industry is growth, and eBay's total sales from all its businesses had been growing by about 30 percent per year. At that figure, compounded, revenues doubled every 2.4 years. Such a rate would be very difficult to sustain over eBay's (or any other company's) second and third decades.

Pierre Omidyar, eBay's founder, established in the twenty-first century a part-philanthropic, part for-profit "Network" devoted to microlending and other locally based initiatives. His aim was to "enable individual self-empowerment on a global scale." This is the same principle that underlies eBay. The distinctive glory of the company has been its proficiency in affording *anyone* the chance to become an entrepreneur. For the first time in history, very large numbers of people, even those with severe disabilities, can go online and market their goods. Apart from earning money, the psychological benefits of this kind of empowerment are beyond calculation, and they apply to many more people than one might at first think.

3. *Google*. Google had its origins at Stanford University in 1995, with the meeting of two graduate students in computer science. One, a math prodigy named Sergey Brin, was showing some new students around the campus, and among the group was Larry Page. When Larry met Sergey, he thought him an arrogant snob. Sergey found Larry irritating as well, but their mutual dislike didn't last very long.

The two had a great deal in common. Both were 22 years old and sons of academic parents. Sergey Brin had emigrated from Russia at the age of six. His parents, mathematicians who had graduated from Moscow State University, were Jews seeking a better life in the West. Sergey's father had become a professor of math at the University of Maryland, where Sergey himself received his B.S. degree in 1993, just before his 20th birthday. He then won a graduate fellowship from the National Science Foundation to study computer science at Stanford. Although he was five months younger than Larry Page, he had come to Stanford a year earlier because he had skipped a grade in high school.

Page's father was a professor of computer science at Michigan State, and his mother taught computer programming at the same university. Page attended the University of Michigan in Ann Arbor, where he received his degree in computer science in 1995. Both he and Sergey Brin quickly became fascinated with the limitless possibilities of the World Wide Web, and they began to think about how it could be made easier for people to use. Page planned to write a dissertation in which he would develop tools for analyzing the linking of websites. The number of sites was already growing so fast that they were becoming hard even to count, let alone to link systematically with one another. Page and Brin sensed that the linking of related sites would become a key to many uses for the web, such as citations to academic papers, articles, and books. At first neither of the two students thought much about how they might commercialize their work.

Page named his research project "BackRub"—wordplay for the manipulation of website backlinks. Before long his friend Sergey Brin, seeing the unique possibilities in the project, joined Page, bringing his singular mathematical skills to bear on a very complex problem. The crux of the problem lay in how to differentiate the importance of one link as compared with another—or, more precisely, of several thousand sites as compared to several thousand others, and eventually several million. It might be compared to looking at 100 acres of mixed fragments of glass, rhinestones, zircons, and diamonds, and trying to figure out how to pick out the diamonds. And once that tedious job was done, how to rank each according to size, color, and other traits that make one diamond worth a thousand dollars whereas another might be so flawed as to be worth only a few cents. And, finally, how to link only the valuable diamonds with one another so as to produce a necklace worth a million dollars.

The making of jewelry, of course, is a physical process that cannot be done mathematically. But the counting, sorting, and ranking of websites *can,* though only with great difficulty. The essential problem is to develop a series of algorithms that will accomplish several steps sequentially: first, "webcrawling" (the gathering of sites through automated browsing); then, indexing (putting each site into one or more categories); and finally, ranking (finding which sites are more important than others). This last step is by far the most difficult, and it was here that Page and Brin made their breakthrough. They developed the PageRank algorithm, so named for both Larry Page and the function that the new algorithm performed.

Their system proved far superior to any other "search engine" then in existence—that is, any other combination of webcrawler, indexer, and ranking tool. In August of 1996 Page and Brin made their discovery available on the Stanford website. They were urged to publish a scientific paper, but they delayed because they had begun to see that their method had real commercial potential. (Eventually, they did publish the paper, titled "The Anatomy of a Large-Scale Hypertextual Web Search Engine," which became one of the most widely cited articles in the field.) Other search engines were going on the market, and were fast becoming one of the hottest products of the 1990s Internet craze. The situation was much like that Henry Ford faced when he went into the automobile business and competed with hundreds of other young companies. The result for Page and Brin resembled the spectacular early success of the Ford Motor Company.

The scientific key to their triumph was the "scalability" of their system—again analogous to Ford's matching of his assembly line to his millions of potential customers, and also to Ray Kroc's standardized system for organizing thousands of McDonald's restaurants. The bigger the World Wide Web grew, the more valuable Page and Brin's system would become to those who used it, both for business and personal items. If their search engine could rank millions of websites as effectively as it could hundreds or thousands—and, given enough computer resources, it could do just that—then there seemed no limit to what they could accomplish. In 1997, the immense numbers involved in their work inspired Page and Brin to name their system Google—a play on the mathematical term *googol*, which means ten to the hundredth power, or the number one followed by a hundred zeroes.

Because of the growing number of websites that had to be searched, Page and Brin's experiments required enormous amounts of computing power. Both students gradually filled up their dorm rooms with equipment. Then they managed to persuade Stanford officials to let them use what ultimately became about half of the university's huge bandwidth to continue their operations. As Page later put it in a considerable understatement, "We're lucky there were a lot of forward-looking people at Stanford. They didn't hassle us too much about the resources we were using." During the Fall of 1996, Stanford's entire Internet connection frequently crashed because of the overload from Page and Brin's webcrawler.

Although commercial possibilities beckoned, neither student wanted to disappoint his parents by dropping out of school, as Bill

Gates had done at Harvard and Michael Dell at the University of Texas. Brin recalled that when he asked his adviser what he should do, the professor replied, "Look, if this Google thing pans out, then great. If not, you can return to graduate school and finish your thesis. I said Yeah, OK, why not? I'll just give it a try." The try, of course, turned into one of the greatest successes in the history of business. Meanwhile, both Brin and Page were listed as "on leave" from their Ph.D. programs, as they remain to this day.

At the World Wide Web Conference of 1998, Brin and Page presented their new method to an expert audience. Andy Bechtolsheim, the cofounder of Sun Microsystems, contributed $100,000 to their enterprise (which was not yet incorporated), and Stanford University made a larger contribution. In 1999 Brin and Page founded Google as a private company. The important money—investments totalling $40.2 million—came during 1999 and 2000, from the venture capital firms Kleiner Perkins and Sequoia Capital.

These financial backers well knew that the youthful Brin and Page, despite their intellectual gifts, lacked the knowledge and experience to develop a business model commensurate with the potential of their discoveries. The well-known venture capitalist John Doerr, a partner at Kleiner Perkins, strongly advised them to find a seasoned manager to run their company. The executive search firm Heidrick & Struggles turned up Eric E. Schmidt.

Schmidt, 46 years old in 2001, understood both the technical and the business sides of the IT industry. He had a B.S. in electrical engineering from Princeton, and an M.S. and Ph.D. in Electrical Engineering and Computer Science from Berkeley. He had worked at Bell Labs and other research centers, then at Sun Microsystems, and finally as CEO of Novell before it was acquired by Cambridge Technology Partners. Brin and Page interviewed Schmidt, liked him, and hired him to run Google as CEO. Page, who had held that title, became president in charge of products, and Brin president in charge of technology. In the final workout after the IPO of stock in 2004, the two founders each owned about 30 percent of the company, and Eric Schmidt 5 percent. On the occasion of the IPO, all three men became instant billionaires.

Under the leadership of Schmidt, Page, and Brin, Google developed many products. But from the beginning, its principal business has been advertising, which has generated practically all of its revenues. The Google search engine guides advertisers to the sites and web pages where they are likely to get the best returns for their money. It does this with remarkable precision because of the sophistication of its ranking system: site A is more lucrative than site B, and so on down the line—not only because of more visits to a particular site but also because of the links of that site to others, each of which has its own rank; and then to still other sites, in an almost infinite progression that grows exactly as fast as does the World Wide Web. Most of the millions of ads posted by Google not only tout a customer's product but also provide a link back to the customer's own website. Typical postings under Google's system are brief text ads, as opposed to the pictures and graphics employed by Yahoo!, Google's main search-engine competitor. Google has refused to do pop-up ads of any kind.

The company charges its customers either on a cost-per-view or cost-per-click basis, each view or click being inexpensive, but their aggregate numbers adding up to very large sums. The possibility exists of "click fraud," done by either renegades trying to help Google or to hurt the companies being advertised. In 2006 one analyst estimated that 14–20 percent of all clicks were fraudulent—a figure impossible either to substantiate or disprove.

From the beginning, Google cultivated an image of social responsibility. Its motto, "Don't be evil," pervades its corporate culture to this day. The journalist John Battelle interviewed Eric Schmidt at length for an article that later became part of Battelle's excellent book, *The Search: How Google and Its Rivals Rewrote the Rules of Business and Transformed Our Culture* (2005). When Schmidt was hired as CEO in 2001 to provide what Battelle calls "adult supervision" of the youthful Brin and Page, they told him "Don't be evil." He replied, "'You've got to be kidding.' Then one day, very early on, I was in a meeting where an engineer said, 'That would be evil.' It was as if he'd said there was a murderer in the room." But within the company, Schmidt went on to say, "That kind of story is repeated every hour now with thousands of people. Think of 'Don't be evil' as an organizing principle about values. You and I may disagree on the definition of what is evil, but at least it gives us a way to have a very healthy debate." Schmidt compared the slogan with the famous practice in Japanese factories of empowering every person working on an assembly line to stop the line if he or she sees something amiss.

Of course, the slogan can backfire, and sometimes it has. The immense amount of personal information stored in Google's data banks and those of other Internet companies raises serious questions about privacy—questions that are unlikely ever to disappear. Then, too, Google Maps—one of its many products, in this case partly satellite-based—are so detailed that they can "see" almost anything in the world, from pedestrians to weapons stockpiles. Google's proposal to digitize all books ever published caused an uproar among authors, publishers, and defenders of intellectual property. The company's vast networks of computers and servers—some estimates run as high as half a million machines— consume tremendous quantities of electricity, and contribute to global warming. Google has also consented to Internet censorship in China. Some critics have wondered how these issues should be gauged on the "Don't be evil" scale.

Despite such controversies, Google's good-guy image has remained mostly intact. The company has consistently ranked number one in *Fortune*'s annual list of best places to work. The amenities it offers employees at Googleplex, its headquarters in Mountain View, California (a small city in Silicon Valley) are extraordinarily generous by any measure. Then, too, there is the 70-20-10 rule, closely identified with Eric Schmidt. Everyone at Google should spend 70 percent of his or her working time on the firm's core business, 20 percent on related projects, and 10 percent on unrelated new initiatives—the latter including staring out the window, building castles in the air, or not even showing up for work. And, like those of many other Silicon Valley firms, most of Google's offices are unpretentious cubicles that tell the observer almost nothing about the occupant's rank.

Schmidt has said that "Virtually everything new seems to come from the 20 percent of their time engineers here are expected to spend on side projects." The new ideas "certainly don't come out of the management team." In management, "We spend 70 percent of our time on core search and ads [and] 20 percent on adjacent businesses, ones related to the core business in some interesting way. Examples of that would be Google News, Google Earth, and Google Local. And then 10 percent of our time should be on things that are truly new," such as Google Print, "the world's largest card catalog." Schmidt emphasizes that "We're not in the portal business, we're in the business of making all the world's information accessible and useful."

In 2003, for example, Google purchased Pyra Labs, the originator of Blogger (Web logging tools — that is, how to set up a blog). Over the next few years, Google improved the technology and offered the service for free, thereby helping millions of people start their own blogs. In 2006, Google bought YouTube to complement its own Google Video. Soon YouTube was uploading thousands of items every day. How it would eventually relate to Google Video, whose offerings were typically longer and of higher resolution, remained uncertain. In the meantime, however, YouTube became one of the Web's most popular sites.

The company's overall growth was phenomenal. In 2007, its sales were $16.6 billion, a 57 percent increase from 2006. Its net income was $4.2 billion, a 37 percent one-year growth. It employed 17,000 people, an increase of 57 percent from 2006; and the number had grown to more than 19,000 employees by March 2008. These are startlingly high growth figures, and they make any portrait of Google a snapshot in time that is almost certain to change quickly. Even in national recessions Google continues to grow, partly because of its international sales. In 2008, for the first time in the company's brief history, it received more of its revenues from abroad than from the United States. Worldwide, Google came to dominate web searching. The market shares of search-engine firms in 2007 were:

Google: 46.5 percent
Yahoo!: 17.2 percent
Baidu (China): 13.8 percent
Microsoft: 12.9 percent
Others: 9.6 percent

Not many companies see their names become verbs put into dictionaries, but Google is one of them. Just as "to xerox" used to mean to photocopy a document, "to google" means to search for information about a topic or an individual on the World Wide Web. In 2007, the magazine *PC World* ranked Schmidt, Brin, and Page jointly as number one on its list of the most important people on the Web. In the same year, Brin and Page, each with a net worth of about $17 billion, were ranked by *Forbes* as the fifth richest individuals in the United States. Eric Schmidt, with $6.8 billion, ranked number 129. The fortunes of all three men were based on their holdings of shares in Google, Inc.

From the beginning of the company in 1998 through its first decade, Google tried to maintain a fun-loving culture. The very name Google was the start of its playful public face. When Google made its IPO in 2004 (one of the most lucrative in the history of business), it floated 19.6 million shares at a price of $85 each. Of these, about 5.5 million were offered by existing shareholders. The number of other shares, 14,142,135 was chosen by Brin and Page because the square root of the number 2 is 1.4142135. Follow-on equity offerings yielded $4.4 billion in 2005 and $2.1 billion in 2006. After the IPO, Brin, Page, and Schmidt paid themselves annual salaries of $1.

Meanwhile, the company's tradition of sophomoric pranks continued. In 2004, "Google Lunar" was ostensibly launched, offering jobs on the moon. In 2005 came Google Gulp, a soft drink to augment brainpower. In 2007, TiSP (Toilet Internet Service Provider), to be installed by flushing a fiber optic cable and waiting an hour for it to be connected to the Internet by a PHD (Plumbing Hardware Dispatcher). As Larry Page said, "We think a lot about how to maintain our culture and the fun elements."

It would be a mistake, however, to regard Google as a collection of lucky Peter Pans with a magic machine. No company is more serious or more fixated on its purpose. In 2004 it announced "Ten things Google has found to be true." The first four were: "Focus on the user and all else will follow," "It's best to do one thing really, really well," "Fast is better than slow," and "Democracy on the web works."

Corporate credos and mission statements of this sort are a dime a dozen, but Google seems to have understood its goals and followed its principles better than have most other companies. For example, its discussion of the fourth principle, "Democracy on the web works," goes on to say that the company has succeeded "because it relies on the millions of individuals posting websites"; and that "by analyzing the full structure of the web, Google is able to determine which sites have been 'voted' the best sources of information by those most interested in the information they offer." Much of this success was made possible by the simple revolution through which any company, person, or group could design a website with links to other sites.

In the broadest sense, as we have seen throughout this chapter, never before in history have so many people been so enabled to do so many different things. Everyone in the world with access to the Internet can now gather reams of information, find markets and customers, communicate with one another, and proclaim their opinions—all with an ease that would have been inconceivable before the revolution in information technology—before IT became "It."

*Left: John Johnson, the Chicago businessman whose company published Ebony and Jet and later branched into real estate, beauty products, and other fields. This picture appeared in Black Enterprise in 1987, announcing Johnson's selection as Entrepreneur of the Decade.* Courtesy of Johnson Publishing Company, Inc.

*Right: Mary Kay Ash in 1978. Ash founded Mary Kay Cosmetics in 1963 and quickly built it into a thriving business based on energetic marketing by thousands of part-time sales agents working on commission.* Corbis/Bettmann-UPI.

*Left: Oprah Winfrey—TV talk-show host, actor, entertainment entrepreneur, and one of the most famous Americans at the start of the twenty-first century.* Mitchell Gerber/Corbis.

*Right: Roberto Goizueta, chairman of the Coca-Cola Company and the most prominent Hispanic businessperson in the U.S. of his time. Here, in 1985, he announces the introduction of "Classic Coke" and takes a sip.* AP/WIDE WORLD PHOTOS.

Right: Michael Milken (center, with curly toupee), financial genius and convicted felon, leaving the U.S. District Court in Manhattan in 1990 after a pre-sentencing hearing. Indicted on 98 counts of racketeering, securities fraud, and other crimes, he avoided trial by pleading guilty to six of the charges. He was sentenced to ten years in prison but paroled after serving less than two. He was fined $200 million and ordered to pay $400 million in restitution to shareholders whom his actions had damaged. AP/WIDE WORLD PHOTOS.

Above: Jeffrey Skilling, former CEO of the mammoth energy trading company Enron, testifying before Congress in 2002, denying the numerous charges against him. At his subsequent trial in federal court, he was indicted on a total of 35 counts of securities fraud, making false statements to auditors, insider trading, and conspiracy, and found guilty of 19. In 2006 he was sentenced to 24 years in prison and fined $45 million. AP/WIDE WORLD PHOTOS.

*Left: Dennis Kozlowski (second from right), former CEO of the conglomerate Tyco Internatioal, leaving New York criminal court in 2002. Known for his extremely lavish lifestyle, Kozlowski was convicted in 2005 for a series of crimes—principally 22 counts of grand larceny in the misappropriation of his company's funds. He received a prison sentence of 8 to 25 years.* AP/WIDE WORLD PHOTOS.

*Below: Bernie Ebbers (center), former CEO of the telecom giant WorldCom, leaving New York's Javitz Federal Building in 2004 after turning himself in for making false statements to the Securities and Exchange Commission and conspiring to commit securities fraud. WorldCom admitted to $11 billion in accounting misstatements--the largest among hundreds of such cases involving large corporations at that time. Ebbers was found guilty on all charges and sentenced to 25 years in prison.* AP/WIDE WORLD PHOTOS.

*Above: The IBM System/360 mainframe computer, brought out in 1964 and one of the most important industrial products of the twentieth century.* Courtesy of IBM Archives.

*Below: Left to right: Steve Jobs, John Sculley, and Steve Wozniak, unveiling the Apple IIc "briefcase-sized" personal computer in 1984. Jobs and Wozniak founded the company in the 1970s and later brought in the professional manager Sculley from PepsiCo to help run it.* Corbis/Bettmann-UPI.

*Left: Bill Gates of Microsoft in 1992, on the eve of the Internet revolution.* Corbis/Reuters.

*Below: Jeff Bezos, founder and CEO of amazon.com. Here, in 2007, he is introducing the Kindle, the company's device for reading books and magazines electronically.* AP/WIDE WORLD PHOTOS.

*Above: Meg Whitman, CEO of eBay from 1998 to 2008. Much like John Sculley of Apple, Whitman was a management professional brought in to run the company as it grew from an entrepreneurial startup to a large firm. She had much more success than Sculley. This picture was taken in 2005.* AP/WIDE WORLD PHOTOS.

*Below: Larry Page (left) and Sergey Brin, the Stanford graduate students who co-founded Google. The company's IPO of 2004 made each of them an immediate multi-billionaire. At that time, when they posed for this photo, they were 31 years old.* © Google Inc. Used with permission.

*Above: CEO Steve Jobs introducing Apple's iPhone at the MacWorld Conference in 2007, 23 years after he and Steve Wozniak had launched the Apple II personal computer. Jobs is one of very few top entrepreneurs in American business history to make a powerful comeback at the same company after being ousted from his post.* AP/WIDE WORLD PHOTOS.

# EPILOGUE

The outburst of information technology capped a century-long trend in which decision making moved downward within business hierarchies. At many companies, the availability of computers and electronic databases gave employees ready access to oceans of information. The advent of e-mail made communication instantaneous, interactive, and inexpensive, even over long distances. With a few strokes of the keyboard, supervisors could deliver fresh news to particular individuals, to selected subgroups, to large divisions, or to everyone in the company.

Enhanced communication through IT could, of course, facilitate either centralized management from above or decentralized decision making from below. Adjustments varied according to the needs of the company and the philosophies of its top executives. On balance, however, the clear trend was toward decentralization. With e-mail and corporate-sponsored blogs, even employees at low levels became more likely to express themselves within the firm. They sent more messages laterally and upward than they had even a short time before using telephones, voice-mail, printers, and fax and copy machines. Something about e-mail and blogs seemed to affect the psychology of hierarchies—to instill an egalitarian spirit that encouraged frequent (and, in the view of critics, excessive) communication.

With so much communication going on, it often became possible to eliminate layers of management within hierarchies themselves. Although an irreducible minimum of bureaucratic procedures remained essential for the orderly conduct of business in any company, layers of authority began to diminish in number. Rather than eight or nine levels, many firms ratcheted down to three or four. At the same time, each manager's supervisory reach ("span of control") began to broaden. With a far greater amount of data at a manager's fingertips, he or she could keep track of what was happening in more and more departments. This, too, could result in either more centralization or less, depending on the circumstances and the aims of top management.

As a second-order effect, the gains in IT began to whittle down the number of essential middle managers—the first time since the rise of modern business that this had occurred on a broad scale. The extension of spans of control and the flattening of hierarchies made it possible to "re-engineer" or "downsize" the staffs of numerous companies. At the executive level, these words meant the reassignment or dismissal of middle managers whose roles were no longer necessary.

Decision making, which had been moving downward for several decades, by the twenty-first century had become more localized than ever. "Employee empowerment," a phrase that became clichéd during the 1990s, expressed this phenomenon. However trite the phrase, the new situation was no illusion.

## Centralization and Decentralization

The relentless gains in IT enabled many firms to aspire to something like what Ray Kroc had accomplished at McDonald's. Kroc had deliberately divided authority and pushed certain kinds of decision making downward. Even at corporate headquarters, where a great deal of centralized control over the far-flung McDonald's system remained, Kroc had recognized that for the good of the company he should share control with June Martino, Harry Sonneborn, and Fred Turner. In the field, Kroc deliberately placed power in the hands of suppliers, master franchisees, regional managers, and individual franchisees. Each McDonald's outlet benefited from the reputational forces of Quality, Service, and Cleanliness built up at every other outlet, and from the constant flow of information up and down the system.

The stories of Alfred Sloan, Neil McElroy, Ferdinand Eberstadt, Ray Kroc, Jeff Bezos, Meg Whitman, Larry Page, Sergey Brin, and Eric Schmidt provide examples of innovative responses by high-ranking executives who faced continual tradeoffs between centralized and decentralized decision making. These entrepreneurs constantly had to adjust the ways in which people at different levels of their organizations related to one another.

Without continual adjustments, disaster could come at any time, as in the case of Henry Ford. During the 1920s and 1930s, Ford's solo rule made it much easier for General Motors to defeat the Ford Motor Company in the epic contest for market share. While Henry Ford was gathering complete control over his company into his own hands, Alfred Sloan was systematically delegating authority at GM. Sloan created a new corporate structure in which dozens of product-division heads wielded great power within their own bailiwicks. In formulating the multi-divisional structure, Sloan worked out a way in which General Motors could benefit from the best of both worlds—"coordinated decentralization," as he liked to call it.

At Procter & Gamble during the 1930s, Neil McElroy's system of brand management accomplished a similar decentralization of authority. Brand managers were responsible to P&G's top executives, but they themselves now had new power over those working under their direction. Others in the Procter & Gamble organization, such as Doc Smelser and his market researchers, performed vital staff functions; but they stood outside the hierarchy of people with profit-and-loss responsibility for particular brands, divisions, or the company as a whole.

During World War II, Ferdinand Eberstadt created yet another system of decentralized decision making, on the largest industrial scale we have seen in this book. The Controlled Materials Plan allocated steel, copper, and aluminum to the Army, Navy, and other claimant agencies on the basis of their own estimates of what they and their primary contractors needed. Where necessary, the claimants could then divert materials from one use to another. They had the authority to do this because Eberstadt, through his "vertical" design of the Plan, had pushed downward the power to make these transfers. The Plan constituted an almost flawless example of placing decisions in the hands of the people with the best information.

It was hardly coincidental that Eberstadt devised this system during a full-fledged national emergency. The unprecedented scale of World War II–related activities made it more important than ever that decision making be thrust downward along numerous fronts at once: the Controlled Materials Plan, the localized conscription system for drafting people into the armed forces, and the community-level rationing boards overseeing the distribution of scarce consumer goods. In all three cases, urgent necessity gave birth to organizational invention—affecting tens of millions of people.

The story of David Sarnoff and RCA illustrates both the good and bad results that can come from a deliberately *centralized* organization. In the early years of radio it made sense for one executive to supervise the development of broadcasting, research, and the manufacture and marketing of equipment. Radio was a systems innovation, and having a person of Sarnoff's great abilities in charge helped to move these many elements forward simultaneously.

When RCA grew larger, however, and powerful competitors entered the game, it was no longer appropriate to have so much power concentrated in the hands of one person, no matter how talented. But Sarnoff, like Henry Ford before him, refused to change the structure of his company. He would not delegate decision making, and he neglected the issue of management succession. Sarnoff assumed much too heavy a burden, and the quality of his decisions began to deteriorate. Even before he passed the CEO's job to his son, RCA had entered a downward spiral.

## Other Themes since 1920

In addition to the growing need to decentralize management decisions, other big changes stand out. So do some continuities.

First, consumers gained power—relentlessly—often at the expense of producers and retailers. They enjoyed far more discretionary income in the twenty-first century than they had in 1920, and they came to demand a much broader choice of goods and services. Consumers acquired this new strength despite ceaseless attempts to manipulate them through advertising; indeed the rapid progress of information technology itself—including advertising—helped to empower them. More than ever before, consumers knew much more about the relative merits of particular products—from laundry detergent to computers to prescription drugs. By the 1990s many Americans were buying online, at whatever times of day were most convenient for them. Their power also grew because of rising competitive pressures on producers. If a certain producer did not cater to consumers' preferences, then other companies would drive the holdout from the market, as happened with RCA.

Second, intensified competition made the task of management more difficult. Between 1920 and the early twenty-first century, the number of American companies grew at a much faster rate than the population as a whole. In 1920 about 346,000 U.S. corporations were doing business; 90 years later this number had reached 4.5 million, some 13 times the 1920 total. Meanwhile, the population had increased by a factor of 2.9, from 105 million to 305 million.

Not only were far more competitors in the game, but in the case of publicly traded companies an additional force had emerged in the form of mutual funds and pension funds. These institutional investors now exerted constant pressure on managers to increase profits and thereby raise the share prices of their companies' stock. And even newer institutions (hedge funds and other kinds of private equity funds) turned up the pressure for even higher profits. This trend represents an exception to the general theme of decentralization in decision making set forth in this book—an exception mentioned earlier in connection with the crisis in home mortgages that began in 2007, but broader than in that sector alone. In business generally, the incessant drive for higher profits could encourage either decentralization or centralization. In finance it caused greater centralization, and the consequences, as in the cases of Henry Ford and David Sarnoff, were mostly negative.

Still another force for intensified competition was the globalization of business. Beginning in the 1970s, this phenomenon brought acute new competition to several industries in which

American managers had assumed that U.S. firms would permanently reign as world champions. In machine tools, rubber tires, consumer electronics, and automobiles, leadership passed to companies headquartered in Europe or Japan. In other areas—including franchised systems, computer hardware and software, aircraft, and many branded and packaged consumer products—American-based companies were still on top in 2009.

Third, many U.S. firms were able to stay ahead in part because of their good fortune in having the world's best support system. This multilayered infrastructure encompassed physical facilities such as highways, railroads, airports, electric utilities, and telecommunications. It also included an advanced legal system with sophisticated laws pertaining to contracts, corporations, torts, and intellectual property. In several categories, however, the nation's politicians—local, state, and federal—had allowed the infrastructure to deteriorate. By the end of the first decade of the twenty-first century, airports, highways, bridges, and railroads were in worse shape than they had been in many years. And the skyrocketing price of oil made it more difficult than ever to impose higher taxes on gasoline and diesel fuel. These taxes had long comprised the chief source of funds for highway maintenance.

Broadly conceived, the business infrastructure also embraced a complex network of companies and other institutions providing financial and informational services to the core systems of production and distribution. On the financial side, these supporting institutions included securities exchanges, commercial banks, insurance companies, investment banks, venture-capital firms, and mutual funds. On the information side, they included law firms, consulting companies, accounting firms, and a broad array of enterprises engaged in the processing and storage of data. But here again, the government had abrogated its proper role, and the regulatory system had decayed—in some cases dangerously so, most conspicuously in finance. As the financial condition of the country continued on a downward path, a daunting job of catch-up confronted public officials.

Fourth, infrastructural enterprises were themselves operating under far greater competitive pressures than those faced by their counterparts in 1920. Here, one of the strongest forces was not globalization but deregulation. Companies in domestic airlines, railroads, trucking, electric utilities, and some types of tele-communications were largely immune to threats from overseas competitors. So too, though to a lesser degree, were most accounting, engineering, and consulting firms, both big and small. In these latter professions, however, the outsourcing of functions to overseas offices ("offshoring") had become possible through spectacular advances in information technology. These functions included bookkeeping, technical support, and customer services, among others.

Nearly all kinds of firms in this broad variety of infrastructural industries felt the hot breath of new competition. One by one, industries were deregulated and exposed to the discipline of the marketplace. Air carriers became much more competitive with one another after passage of the Airline Deregulation Act of 1978. The same thing happened to railroads starting in the 1970s, and to firms in trucking, telecommunications, and financial services beginning in the 1980s. The tremendous growth of IT during the 1980s and 1990s would not have been nearly so strong without the concurrent deregulation of telecommunications. Milestones in this process included the breakup of AT&T's monopolistic Bell System in 1984, the proliferation of new telephone and cable TV companies during the 1980s and 1990s, and the privatization of the Internet in 1995.

Even the "self-regulating" professions of law and medicine grew more competitive. Law firms, medical clinics, and hospitals mostly abandoned their traditional forbearance toward unproductive colleagues and slow-moving procedures. Instead these enterprises became more like conventional businesses: profit-oriented, hard-driving, and alert for any edge that would take market share from rivals. Again, each business entity was tempted by market competition to move offshore certain functions such as reading x-rays, CT scans, and MRIs; and transcribing legal depositions and judicial opinions.

Fifth, the new competitive pressures, while reinvigorating American business, often took a heavy human toll. Starting in the 1980s and accelerating over the next three decades, intensified competition led many companies to "cut the fat" from their employment rolls, in wave after wave of "re-engineering" and "downsizing." All of these words were euphemisms not only for the elimination of middle-management positions but also for mass layoffs of lower-level workers. A few firms went too far, cutting not only fat but corporate muscle. The middle class, so critical to the nation's economic and political identity, was itself downsized.

Inevitably, institutional loyalty began to decline. From top to bottom within company hierarchies, employees began to recognize that a different working environment had now evolved. Even the most efficient firms, though taking steps to empower employees in day-to-day operations, could not assure that these same people would have long-term employment at the firm—let alone steady increases in pay and fringe benefits. In earlier years, it had been easy for everyone to forget that in the actual experience of Schumpeterian "creative destruction," the destruction is just as real as the creation. In the 1980s and afterward, that lesson became palpable.

Sixth, despite its painful side, creative destruction did make the American business system more efficient. In so doing, it improved material standards of living. From 1920 to the early twenty-first century, the amount of time most people were compelled to spend working for pay shrank drastically. Many still put in long hours and worked hard, of course, and at the very end of the twentieth century the American workweek again began to lengthen. But large numbers of people could now afford to spend as much time in leisure activities as in the combined tasks of running a household and working outside the home. In the United States, one hour's work at the end of the century would buy, on average, four or five times the goods and services it bought in 1920. In this situation some people even had trouble finding meaningful activity to fill their free hours.

Seventh, in part because so much leisure time was devoted to watching television and surfing the net—particularly by young people—Americans were exposed to an astronomical number of commercial advertisements. By 2001, nearly all households had at least one TV set, and three-fourths had two or more. In the average home a set was on for 7 hours each day, delivering endless commercials designed to increase viewers' feelings of need for "new and improved" products.

This situation in itself carried a profound message about capitalism. As the sociologist Emile Durkheim had written early in the twentieth century, "Our needs are unlimited. The more one has the more one wants." He was right. The ultimate basis of capitalism has been, and still is, the insatiability of human wants.

Eighth, between the years 1920 and 2010, Americans in general embraced the capitalist system more wholeheartedly than did people in most other countries. They were decidedly more entrepreneurial, as reflected both in their business behavior and in the enabling laws enacted by their national and state legislatures. They took collective action against the capitalist system less often than was the norm elsewhere, either through their votes or through radical political movements. They had a smaller rate of worker unionization. They showed little tendency to become socialists. They were openly competitive with each other and far more willing to run their rivals out of business.

But Americans were also more forgiving of failure. They had little fear of going into debt (ultimately far too little), and they were remarkably tolerant of bankruptcy, by both businesses and individuals. In much of the world bankruptcy represented a permanent stigma, but in America it was often regarded as a phase through which entrepreneurs routinely passed on their way to eventual riches. Over most of the nation's history, and again in comparison to other countries, the dominant assumption seemed to be that prosperity at one extreme and destitution at the other were matters of individual responsibility, even personal choice. They were not determined chiefly by luck or social context—or so most citizens apparently believed.

Americans endured economic turmoil more readily than did other people, again speaking generally. Over a national history of more than 230 years, as the business cycle moved up and down, the U.S. economy, like capitalist economies everywhere, went through frequent recessions. The country also suffered a few deep depressions—during the 1780s, early 1800s, 1830s, 1850s, 1870s, 1890s, and early 1920s. The worst downturn of all, the Great

Depression of the 1930s, was a good deal more severe in the United States than it was elsewhere. Yet it provoked less political radicalism in America than it did in France, Germany, Italy, Japan, and many other countries.

By the late twentieth century, the United States, like all leading industrial nations, had a thoroughly "mixed" economy with very substantial government expenditures: about one-third of GNP, up from one-ninth in 1920. These outlays included large transfer payments in the form of Social Security, Medicare, and unemployment benefits. Among their many results, such measures—along with sophisticated monetary and fiscal policies—tended to flatten the business cycle. They made swings of prosperity and recession a lot less violent than had been the case before World War II.

In comparison with Europeans, Americans had been noticeably late to develop most of these systems of social welfare. Nor did they enact unemployment, health, and welfare laws of such extensive reach, or spend such a high proportion of public revenue on them. In the early twenty-first century, the total tax burden in the United States, as a percentage of income, was less than that in almost all other industrialized countries, despite huge military expenditures by the U.S. government. The individualistic, tax-averse, "free-market" ideology of the United States had proved to be invaluable for promoting entrepreneurship and unleashing economic energy.

But there was a downside. As viewed by numerous analysts abroad, and also by many critics at home, American-style capitalism carried unacceptably high social costs. In many sectors, most notably the financial services and electric power industries, deregulation had gone much too far, beginning in the 1980s. The U.S. business system in general tolerated wholesale layoffs of employees by large companies and frequent failures by small ones. It offered little succor to those who found it hard to compete. By most accounts, the nation's health-care system was a mess, leaving tens of millions of citizens without insurance or hope of timely medical treatment. This situation derived in part from the American custom of splitting welfare functions between the public and private sectors. In most industrialized countries, health care and pensions were managed by the central government and paid for by tax revenues. In the United States, these benefits were partly public (Medicare, Social Security) and partly private (health insurance paid through private employers, and pensions and 401(k) programs offered by some companies to their employees). The result was an additional financial burden on businesses subject to international competition—sometimes a heavy burden, as in the auto industry; and a very uneven array of benefits for different categories of citizens. Then, too, the gap between rich and poor stretched wider than in comparable countries—and it was continuing to grow, reversing prior trends and calling into question some of the nation's proudest traditions.

In the broadest sense, the question of whether the economic gains from the new style of American capitalism that emerged in the 1980s were worth the social costs does not have a self-evident answer. Nor does the precise mechanism by which the gains and costs are connected. This book has not addressed most of those issues directly, because its central focus has been on something else: the internal workings of the business system. But it does take note that the relative speed at which creative destruction is permitted to go forward within any country is in large part a political choice by those who control national priorities, and that the remarkable economic success of American business was not, by itself, cause for unconditional celebration by everyone involved.

Nor, by any means, could the country's future economic prosperity be taken for granted. In polling data gathered during 2008, an astonishing 82 percent of the American people judged the nation as headed in the wrong direction. As the first decade of the twenty-first century came to an end, issues of re-ordering national priorities and restoring the country's cherished traditions loomed very large.

# BIBLIOGRAPHICAL ESSAY

## Overview of the Field

The information available on twentieth-century American business is almost overwhelming. In addition to the selected sources listed below for the book as a whole and for each chapter, multitudes of primary and secondary materials are available in libraries and online databases, covering both historical and contemporary business affairs in great depth. Researchers can save themselves a lot of time by consulting a capable reference librarian for guidance across a vast sea of data.

One of the best sources on individual companies is *Hoover's* series of business reports, a brief version of which is free online. Much more detailed *Hoover's* analyses, which contain short corporate histories, are available through research libraries. Articles on individual companies in *Wikipedia*, the online encyclopedia, are often useful but are of very uneven quality and accuracy. Most companies maintain websites and corporate archives, the former usually putting companies in the best possible light, the latter often closed to independent researchers. Firms also issue to government authorities "10-K's" and similar reports (which must, by law, be accurate), annual reports to stockholders, and an imposing array of other publications. Almost every industry has trade papers and magazines, which are often very useful sources. (The magazine *Wired,* which covers information technology, is a good example.) General business publications such as *The Economist, Fortune,*

*Business Week, Forbes, The Wall Street Journal, The Conference Board Review,* and *The Harvard Business Review* provide valuable information for historical research as well as on current trends.

For part of the period covered by this book, particularly the 1930s through the 1960s, the most readable single source is the magazine *Fortune.* During most of those four decades, *Fortune* was an elite monthly filled with long, in-depth articles, usually unsigned, by a stable of important writers such as James Agee, Daniel Bell, John Kenneth Galbraith, Alfred Kazin, Archibald MacLeish, and Dwight Macdonald. *Fortune*'s articles for those years represent, in aggregate, perhaps the most distinguished sustained body of business journalism ever produced in any country.

Rigorous scholarly coverage is best represented by the *Business History Review,* published quarterly by the Harvard Business School; *Enterprise and Society,* issued quarterly by the Business History Conference (before the year 2000 this publication was called *Business and Economic History* and appeared annually); and *Essays in Economic and Business History,* published each year by the Economic and Business Historical Society. All three of these periodicals cover other countries in addition to the United States. A fourth journal, the British quarterly *Business History,* often contains articles on American business.

## Statistical References

Again there's an embarrassment of riches. All major industries keep detailed statistical series containing a welter of data on the state of product markets and companies' performance. Most of these reports are published through industry trade associations, of which there are too many to name here but which can be easily traced through libraries.

For more general statistical references, five publications are indispensable for twentieth-century business, economic, and social history: U.S. Bureau of the Census, *Historical Statistics of the United States: Colonial Times to 1970,* 2 vols. (Washington, D.C.: Government Printing Office, 1975); *Statistical Abstract of the United States* (Washington, D.C.: Government Printing Office, annual editions); *Economic Report of the President* (Washington, D.C.: Government Printing Office, annual editions); Angus Maddison, *Phases of Capitalist Development: A Long-Run Comparative View* (Oxford: Oxford University Press, 1991), a vital source for placing the American experience in cross-national perspective, updated by the same author's subsequent publications on the subject; and Stanley Lebergott, *Pursuing Happiness: American Consumers in the Twentieth Century* (Princeton, N.J.: Princeton University Press, 1993), a brief and charming treasury of information, full of good sense as well as reams of useful numbers.

## Syntheses and Bibliographies

Several specialized encyclopedias, textbooks, and other references are helpful not only in their contents but also for the extensive bibliographies they contain. The most important include Geoffrey Jones and Jonathan Zeitlin, eds., *The Oxford Handbook of Business History* (Oxford, U.K.: Oxford University Press, 2008), which covers the entire field, not just the United States; Stanley Engerman and Robert Gallman, eds., *The Cambridge Economic History of the United States* (New York: Cambridge University Press, 1996–2000), a reference book that examines the nation's entire economic history; Stanley I. Kutler, ed., *Encyclopedia of the United States in the Twentieth Century* (New York: Simon & Schuster, 1996). Volume III of this work, which I edited, is devoted to economics and business. It contains 18 long articles on broad topics, written by leading historians. All of those articles were useful to me in the writing of this book, particularly those on Consumption (by Susan Strasser), Marketing (Richard S. Tedlow), Industrial Production (Alfred D. Chandler, Jr.), Economic Performance (Richard H. K. Vietor), Infrastructure (William R. Childs), The Professions (Kenneth Lipartito and Paul Miranti), and Capital Markets (George David Smith and Richard Sylla). In addition to Volume III, portions of Volume II, which includes Science and Technology, have also been useful, particularly the essays on Industrial Research and Manufacturing Technology (David A. Hounshell), Computer and Communications Technology (Steven W. Usselman), and Aerospace Technology (Roger E. Bilstein). Another sweeping and helpful source, which covers not just the twentieth century but the whole of the nation's economic history, is Glenn Porter, ed., *Encyclopedia of American Economic History* (New York: Scribner's, 1980), which is presented in three thick volumes.

Useful textbooks, all of which contain ample bibliographies or source notes, include Mansel G. Blackford and K. Austin Kerr, *Business Enterprise in American History* (Boston: Houghton Mifflin, 3rd ed., 1994); Alfred D. Chandler, Jr., Thomas K. McCraw, and Richard S. Tedlow, *Management Past and Present: A Casebook on the History of American Business* (Cincinnati: South-Western, 1996); and Thomas K. McCraw, ed., *Creating Modern Capitalism: How Entrepreneurs, Companies, and Countries Triumphed in Three Industrial Revolutions* (Cambridge, Mass.: Harvard University Press, 1997), which covers Great Britain, Germany, Japan, and the United States.

Some important reference works are John N. Ingham, *Biographical Dictionary of American Business Leaders*, 4 vols. (Westport, Conn.: Greenwood Press, 1983); Thomas Derdak et al., eds., *International Directory of Company Histories*, 76+ vols. (Chicago: St. James Press, 1988– ); and Susan Boyles Martin, ed., *Notable Corporate Chronologies*, 2 vols. (New York: Gale Research, 1995).

## Standard Works

Because this book is restricted to the period since 1920, only a few standard works on business history can be mentioned here, and even for that period the following list cannot be complete, only representative. These works include three books by Alfred D. Chandler, Jr., a prolific scholar who redefined the field of business history: *Strategy and Structure: Chapters in the History of the American Industrial Enterprise* (Cambridge, Mass.: MIT Press, 1962); *The Visible Hand: The Managerial Revolution in American Business* (Cambridge, Mass.: Harvard University Press, 1977); and *Scale and Scope: The Dynamics of Industrial Capi-*

*talism* (Cambridge, Mass.: Harvard University Press, 1990). The standard book on strategic marketing is Richard S. Tedlow, *New and Improved: The Story of Mass Marketing in America* (Boston, Mass.: Harvard Business School Press, 1996, first published in 1990). Indispensable on the production side is David A. Hounshell, *From the American System to Mass Production, 1800–1932: The Development of Manufacturing Technology in the United States* (Baltimore: Johns Hopkins University Press, 1984). A useful historiographical survey of the entire field of business history, taking as its point of departure the work of Chandler, is Richard R. John, Jr., "Elaborations, Revisions, Dissents: Alfred D. Chandler's *The Visible Hand* after Twenty Years," *Business History Review,* 71 (Summer 1997). A collection that combines social, economic, and political history is Nelson Lichtenstein, ed., *American Capitalism: Social Thought and Political Economy in the Twentieth Century* (Philadelphia: University of Pennsylvania Press, 2006).

On government-business relations, which has received far more coverage in the scholarly literature than it is possible even to summarize here, a short list of standard works would include Ellis W. Hawley, *The New Deal and the Problem of Monopoly: A Study in Economic Ambivalence* (Princeton, N.J.: Princeton University Press, 1966); Thomas K. McCraw, *Prophets of Regulation* (Cambridge, Mass.: Harvard University Press, 1984); Louis Galambos and Joseph Pratt, *The Rise of the Corporate Commonwealth: U.S. Business and Public Policy in the Twentieth Century* (New York: Basic Books, 1988); Morton Keller, *Regulating a New Economy: Public Policy and Economic Change in America, 1900–1933* (Cambridge, Mass.: Harvard University Press, 1990); Richard H. K. Vietor, *Contrived Competition: Regulation and Deregulation in America* (Cambridge, Mass.: Harvard University Press, 1994); and William R. Childs, *The Texas Railroad Commission: Understanding Regulation in America to the Mid-Twentieth Century* (College Station: Texas A&M University Press, 2005). Two books that take opposite positions on the proper role of government are Robert Higgs, *Depression, War, and Cold War: Studies in Political Economy* (New York: Oxford University Press, 2006), which is a view from the Right; and, from the Center-Left, Richard M. Abrams, *America Transformed: Sixty Years of Revolutionary Change, 1941–2001* (New York: Cambridge University Press, 2006), which engages cultural topics as well as business-government relations.

For a counterpoint to the "Chandlerian" emphasis on big business, see Philip Scranton, *Figured Tapestry: Production, Markets, and Power in Philadelphia Textiles, 1885–1941* (New York: Cambridge University Press, 1989) and the same author's *Endless Novelty: Specialty Production and American Industrialization, 1865–1925* (Princeton, N.J.: Princeton University Press, 1997). A thoughtful discussion of small business with a thorough citation of relevant works may be found in Mansel G. Blackford, "Small Business in America: A Historiographic Survey," *Business History Review,* 65 (Spring 1991): pp. 1–26. See also Mansel G. Blackford, *A History of Small Business in America,* 2d ed. (Chapel Hill: University of North Carolina Press, 2003); and Stuart Bruchey, ed., *Small Business and American Life* (New York: Columbia University Press, 1980). On social history, Olivier Zunz's *Making America Corporate, 1870–1920* (Chicago: University of Chicago Press, 1990), like Chandler's *Visible Hand* and Scranton's *Endless Novelty,* almost stops as it reaches the 1920s, where this book begins, but like them is important for its methodological contributions.

Theoretical evaluations of capitalism are explored in many books by economists, of which the following have unusual relevance to American business history: Joseph A. Schumpeter, *Capitalism, Socialism and Democracy* (New York: Harper, 1942, new edition 2008); Oliver E. Williamson, *The Economic Institutions of Capitalism: Firms, Markets, Relational Contracting* (New York: Free Press, 1985); Douglass C. North, *Institutions, Institutional Change, and Economic Performance* (Cambridge, U.K.: Cambridge University Press,1990); and William Lazonick, *Business Organization and the Myth of the Market Economy* (Cambridge, U.K.: Cambridge University Press, 1991). Three influential works by Michael E. Porter provide both theoretical and practical guides to the analysis of business behavior: *Competitive Strategy* (New York: Free Press, 1980); *Competitive Advantage* (New York: Free Press, 1985); and *The Competitive Advantage of Nations* (New York: Free Press, 1990). The morphology of decision making in business is ably analyzed in Michael C. Jensen, *Foundations of Organizational Strategy* (Cambridge, Mass.: Harvard University Press, 1999).

## Selected Sources for Chapter One
## Decentralization in the 1920s: GM Defeats Ford

An invaluable collection of statistics and other primary materials is Alfred D. Chandler, Jr., comp. and ed., *Giant Enterprise: Ford, General Motors, and the Automobile Industry: Sources and Readings* (New York: Harcourt, Brace & World, 1964). See also the relevant chapters in Chandler, *Strategy and Structure: Chapters in the History of the American Industrial Enterprise* (Cambridge, Mass.: MIT Press, 1962); Richard S. Tedlow, *New and Improved: The Story of Mass Marketing in America* (Boston, Mass.: Harvard Business School Press, 1996, first published in 1990); and David A. Hounshell, *From the American System to Mass Production, 1800–1932: The Development of Manufacturing Technology in the United States* (Baltimore: Johns Hopkins University Press, 1984).

On the automobile industry in general, an excellent contemporary study is the Federal Trade Commission's *Report on the Motor Vehicle Industry* (Washington, D.C., U.S. Government Printing Office, 1939). Other standard sources include James J. Flink, "Automobile," in Glenn Porter, ed., *Encyclopedia of American Economic History* (New York: Scribner's, 1980), pp. 1168–93; Flink, *The Car Culture* (Cambridge, Mass.: MIT Press, 1975); John B. Rae, *The American Automobile* (Chicago: University of Chicago Press, 1965); James M. Rubenstein, *Making and Selling Cars: Innovation and Change in the U.S. Automotive Industry* (Baltimore: Johns Hopkins University Press, 2001), a narrative overview; and the very careful analysis by Sally H. Clarke, *Trust* and Power: Consumers, the Modern Corporation, and the Making of the United States Automobile Market (New York: Cambridge University Press, 2007). The best introduction to the reasons behind the successful Japanese challenge later in the twentieth century is Michael A. Cusumano, *The Japanese Automobile Industry: Technology and Management at Nissan and Toyota* (Cambridge, Mass.: Harvard University Press, 1985).

The vast literature on Henry Ford includes several autobiographical statements, the most useful being two books Ford prepared in collaboration with Samuel Crowther, *My Life and Work* (Garden City, N.Y.: Doubleday, 1923), and *Moving Forward* (Garden City, N.Y.: Doubleday, 1931). A key associate of Ford provided an alternative account in his own autobiography: Charles E. Sorensen, with Samuel T. Williamson, *My Forty Years with Ford* (New York: Norton, 1956). A thorough company-sponsored history, with some but not all of the ugliness downplayed, is the three-volume study by Allan Nevins with the collaboration of Frank Ernest Hill: *Ford: The Times, the Man, the Company* (New York: Scribner's, 1954); *Ford: Expansion and Challenge 1915–1933* (New York: Scribner's, 1957); and *Ford: Decline and Rebirth 1933–1962* (New York: Scribner's, 1963).

Other useful studies include Keith Sward, *The Legend of Henry Ford* (New York: Holt, Rinehart and Winston, 1948); John B. Rae, ed., *Henry Ford* (Englewood Cliffs, N.J.: Prentice-Hall, 1960); Reynold M. Wik, *Henry Ford and Grass Roots America* (Ann Arbor: University of Michigan Press, 1972); David L. Lewis, *The Public Image of Henry Ford: An American Folk Hero and His Company* (Detroit: Wayne State University Press, 1976); Stephen Meyer III, *The Five Dollar Day: Labor, Management, and Social Control in the Ford Motor Company, 1908–1921* (Albany: State University of New York Press, 1981); and Douglas Brinkley, *Wheels for the World: Henry Ford, His Company, and a Century of Progress* (New York: Viking, 2003), a company-sponsored history of the firm's first century. A superb brief overview of the literature on Ford and his company is Dmitry Anastakis, "Review Essay," *Business History Review*, 80 (Spring 2008).

The literature on Sloan is much less voluminous, partly because he wanted it that way. But see especially *Fortune*, "Alfred P. Sloan Jr.: Chairman," April 1938; Sloan in collaboration with Boyden Sparkes, *Adventures of a White Collar Man* (New York: Doubleday, 1941); the very important Sloan, *My Years With General Motors* (New York: Doubleday, 1963); Arthur J. Kuhn, *GM Passes Ford, 1918–1938: Designing the General Motors Performance-Control System* (University Park: Pennsylvania State University Press, 1986); Daniel M. G. Raff, "Making Cars and Making Money in the Interwar Automobile Industry: Economies of Scale and Scope and the Manufacturing behind the Marketing," *Business History Review*, 65 (Winter 1991); Walter Friedman, "A Car for Her: Selling Consumer Goods in the 1920s," in Friedman, *Birth of a Salesman: The Transformation of Selling in America* (Cambridge, Mass.: Harvard University Press, 2004); David Farber, *Sloan Rules: Alfred P. Sloan and the Triumph of General Motors* (Chicago: University of Chicago Press, 2002); and John McDonald, *A Ghost's Memoir: The Making of Alfred P. Sloan's* My Years with General Motors (Cambridge, Mass.: MIT Press, 2002), a brief account of the composition of Sloan's landmark autobiography.

The sociologist Robert F. Freeland, in *The Struggle for Control of the Modern Corporation: Organizational Change at General Motors, 1924–1970* (New York: Cambridge University Press, 2001), poses a challenging argument that the multidivisional structure did not operate at GM as I (and almost all other scholars) have described it—that is, as a force for decentralized decision making in a giant corporation. Freeland's point applies more to the organizational sociology within GM than to the relative decentralization of GM compared to that of the Ford Motor Company. Nor does it satisfactorily explain GM's superior economic performance for six decades, and the relentless adoption of the multidivisional structure by large companies throughout the world. Even so, it is an important book that challenges much conventional wisdom about what the author calls "the textbook M-form." Freeland's argument is less with Sloan's management style than with the theories of other scholars, in particular the economist Oliver Williamson.

## Selected Sources for Chapter Two
## Brand Management in the 1930s:
## Decentralization at Procter & Gamble

The Great Depression is the subject of a large academic literature, but scholars have not come to consensus about its causes. Two fundamental books are John Maynard Keynes, *The General Theory of Employment, Interest, and Money* (New York: Macmillan, 1936), and Milton J. Friedman and Anna Schwartz, *A Monetary History of the United States, 1867–1960* (Princeton, N.J.: Princeton University Press, 1963). Other basic works include John Kenneth Galbraith, *The Great Crash: 1929* (Boston: Houghton Mifflin, 1972 edition); Charles P. Kindleberger, *The World in Depression: 1929–1939* (Berkeley: University of California Press, 1973); Robert M. Collins, *The Business Response to Keynes: 1929–1964* (New York: Columbia University Press, 1981); Michael A. Bernstein, *The Great Depression: Delayed Recovery and Economic Change in America, 1929–1939* (New York: Cambridge University Press, 1987); Robert S. McElvaine, ed., *Encyclopedia of the Great Depression*, 2 vols. (New York: Macmillan, 2003), a thorough and accessible reference work; and Randall E. Parker, *Reflections on the Great Depression* (Northampton, Mass.: Edward Elgar, 2003), an annotated collection of interviews with leading economists.

A well-written analysis of the subject described in its title is David E. Kyvig, *Daily Life in the United States, 1920–1940: How Americans Lived through the Roaring Twenties and the Great Depression* (New York: Ivan Dee, 2004), which is especially good on automobiles, electricity, and the movies. On the latter, see also Virginia Wright Wexman, *A History of Film*, 6th ed. (Boston: Allyn and Bacon, 2005); John Baxter, *Hollywood in the Thirties, 1929–1939* (New York: A. S. Barnes, 1968, 1980); and Martin Quigley et al., eds., *International Motion Picture Almanac* (New York: Quigley, annual), which contains detailed information on revenues, industry structure, movie attendance, and much else about the industry during the thirties and subsequent decades.

Sources on Procter & Gamble include two articles published in *Fortune* during the 1930s: "Procter & Gamble," IV (Dec. 1936), and especially "99 44/100% Pure Profit Record," XIX (April 1939). Alfred Lief, *"It Floats": The Story of Procter & Gamble* (New York: Rinehart, 1958), is a breezy informal history. A book put together by the editors of *Advertising Age*, entitled *Procter & Gamble: The House that Ivory Built* (Lincolnwood, Ill.: NTC Business Books, 1988), is a sympathetic and thorough analysis. Alecia Swasy, *Soap Opera: The Inside Story of Procter & Gamble* (New York: Times Books, 1993), is a muckraker's account of the company's then recent history. Davis Dyer, Frederick Dalzell, and Rowena Olegario, *Rising Tide: Lessons from 165 Years of Brand Building at Procter & Gamble* (Boston: Harvard Business School Press, 2004), provides a good company-sponsored analysis of P&G's history, emphasizing the period since World War II. Susan Strasser, *Satisfaction Guaranteed: The Making of the American Mass Market* (New York: Pantheon, 1989) is excellent on P&G's initial Crisco marketing campaign, and on the subject of general mass marketing at the point where the consumer perceived the product. An account of the important changes at Procter & Gamble starting in 2000 is A. G. Lafley and Ram Charan, *The Game-Changer: How You Can Drive Revenue and Profit Growth with Innovation* (New York: Crown Business, 2008). Lafley became CEO of Procter & Gamble in 2000, and this book analyzes his own company and several others.

Insightful analyses of advertising include Daniel Pope, *The Making of Modern Advertising* (New York: Basic Books, 1983); Roland Marchand, *Advertising the American Dream: Making Way for Modernity, 1920–1940* (Berkeley: University of California Press, 1985); and Michael Schudson, *Advertising, the Uneasy Persuasion: Its Dubious Impact on American Society* (New York: Basic Books, 1984). Walter Friedman, "Selling Salesmanship: Public Relations and the Great Depression," in Friedman, *Birth of a Salesman* (Cambridge, Mass.: Harvard University Press, 2004), sheds new light on the subject of its title. Lizabeth Cohen's *Making a New Deal: Industrial Workers in Chicago, 1919–1939* (Cambridge, U.K.: Cambridge University Press, 1990) is a wide-ranging analysis that includes a discussion of patterns of consumer behavior. On this complex subject, see also Gary Cross, *An All-Consuming Century: Why Commercialism Won in Modern America* (New York: Columbia University Press, 2000); Kathleen G. Donahue, *Freedom from Want: American Liberalism and the Idea of the Consumer* (Baltimore: Johns Hopkins University Press, 2003); Meg Jacobs, *Pocketbook Politics: Economic Citizenship in Twentieth-Century America* (Princeton, N.J.: Princeton University Press, 2005) Charles McGovern, *Sold American: Consumption and Citizenship, 1890–1945* (Chapel Hill: University of North Carolina Press, 2006); and Inger L. Stole, *Advertising on Trial: Consumer Activism and Corporate Public Relations in the 1930s* (Urbana: University of Illinois Press, 2006).

My brief treatment of brands in this chapter has been influenced by conversations with and presentations by my Harvard Business School colleagues Alvin Silk, Nancy F. Koehn, and Susan Fournier. Here is a sample of relevant texts culled from many significant works: Kevin Lane Keller, *Strategic Brand Management*, 3rd ed. (Upper Saddle River, N.J.: Prentice-Hall, 2007); David A. Aaker, *Brand Portfolio Strategy: Creating Relevance, Differentiation, Energy, Leverage, and Clarity* (New York: Free Press, 2004); Jean-Noel Kapferer, *The New Strategic Brand Management: Creating and Sustaining Brand Equity Long Term*, 4th ed. (London: Kogan Page, 2008); and Philip Kotler and Gary Armstrong, *Principles of Marketing*, 11th ed. (Upper Saddle River, N.J.: Prentice-Hall, 2005). See also Allen P. Adamson, *BrandSimple: How the Best Brands Keep It Simple and Compete* (New York: Palgrave Macmillan, 2007); and Allen P. Adamson, *BrandDigital: Simple Ways Top Brands Succeed in the Digital World* (New York: Palgrave Macmillan, 2008), which emphasizes new opportunities raised by information technology.

## Selected Sources for Chapter Three
## The New Deal and World War II, 1933–1945:
## Decentralizing Regulation and War Mobilization

The most thorough engagement of the period covered by this chapter is David M. Kennedy's superb *Freedom from Fear: The American People in Depression and War, 1929–1945* (New York:

Oxford University Press, 1999). The vast historical literature on Franklin D. Roosevelt and the New Deal begins with the sympathetic treatments in Arthur M. Schlesinger, Jr.'s trilogy The Age of Roosevelt (Boston: Houghton Mifflin, 1957–60): *The Crisis of the Old Order, The Coming of the New Deal, and The Politics of Upheaval.* The best one-volume syntheses are William E. Leuchtenburg's thorough *Franklin D. Roosevelt and the New Deal, 1933–1940* (New York: Harper & Row, 1963), and Paul K. Conkin's brief and critical *The New Deal,* 3d ed. (Arlington Heights, Ill.: Harlan Davidson, Inc., 1992). One of the most important books on New Deal economic policy is Ellis W. Hawley, *The New Deal and the Problem of Monopoly: A Study in Economic Ambivalence* (Princeton, N.J.: Princeton University Press, 1966). On reforms in the capital markets, see Michael E. Parrish, *Securities Regulation and the New Deal* (New Haven, Conn.: Yale University Press, 1970); Chapters 2 and 3 of Joel Seligman, *The Transformation of Wall Street: A History of the Securities and Exchange Commission and Modern Corporate Finance* (Boston: Houghton Mifflin, 1982); and Chapter 5 of Thomas K. McCraw, *Prophets of Regulation* (Cambridge, Mass.: Harvard University Press, 1984).

Recent scholarship on the New Deal includes Colin Gordon, *New Deals: Business, Labor, and Politics in America, 1920–1935* (Cambridge, U.K.: Cambridge University Press, 1994), Alan Brinkley, *The End of Reform: New Deal Liberalism in Recession and War* (New York: Knopf, 1995); Eliot A. Rosen, *Roosevelt, the Great Depression, and the Economics of Recovery* (Charlottesville: University of Virginia Press, 2005); Alan Lawson, *A Commonwealth of Hope: The New Deal Response to Crisis* (Baltimore: Johns Hopkins University Press, 2006); and Jason Scott Smith, *Building New Deal Liberalism: The Political Economy of Public Works, 1933–1956* (New York: Cambridge University Press, 2006).

On the Roosevelts' wartime role, see Doris Kearns Goodwin, *Franklin and Eleanor Roosevelt: The Home Front in World War II* (New York: Simon and Schuster, 1994). Of the numerous works on the American military during World War II, one of the best and most thorough is Williamson Murray and Alan R. Millett, *A War To Be Won: Fighting the Second World War* (Cambridge, Mass.:

Harvard University Press, 2000). A useful summary discussion of the economic dimensions of American wars is Claudia D. Goldin, "War," in Glenn Porter, ed., *Encyclopedia of American Economic History* (New York: Scribner's, 1980), pp. 935–57. On mobilization for World War II, see the thorough compilation by the U.S. Department of Commerce, Bureau of the Budget, *The United States at War: Development and Administration of the War Program by the Federal Government* (Washington, D.C.: Government Printing Office, 1946); also Donald Nelson, *Arsenal of Democracy* (New York: Harcourt, Brace, 1946); Eliot Janeway, *The Struggle for Survival: A Chronicle of Economic Mobilization in World War II* (New Haven, Conn.: Yale University Press, 1951); Richard Polenberg, *War and Society: The United States, 1941–1945* (Philadelphia: J. B. Lippincott, 1972); John Morton Blum, *V Was for Victory: Politics and American Culture during World War II* (New York: Harcourt Brace Jovanovich, 1976); Harold G. Vatter, *The U.S. Economy in World War II* (New York: Columbia University Press, 1985); Paul A. C. Koistenen, *Arsenal of World War II: The Political Economy of American Warfare, 1940–1945* (Lawrence: University Press of Kansas, 2004); and Richard E. Holl, *From the Boardroom to the War Room: America's Corporate Liberals and FDR's Preparedness Program* (Rochester, N.Y.: University of Rochester Press, 2005).

On research and development during World War II, see Ronald Kline, "R&D: Organizing for War," *IEEE Spectrum*, November 1987, a cross-national study. A provocative interpretation of the relationship between mobilization and the nation's economic recovery from the Great Depression is Robert Higgs, "Wartime Prosperity? A Reassessment of the U.S. Economy in the 1940s," *Journal of Economic History*, 52 (March 1992). See also Hugh Rockoff, "From Plowshares to Swords: The American Economy in World War II," *National Bureau of Economic Research Historical Paper* 77 (December 1995). For the social impact of the war as viewed by contemporaries, see the collection of articles edited by Richard Polenberg, *America at War: The Home Front, 1941–1945* (Englewood Cliffs, N.J.: Prentice-Hall, 1968). On the control of prices, see Harvey C. Mansfield, *Historical Reports on War Administration: Office of Price Administration*, vol. XV of which is

*A Short History of OPA* (Washington, D.C.: Government Printing Office, 1947); Andrew H. Bartels, "The Office of Price Administration and the Legacy of the New Deal, 1939–1946," *Public Historian*, 5 (Summer 1983), pp. 5–29; and Meg Jacobs, "'How About Some Meat?' The Office of Price Administration, Consumption Politics, and State Building from the Bottom Up," *Journal of American History*, 84 (December 1997). A brilliant cross-national analysis of all aspects of World War II, from economic and military mobilization to tactics and leadership, is Richard Overy, *Why the Allies Won* (New York: Norton, 1995).

On Ferdinand Eberstadt and the Controlled Materials Plan, see Robert C. Perez and Edward F. Willett, *The Will to Win: A Biography of Ferdinand Eberstadt* (New York: Greenwood Press, 1989); Jeffrey M. Dorwart, *Eberstadt and Forrestal: A National Security Partnership, 1909–1949* (College Station: Texas A&M University Press, 1991); "Ferdinand Eberstadt," *Fortune*, 19 (April 1939); and especially Calvin Lee Christman, "Ferdinand Eberstadt and Economic Mobilization for War, 1941–1943," Ph.D. dissertation (history), Ohio State University, 1971. A useful but in my judgment mistaken analysis by Hugh Rockoff entitled "The Paradox of Planning in World War II" and published as *National Bureau of Economic Research Historical Paper* 83 (May 1996), argues that the positive impact of the Controlled Materials Plan has been overrated, and that the mobilization miracle might more accurately be viewed as a "gold rush" by American business in response to lavish federal funding. In my own interpretation of the Plan, I have relied, in addition to my own research, on the other works mentioned, on conversations with the late Robert D. Cuff, and on his case study, "Organizational Capabilities and U.S. War Production: The Controlled Materials Plan of World War II," (Boston, Mass.: Harvard Business School Case #390166, 1997).

Statistics on American population movements, the growth of cities, employment, and consumption patterns may be found in *The Impact of the War on Civilian Consumption in the United Kingdom, the United States and Canada: A Report to the Combined Production and Resources Board from a Special Combined Committee on Nonfood Consumption Levels* (Washington, D.C.:

Government Printing Office, 1945). See also Gerald D. Nash, *The American West Transformed: The Impact of World War II* (Bloomington, Ind.: Indiana University Press, 1985); Jacob Vander Meulen, "World War II Aircraft Industry in the West," *Journal of the West,* 36 (July 1997): pp. 78–84, and Carl Abbott, *The New Urban America: Growth and Politics in Sunbelt Cities* (Chapel Hill: University of North Carolina Press, 1981). A thorough analysis of the spread of defense-related industry during and especially after the war is Ann Markusen, Scott Campbell, Peter Hall, and Sabina Deitrick, *The Rise of the Gunbelt: The Military Remapping of Industrial America* (New York: Oxford University Press, 1991).

On the entry of women into the workforce outside the home, see Gregory Chester, *Women in Defense Work during World War II: An Analysis of the Labor Problem and Women's Rights* (New York: Exposition Press, 1974); Sherna Berger Gluck, *Rosie the Riveter Revisited: Women, the War, and Social Change* (Boston: Twayne, 1987); Ruth Milkman, *Gender at Work: The Dynamics of Job Segregation by Sex during World War II* (Urbana: University of Illinois Press, 1987); and D'Ann Campbell, *Women at War with America: Private Lives in a Patriotic Era* (Cambridge, Mass.: Harvard University Press, 1984).

On the evolution of the federal tax system, see W. Elliot Brownlee, *Federal Taxation in America: A Short History* (New York: Cambridge University Press, 1996); and Carolyn C. Jones, "Class Tax to Mass Tax: The Role of Propaganda in the Expansion of the Income Tax during World War II," *Buffalo Law Review,* 37 (Fall 1988/89). On the extraordinary effects of the war on postwar global economic development, see—among many other important books—Patrick J. Hearden, *Architects of Globalism: Building a New World Order during World War II* (Fayetteville: University of Arkansas Press, 2002).

The role of individual industries and companies during the war may be traced in a very large number of specialized books and articles. Representative of this literature are William M. Tuttle, Jr., "The Birth of an Industry: The Synthetic Rubber 'Mess' in World War II," *Technology and Culture,* 22 (January 1981); and, for the aluminum industry, which the war changed from a monopoly to a three-firm oligopoly of Alcoa, Kaiser, and Reynolds, George David Smith, *From Monopoly to Competition: The Transformations of Alcoa, 1888–1986* (New York: Cambridge University Press, 1988). On the remarkable achievement in producing ships, see Frederic C. Lane, *Ships for Victory: A History of Shipbuilding under the U.S. Maritime Commission in World War II* (Baltimore: Johns Hopkins University Press, 1951).

For statistics and other information on aircraft procurement, see I. B. Holley, Jr.'s thorough *Buying Aircraft: Matériel Procurement for the Army Air Forces* (Washington, D.C.: Government Printing Office, 1964). An outstanding analysis of business-government interplay is Robert D. Cuff, "Organizing U.S. Aircraft Production for War, 1938–1944: An Experiment in Group Enterprise," in Jun Sakudo and Takao Shiba, eds., *World War II and the Transformation of Business Systems* (Tokyo: University of Tokyo Press, 1994), a book that is itself a good source for comparative analysis. See also Tom Lilley et al., *Problems of Accelerating Aircraft Production during World War II* (Boston: Harvard University Graduate School of Business Administration, 1947); and Jonathan Zeitlin, "Flexibility and Mass Production at War: Aircraft Manufacture in Britain, the United States, and Germany, 1939–1945," *Technology and Culture*, 36 (January 1995).

On aviation more generally, see Roger E. Bilstein, *The American Aerospace Industry: From Workshop to Global Enterprise* (New York: Twayne, 1996); John B. Rae, *Climb to Greatness* (Cambridge, Mass.: MIT Press, 1968); Michael S. Sherry, *The Rise of American Air Power: The Creation of Armageddon* (New Haven, Conn.: Yale University Press, 1987); Jacob Vander Meulen, *The Politics of Aircraft: Building an American Military Industry* (Lawrence: University Press of Kansas, 1991); and Ronald Shaffer, *Wings of Judgment: American Bombing in World War II* (New York: Oxford University Press, 1985). A devastating critique of bombing campaigns against Axis cities by the British and Americans is a work by the philosopher A. C. Grayling, *Among the Dead Cities: The History and Moral Legacy of the WWII Bombing of Civilians in Germany and Japan* (New York: Walker, 2006).

Data on the aircraft companies discussed in this chapter come from a variety of sources, including the works cited just above plus the corporate and biographical reference books mentioned on the first pages of this bibliographical essay. See also René J. Francillon, *McDonnell Douglas Aircraft since 1920* (London: Putnam Aeronautical Books, 1979); Peter M. Bowers, *Boeing Aircraft since 1916* (London: Putnam Aeronautical Books, 1989); Harold Mansfield, *Vision: A Saga of the Sky* [Boeing] (New York: Duell, Sloan and Pearce, 1956); *Pedigree of Champions: Boeing Since 1916*, 6th ed. (The Boeing Co., 1985); Robert J. Serling, *Legend and Legacy: The Story of Boeing and Its People* (New York: St. Martin's Press, 1992); H. P. Willmott, *B-17 Flying Fortress* (New York: Prentice-Hall, 1983); Jacob Vander Meulen, *Building the B-29* (Washington, D.C.: Smithsonian Institution Press, 1995); Clive Irving, *Wide-Body: The Triumph of the 747* (New York: Morrow, 1993); Guy Norris and Mark Wagner, *Boeing 777: The Technological Marvel* (Osceola, Wisc.: Zenith Press, 2001), a well-illustrated but relatively superficial book (this publisher specializes in military and aviation books, and also has similar volumes on the Boeing 737, 757, 767, 787 and other aircraft); the anti-Boeing volume by Philip K. Lawrence and David Weldon Thornton, *Deep Stall: The Story of Boeing Commercial Airplanes* (Aldershot, U.K.: Ashgate, 2006); and the much fairer and more informative John Newhouse, *Boeing versus Airbus: The Inside Story of the Greatest International Competition in Business* (New York: Knopf, 2007).

## Selected Sources for Chapter Four
## Science and R&D: Color TV, Chemicals, and Pharmaceuticals Strengthen Postwar Prosperity

A concise analysis and interpretation of the American economy's unprecedented prosperity during the postwar period is Richard H. K. Vietor, "Economic Performance," in Stanley I. Kutler, ed., *Encyclopedia of the United States in the Twentieth Century*, III (New York: Scribner & Sons, 1995), pp. 1155–81. Also in the same volume, see especially the following essays: Alfred D. Chandler, Jr., "Industrial Production," pp. 1127–54; Susan

Strasser, "Consumption," pp. 1017–35; and William R. Childs, "Infrastructure," pp. 1331–55. I have also relied on two other essays, which appear in Volume II of the encyclopedia: David A. Hounshell, "Industrial Research and Manufacturing Technology," pp. 831–57; and Steven W. Usselman, "Computer and Communications Technology," pp. 799–829. On the broad theme of consumption, see Lizabeth Cohen, *A Consumers' Republic: The Politics of Mass Consumption in Postwar America* (New York: Knopf, 2003).

An outstanding general overview of American manufacturing may be found in Alfred D. Chandler, Jr., "The Competitive Performance of U.S. Industrial Enterprises since the Second World War," *Business History Review*, 68 (Spring 1994). On the evolution of air conditioning, see Raymond Arsenault, "The End of the Long Hot Summer: The Air Conditioner and Southern Culture," *Journal of Southern History*, 50 (November 1984); and Gail Cooper, *Airconditioning America: Engineers and the Controlled Environment 1900–1960* (Baltimore: Johns Hopkins University Press, 1998).

On aspects of R&D during the postwar period, S. M. Amadae, *Rationalizing Capitalist Democracy: The Cold War Origins of Rational Choice Liberalism* (Chicago: University of Chicago Press, 2003) recounts the influence of the Cold War and the RAND Corporation on the thinking of economists and intellectuals. On the origins and early development of radio, the standard source is Hugh G. J. Aitken, *The Continuous Wave: Technology and American Radio, 1900–1932* (Princeton, N.J.: Princeton University Press, 1985), which has excellent material on the formation of RCA. For a cultural historian's approach, see Susan Smulyan, *Selling Radio: The Commercialization of American Broadcasting* (Washington, D.C.: Smithsonian Institution Press, 1994). Michele Hilmes, *Radio Voices: American Broadcasting, 1922–1952* (St. Paul: University of Minnesota Press, 1998) examines the intersection of technology, advertising, and program content. Kathy M. Newman, *Radio Active: Advertising and Consumer Activism, 1935–1947* (Berkeley: University of California Press, 2004), presents radio listeners as actively resisting commercialism. Elizabeth Fones-Wolf, *Waves of Opposition: Labor and the Struggle for*

*Democratic Radio* (Champaign: University of Illinois Press, 2006), is an excellent account of organized labor's struggle for airtime from the 1920s to the 1960s. An outstanding introduction to the nature of the electronics industry and its history through the 1950s and into the early 1960s is Stanley S. Miller et al., *Manufacturing Policy: A Casebook of Major Production Problems in Six Selected Industries* (Homewood, Ill.: Irwin, 1957; 2d ed., 1964). In this volume, the materials on television and the electronics industry were written by my Harvard Business School colleague Richard Rosenbloom. Another important study of R&D is Stuart W. Leslie, *The Cold War and American Science* (New York: Columbia University Press, 1993), which focuses on Stanford University and MIT.

The best source on the career of David Sarnoff is Kenneth Bilby, *The General: David Sarnoff and the Rise of the Communications Industry* (New York: Harper & Row, 1986); Bilby was a close associate of Sarnoff and himself a high-ranking RCA executive. See also David Sarnoff, *Looking Ahead: The Papers of David Sarnoff* (New York: McGraw-Hill, 1968); Carl Dreher, *Sarnoff: An American Success* (New York: Quadrangle, 1977), written by a technical expert with a long association with Sarnoff and RCA; Eugene Lyons, *David Sarnoff: A Biography* (New York: Harper & Row, 1966), a hagiographic account; and Tom Lewis, *Empire of the Air: The Men Who Made Radio* (New York: HarperCollins, 1991), which covers the careers of Sarnoff, Lee de Forest, Howard Armstrong, and other industry pioneers.

Additional sources on RCA include Margaret B. W. Graham, *RCA and the VideoDisc: The Business of Research* (Cambridge: Cambridge University Press, 1986), an especially insightful analysis; Robert Sobel, *RCA* (New York: Stein and Day, 1986), which contains some useful statistics; and *Fortune*'s frequent articles on RCA and the electronics industry from the 1930s to the 1980s, among which the following are particularly useful: "RCA's Television," *Fortune,* September 1948; Lawrence P. Lessing, "The Electronics Era," *Fortune,* July 1951; "C.B.S. Steals the Show," *Fortune,* July 1953; David Sarnoff, "The Fabulous Future," *Fortune,* January 1955, which contains examples of Sarnoff's overblown rhetoric; William B. Harris, "R.C.A. Organizes for

Profit," *Fortune,* August 1957; Walter Guzzardi, Jr., "R.C.A.: The General Never Got Butterflies," *Fortune,* October 1962; Bro Uttal, "How Ed Griffiths Brought RCA into Focus," *Fortune,* December 31, 1978; Peter Nulty, "A Peacemaker Comes to RCA," *Fortune,* May 4, 1981; and "The Colossus of Conglomerates Moves Away from Smokestacks by Buying RCA," *Fortune,* January 1, 1986.

The literature on television is immense. A good starting point is James L. Baughman, *Same Time, Same Station: Creating American Television, 1948–1961* (Baltimore: Johns Hopkins University Press, 2007). See also Hugh R. Slotten, *Radio and Television Regulation: Broadcast Technology in the United States, 1920–1960* (Baltimore: Johns Hopkins University Press, 2000). Coverage of the many aspects of the influence of TV on American culture lies beyond the scope of this book, but see the following sample of works: Erik Barnouw, *Tube of Plenty: The Evolution of American Television* (New York: Oxford University Press, 1970); Jerry Mander, *Four Arguments for the Elimination of Television* (New York: Quill, 1978); George Comstock et al., *Television and Human Behavior* (New York: Columbia University Press, 1978); Carl Lowe, ed., *Television and American Culture* (New York: H.W. Wilson Co., 1981); and Joseph Turow, *Breaking Up America: Advertisers and the New Media World* (Chicago: University of Chicago Press, 1997).

The theme of American industrial arrogance and consequent decline, exemplified in this chapter through the story of RCA, is set forth in numerous books published during the 1980s. A good example is Robert C. Hayes, Steven C. Wheelwright, and Kim B. Clark, *Dynamic Manufacturing: Creating the Learning Organization* (New York: Free Press, 1988). There is also a plethora of works on the Japanese challenge in electronics and other industries, examples of which include Thomas K. McCraw, ed., *America Versus Japan: A Study in Business-Government Relations* (Boston: Harvard Business School Press, 1986); Philip J. Curtis, *The Fall of the U.S. Consumer Electronics Industry: An American Trade Tragedy* (Westport, Conn.: Quorum Books, 1994); and David Schwartzman, *The Japanese Television Cartel: A Study Based on Matsushita vs. Zenith* (Ann Arbor: University of Michigan

Press, 1993). See also MIT Commission on Industrial Productivity, Commission Working Group on the Consumer Electronics Industries, "The Decline of U.S. Consumer Electronics Manufacturing: History, Hypotheses, and Remedies," in *Working Papers of the MIT Commission on Industrial Productivity*, Vol. 1 (Cambridge, Mass.: MIT Press, 1989); and Richard Rosenbloom and William Abernathy, "The Climate for Innovation in Industry: The Role of Management Attitudes and Practices in Consumer Electronics," *Research Policy*, 11 (1982). A readable account of the consumer-electronics story from the Japanese side is Akio Morita, *Made in Japan* (New York: Dutton, 1986), written by the co-founder and longtime CEO of Sony. For a very good retrospective, see Alfred D. Chandler, Jr., *Inventing the Electronic Century: The Epic Story of the Consumer Electronics and Computer Industries* (New York: Free Press, 2001).

For the chemical industry and the morphology of industrial research, see David A. Hounshell and John Kenly Smith, *Science and Corporate Strategy: Du Pont R&D, 1902–1980* (New York: Cambridge University Press, 1988), which analyzes the theme of centralization versus decentralization in industrial R&D. Broad overviews of both chemicals and pharmaceuticals are Alfred D. Chandler, Jr., *Shaping the Industrial Century: The Remarkable Story of the Modern Chemical and Pharmaceutical Industries* (Cambridge, Mass.: Harvard University Press, 2005), and Louis Galambos, Takashi Hikino, and Vera Zamagni, eds., *The Global Chemical Industry in the Age of the Petrochemical Revolution* (New York: Cambridge University Press, 2007), which covers many countries besides the United States.

On pharmaceuticals, see Jerry Avorn, *The Benefits, Risks, and Costs of Prescription Drugs* (New York: Vintage, 2005), a critical but extremely informative analysis. See also David Schwartzman, *Innovation in the Pharmaceutical Industry* (Baltimore: Johns Hopkins University Press, 1976); and National Research Council, *The Competitive Status of the U.S. Pharmaceutical Industry: The Influences of Technology in Determining International Industrial Competitive Advantage* (Washington, D.C.: National Academy Press, 1983). Current information is available from the *Annual Survey*

*Report* of the Pharmaceutical Manufacturers Association (Washington, D.C.: the Association, annual), and the same association's *Fact Book,* also issued annually. The industry can be followed through other trade publications as well, such as *Pharmacy in History, Drug Topics,* and *Chemist and Druggist.* Also, there are very long entries in Wikipedia under "pharmaceutical industry" and "biotechnology," with links to numerous subtopics, some of them highly technical, others conventional company histories. One of the best books on the history of an important drug firm is Louis Galambos with Jane Eliot Sewell, *Networks of Innovation: Vaccine Development at Merck, Sharp & Dohme, and Mulford, 1895–1995* (New York: Cambridge University Press, 1995). On regulation, see Peter Temin, *Taking Your Medicine: Drug Regulation in the United States* (Cambridge, Mass.: Harvard University Press, 1980); and Philip J. Hilts, *Protecting America's Health: The FDA, Business, and One Hundred Years of Regulation* (New York: Knopf, 2003).

## Selected Sources for Chapter Five
## Franchising and McDonald's

For general discussions of the distribution of both income and wealth see James T. Patterson, "Wealth and Poverty," in Stanley I. Kutler, ed., *Encyclopedia of the United States in the Twentieth Century,* III, pp. 1067–90; Edward Wolff, "Trends in Household Wealth in the United States, 1962–83 and 1983–89," *Review of Income and Wealth,* 40, No. 2 (1994); and Lee Soltow, "Distribution of Income and Wealth," in Glenn Porter, ed., *Encyclopedia of American Economic History,* pp. 1087–1119. See also Andrew Hacker, *Money: Who Has How Much and Why* (New York: Scribner & Sons, 1997); James K. Galbraith, *Created Unequal: The Crisis in American Pay* (New York: Free Press, 1998); John McNeil, "Changes in Median Household Income: 1969 to 1996," U.S. Bureau of the Census, Special Studies, pp. 23–196, July 1998; Edward N. Wolff, *Top Heavy: The Increasing Inequality of Wealth in America and What Can Be Done About It* (New York: The New Press, 1996); and Robert H. Frank and Philip J. Cook, *The*

*Winner-Take-All Society: Why the Few at the Top Get So Much More Than the Rest of Us* (New York: Penguin, 1996). *Business Week* publishes annual statistical surveys of executive compensation. See, for example, "Is Greed Good?" *Business Week*, April 19, 1999, pp. 72–118. I have limited the sources on income inequality listed above mainly to the period covered by this chapter. For additional information on continuing inequality in the twenty-first century, see the Selected Sources for Chapter Seven, below.

Standard analyses of franchising include Thomas S. Dicke, *Franchising in America: The Development of a Business Method, 1840–1980* (Chapel Hill: University of North Carolina Press, 1992); and the pessimistic Peter M. Birkeland, *Franchising Dreams: The Lure of Entrepreneurship in America* (Chicago: University of Chicago Press, 2002). A major source listing numerous articles is B. Elango and Vance H. Fried, "Franchising Research: A Literature Review and Synthesis," *Journal of Small Business Management,* 35 (July 1997). See also the following annual publications: *Franchising in the Economy; The Franchise Annual; The Franchise Opportunities Handbook; Bond's Franchise Guide; Proceedings* of the Society of Franchising, International Franchise Association, and *The Source Book of Franchise Opportunities.* An annual survey of franchising in the magazine *Entrepreneur* has been conducted since the early 1980s, containing information on *Entrepreneur's* "Franchise 500." See also current issues of *Nation's Restaurant News; Franchising World; Restaurant Business; American Journal of Small Business; Women in Franchising*; and *Pizza Today.* Bill Carlino, "75 Years: The Odyssey of Eating Out," *Nation's Restaurant News*, Special Commemorative Issue, January 1994, is full of good anecdotes and other information not only on franchising but on restaurant dining in general. In addition, see Patrick J. Kaufmann and Rajiv P. Dant, eds., *Franchising: Contemporary Issues and Research* (Binghamton, N.Y.: Haworth Press, 1995). Two of several useful websites on the fundamental business model are Franchising.com and Franchising.org.

Rigorous economic analyses may be found in Richard E. Caves and William F. Murphy II, "Franchising: Firms, Markets, and Intangible Assets," *Southern Economic Journal*, 42 (April 1976); Paul H. Rubin, "The Theory of the Firm and the Structure of the Franchise Contract," *Journal of Law & Economics*, 21 (April 1978); Benjamin Klein and Lester F. Saft, "The Law and Economics of Franchise Tying Contracts," *Journal of Law & Economics*, 28 (May 1985); Alan Krueger, "Ownership, Agency, and Wages: An Examination of Franchising in the Fast-Food Industry," *Quarterly Journal of Economics* (February 1991); Paul Steinberg and Gerald Lescatre, "Beguiling Heresy: Regulating the Franchise Relationship," *Penn State Law Review*, 109 (Summer 2004); and Roger D. Clair and Francine Lafontaine, *The Economics of Franchising* (New York: Cambridge University Press, 2005).

On restaurants, see Robert Emerson, *Fast Food: The Endless Shakeout* (New York: Lebhar-Friedman, 1982); Robert Emerson, *The New Economics of Fast Food* (New York: Van Nostrand Reinhold, 1990); and the extremely critical bestseller by Eric Schlosser, *Fast Food Nation* (Boston: Houghton Mifflin, 2001).

John Love, *McDonald's: Behind the Arches* (New York: Bantam, 1986, revised ed. 1995) is by far the most informative source on the history of the company, and I am much indebted to it. Robin Leidner, *Fast Food, Fast Talk: Service Work and the Routinization of Everyday Life* (Berkeley: University of California Press, 1993) is a sociologist's firsthand account of working conditions, especially strong in its evocation of life inside a McDonald's restaurant. James L. Watson, ed., *Golden Arches East: McDonald's in East Asia* (Stanford, Calif.: Stanford University Press, 1997) provides an insightful analysis by anthropologists of the McDonald's experience in Beijing, Hong Kong, Taipei, Seoul, and Tokyo. Ray Kroc with Robert Anderson, *Grinding It Out: The Making of McDonald's* (Chicago: Henry Regnery, 1977) is a brief and serviceable autobiography, characteristically unpretentious and fairly candid. Lisa Bertagnoli, "McDonald's: Company of the Century," *Restaurants and Institutions*, 99 (July 10, 1989); and the same author's "Inside McDonald's," *Restaurants and Institutions*, 99 (August 21, 1989), are excellent articles containing useful information about, among other things, employment of women and minorities. The story of the company's troubles in the early twenty-first century and its subsequent internal reforms is well told in "A Turnaround at McDonald's," *The Economist*, Oct. 14, 2004.

See also Stan Luxenberg, *Roadside Empires: How the Chains Franchised America* (New York: Penguin, 1985); Timothy Bates, "Analysis of Survival Rates among Franchise and Independent Small Business Startups," *Journal of Small Business Management*, 33 (April 1995); and, on motels and franchising, John A. Jakle, Keith A. Sculle, and Jefferson S. Rogers, *The Motel in America* (Baltimore: Johns Hopkins University Press, 1996), Chapters 6 and 7.

## Selected Sources for Chapter Six
## Empowerment of Women and Minorities

1. *Women*. For a superb analysis of career issues common to women and minorities—and to white men as well—see Pamela Walker Laird, *PULL: Networking and Success since Benjamin Franklin* (Cambridge, Mass.: Harvard University Press, 2006). The literature on women in business is not as voluminous as it is for political, social, and cultural topics. It is perhaps stronger for the nineteenth century than the twentieth, and fuller for the early and late parts of the twentieth century than the middle. But scholarly work grew rapidly toward the close of that century, and the following items are especially useful: Angel Kwolek-Folland, *Incorporating Women: A History of Women and Business in the United States* (New York: Twayne, 1998); Mary A. Yeager, ed., *Women in Business*, a three-volume collection of articles with a comprehensive introduction (Northampton, Mass.: Edward Elgar, 1999); Carol H. Krismann, *Encyclopedia of American Women in Business: From Colonial Times to the Present* (Westport, Conn.: Greenwood Press, 2005); Virginia G. Drachman, *Enterprising Women: 250 Years of American Business* (Chapel Hill: University of North Carolina Press, 2002)—a glossy, picture-filled book published in conjunction with an exhibition by the Schlesinger Library at Harvard; Alice Kessler-Harris, *In Pursuit of Equity: Women, Men and*

*the Quest for Economic Citizenship in Twentieth-Century America* (New York: Oxford University Press, 2001); Victoria Sharrow, *A to Z of American Women Business Leaders and Entrepreneurs* (New York: Facts on File, 2002); Claudia Goldin, *Understanding the Gender Gap: An Economic History of American Women* (New York: Oxford University Press, 1990); Kathy Peiss, "'Vital Industry' and Women's Ventures: Conceptualizing Gender in Twentieth Century Business History," *Business History Review,* 72 (Summer 1998); Julia Kirk Blackwelder, *Now Hiring: The Feminization of Work in the United States, 1900–1995* (College Station: Texas A&M University Press, 1997); Sharon Hartman Strom, *Beyond the Typewriter: Gender, Class, and the Origins of Modern Office Work, 1900–1930* (Urbana: University of Illinois Press, 1992); Angel Kwolek-Folland, *Engendering Business: Men and Women of the Corporate Office, 1870–1930* (Baltimore: Johns Hopkins University Press, 1994); Susan Thistle, *From Marriage to the Market: The Transformation of Women's Lives and Work* (Berkeley: University of California Press, 2006); Caroline Bird, *Enterprising Women* (New York: Norton, 1986); Frank Stricker, "Cookbooks and Law Books: The Hidden History of Career Women in Twentieth Century America," in Nancy F. Cott, ed., *History of Women in the United States,* vol. 8: *Professional and White-Collar Employments,* part 2 (Munich: K. G. Saur, 1993); Clark Davis, "'Girls in Grey Flannel Suits': White Career Women in Postwar American Culture," in Elspeth H. Brown, Catherine Gudis, and Marina Moskowitz, eds., *Cultures of Commerce: Representation and American Business Culture, 1877–1960* (New York: Palgrave Macmillan, 2006); Wendy Gamber, *The Female Economy: The Millinery and Dressmaking Trades, 1860–1930* (Urbana: University of Illinois Press, 1997); Rosabeth Moss Kanter, *Men and Women of the Corporation* (New York: Basic Books, 1977); Barbara J. Harris, *Beyond Her Sphere: Women and the Professions in American History* (Westport, Conn.: Greenwood Press, 1978); U.S. Department of Commerce, *The Bottom Line: Equal Enterprise in America: Report of the President's Interagency Task Force on Women Business Owners* (Washington, D.C.: Government Printing Office, 1978); Dawn-Marie Driscoll and Carol R. Goldberg, *Members of the Club: The Coming of Age of Executive Women* (New York: Free Press, 1993); Betsy Morris, "Tales of the Trailblazers: *Fortune* Visits Harvard's Women MBAs of 1973," *Fortune,* 138 (October 12, 1998); Ann Faircloth, Andrew Goldsmith, and Ann Harrington, "The Class of '83," ibid. Some of the statistics about women in the workforce quoted in this chapter come from Andrew J. Cherlin, "By the Numbers," *New York Times Magazine,* April 8, 1998. There are many sources on the Estée Lauder and Mary Kay companies. Both entrepreneurs wrote autobiographies: *Estée: A Success Story* (New York: Random House, 1985); and *Mary Kay: The Story of America's Most Dynamic Businesswoman,* 3rd ed. (New York: HarperPerennial, 1994). Magazine coverage has been extensive; see, as examples, Sandra Mardenfeld, "Mary Kay Ash," *Incentive,* 170 (January 1996); and Nina Munk, "Why Women Find Lauder Mesmerizing," *Fortune,* 137 (May 25, 1998). For cosmetics and other industries, see Kathy Peiss, *Hope in a Jar: The Making of America's Beauty Culture* (New York: Metropolitan Books/Henry Holt, 1998). On Oprah Winfrey, the magazine literature is overwhelming—including Winfrey's own monthly, *O, the Oprah Magazine.* No single book is fully satisfactory in its coverage of this American icon, but Janet Lowe, *Oprah Winfrey Speaks* (New York: Wiley, 2001) is helpful; and Marcia Z. Nelson, *The Gospel According to Oprah* (Louisville, Ky.: Westminster John Knox Press, 2005) is a thoughtful engagement of the religious implications of Winfrey's message.

2. *African Americans.* Scholarly work on African Americans and business also began to grow rapidly toward the close of the twentieth century, and the following items provide a good introduction: John N. Ingham and Lynne B. Feldman, *African-American Business Leaders: A Biographical Dictionary* (Westport, Conn.: Greenwood Press, 1993); Jessie Carney Smith, ed., *Encyclopedia of African American Business* (Westport, Conn.: Greenwood Press, 2006); Rachel Kranz, *African-American Business Leaders and Entrepreneurs* (New York: Facts on File, 2004); Alusine Jalloh and Toyin Falolo, eds., *Black Business and Economic Power* (Rochester, N.Y.: University of Rochester Press, 2002); Juliet E. K. Walker, *The History of Black Business in America: Capital-*

*ism, Race, Entrepreneurship* (New York: Macmillan, 1998), which covers the colonial period to the middle 1990s; and Ronald W. Bailey, ed., *Black Business Enterprise: Historical and Contemporary Perspectives* (New York: Basic Books, 1971).

On specific topics, see Timothy Bates, "Black Business Community," in Jack Salzman, David Lionel Smith, and Cornel West, eds., *Encyclopedia of African-American Culture and History* (New York: Simon & Schuster Macmillan, 1996), pp. 332–46; Juliet E. K. Walker, "Banking," ibid., pp. 246–50, and "Entrepreneurs," ibid., pp. 897–909; Susannah Walker, *Style and Status: Selling Beauty to African American Women, 1920–1975* (Lexington: University Press of Kentucky, 2007); Adam Green, *Selling the Race: Culture, Community, and Black Chicago, 1940–1955* (Chicago: University of Chicago Press, 2006); Jason Chambers, *Madison Avenue and the Color Line: African Americans in the Advertising Industry* (Philadelphia: University of Pennsylvania Press, 2008); John Sibley Butler, *Entrepreneurship and Self-Help among Black Americans: A Reconsideration of Race and Economics* (Albany: State University of New York Press, 1991); Shelley Greene and Paul Pryde, *Black Entrepreneurship in America* (New Brunswick, N.J.: Transaction Publishers, 1990); Timothy Bates, *Black Capitalism: A Quantitative Analysis* (New York: Praeger, 1973), which is especially concerned with the issue of whether black patronage of black businesses was on balance a helpful or limiting phenomenon, as is Russ Rymer, "Integration's Casualties: Segregation Helped Black Business, Civil Rights Helped Destroy It," *New York Times Magazine*, November 1, 1998. See also Paula Mergenhagen, "Black-owned Businesses," *American Demographics*, 18 (June 1996); and any issue of *Black Enterprise*, a periodical established in 1970. An excellent analysis of black managers and the corporate ladder is David A. Thomas and John J. Gabarro, *Breaking Through: The Making of Minority Executives in Corporate America* (Boston: Harvard Business School Press, 1999).

On insurance, good sources are Walter A. Friedman, "Insurance Companies," in Salzman, Smith, and West, eds., *Encyclopedia of African-American Culture and History*, pp. 1365–69; Robert Weems, *Black Business in the Black Metropolis* (Bloomington:

Indiana University Press, 1996), which examines the Chicago Metropolitan Assurance Company; Alexa Henderson, *Atlanta Life Insurance Company: Guardian of Black Economic Dignity* (Tuscaloosa: University of Alabama Press, 1990); Walter Weare, *Black Business in the New South: A Social History of the North Carolina Mutual Life Insurance Company* (Urbana: University of Illinois Press, 1973).

On the intersection of politics and minority business, see George R. LaNoue, "Split Visions: Minority Business Set Asides," *Annals of the American Academy of Political and Social Science,* 523 (September 1992); Dean Kotlowski, "Black Power—Nixon Style: The Nixon Administration and Minority Business Enterprise," *Business History Review,* 72 (Autumn 1998); and the very critical book by Jonathan Bean, *Big Government and Affirmative Action: The Scandalous History of the Small Business Administration* (Lexington: University Press of Kentucky, 2001).

3. *Hispanics.* The literature about Hispanics in U.S. business is, at least for the moment, extremely sparse compared to that about women and African Americans. The best single source is the magazine *Hispanic Business,* whose current and back issues contain useful data in both statistical and narrative forms. Its website, HispanicBusiness.com, has numerous links to specific data. The National Hispanic Business Information Clearing House (nhbic. org) is another rich resource.

Government reports on minority business in general usually contain sections on Hispanic business. Two good examples are Robert W. Fairlie, "Minority Ownership," in *The Small Business Economy 2005: A Report to the President* (Washington, D.C.: Government Printing Office, 2005); and Office of Advocacy, U.S. Small Business Administration, "Minorities in Business: A Demographic Review of Minority Business Ownership" (Washington, D.C., Government Printing Office, April 10, 2007). Both of these sources are filled with helpful statistics, and the same is true of numerous reports on immigration issued by the U.S. Bureau of the Census.

More than 50 Spanish-language newspapers are now published in the United States. Many relevant newspaper articles also appear in English, and are not difficult to research online with the help of a reference librarian. See, for example, the following informative articles—all taken from the year 2006: James Flanigan, "Latino Funds Help Family Businesses with Posterity in Mind," *New York Times*, July 8, 2006, Section C, p. 1; Hubert B. Herring, "A Closer Look at the Hispanic Population," *New York Times*, August 13, 2006, Section 3, p. 2; E. Scott Reckard, "Latino-Owned Banks Seek to Fill Void in L.A.," *Los Angeles Times*, July 23, 2006, part C, p. 1; and James Flanigan, "Champion Boxer [Oscar de la Hoya] and Builder Aim to Help Latinos," *New York Times*, October 14, 2006, Section C, p. 1.

Among prominent Hispanic businesspeople, the most useful biography is David Greising, *I'd Like the World to Buy a Coke: The Life and Leadership of Roberto Goizueta* (New York: Wiley, 1998). The careers of other executives mentioned in this chapter may be researched online by Googling their names: Carlos Gutiérrez, Hector Ruiz, Alain J. P. Belda, William D. Perez, Fernando Aguirre, and Paul Diaz.

## Selected Sources for Chapter Seven
## The Financial System

A good general orientation is Steve Fraser, *Every Man a Speculator: A History of Wall Street in American Life* (New York: HarperCollins, 2005)—a long and thorough cultural history from the beginning of "The Street" to the twenty-first century; Fraser's treatment is especially vivid on financial scandals. See also New York Stock Exchange *Fact Book* (New York: NYSE, annual). Informative historical surveys, many of them stronger on economic analysis than Fraser's book, include George David Smith and Richard Sylla, "Capital Markets," in Stanley I. Kutler, ed., *Encyclopedia of the United States in the Twentieth Century* (New York: Simon & Schuster, 1996), III, pp. 1209–41; Peter Wyckoff, *Wall Street and the Stock Markets: A Chronology, 1644–1971* (Philadelphia: Chilton, 1971); Charles R. Geisst, *Wall Street: A History* (New York: Oxford University Press, 1997); James Grant, *Money of the Mind: Borrowing and Lending in America from the Civil*

*War to Michael Milken* (New York: Farrar Straus Giroux, 1992); Vincent P. Carosso, *Investment Banking in America: A History* (Cambridge, Mass.: Harvard University Press, 1970); Samuel L. Hayes et al., *Competition in the Investment Banking Industry* (Cambridge, Mass.: Harvard University Press, 1983); Jeremy J. Siegel, *Stocks for the Long Run* (New York: McGraw-Hill, 1998); and Richard Sylla, Jack W. Wilson, and Charles P. Jones, "U.S. Financial Markets and Long-Term Economic Growth, 1790–1989," in Thomas Weiss and Donald Schaefer, eds., *American Economic Development in Historical Perspective* (Stanford, Calif.: Stanford University Press, 1994). John Brooks, *Once in Golconda: A True Drama of Wall Street, 1920–1938* (New York: Harper & Row, 1969) is a sprightly account of doings and wrongdoings in the market during a crucial part of its history.

The evolving role of the Federal Reserve System may be traced through books by or about its most influential chairs. See Marriner S. Eccles, *Beckoning Frontiers* (New York: Knopf, 1951); Robert P. Bremner, *Chairman of the Fed: William McChesney Martin Jr. and the Creation of the American Financial System* (New Haven: Yale University Press, 2004); Joseph B. Treaster, *Paul Volcker: The Making of a Financial Legend* (New York: Wiley, 2005); and Alan Greenspan, *The Age of Turbulence: Adventures in a New World* (New York: Penguin, 2007). Eccles served from 1934 to 1948, Martin from 1951 until 1970, Volcker from 1979 until 1982 (especially difficult years during which Volcker led a successful fight against severe inflation), and Greenspan from 1987 until 2006, a period of unprecedented financial innovation, over some of which the Fed—by most accounts—should have exerted tighter regulatory control. See also the very informative Allan H. Meltzer, *History of the Federal Reserve* (Chicago: University of Chicago Press, 2008).

Peter L. Bernstein, *Capital Ideas: The Improbable Origins of Modern Wall Street* (New York: Free Press, 1992) provides, among other insights, a superb intellectual history of finance theory; the same author's *Capital Ideas Evolving*, 2d ed. (New York: Wiley, 2007) updates his analysis. A good introduction to the phenomenon of derivatives is Satyajit Das, *Traders, Guns & Money:*

*Knowns and Unknowns in the Dazzling World of Derivatives* (London: FT Press, 2006). Further theoretical explorations may be followed through current and back issues of academic quarterlies such as the *Journal of Finance, Journal of Financial Economics, Journal of Accounting and Economics,* and *Journal of Accounting Research.*

Critical accounts of the events that changed the nature of the capital markets during the 1980s and 1990s—written mostly by influential journalists—include Connie Bruck, *The Predators' Ball* (New York: Simon & Schuster, 1989); James B. Stewart, *Den of Thieves* (New York: Simon & Schuster, 1991); Jesse Kornbluth, *Highly Confident: The Crime and Punishment of Michael Milken* (New York: Morrow, 1992); George Anders, *Merchants of Debt* (New York: Basic Books, 1993); and Maggie Mahar, *Bull! A History of the Boom, 1982–1999: What Drove the Breakneck Market—and What Every Investor Needs to Know about Financial Cycles* (New York: HarperBusiness, 2003). On private equity, see the practical textbook, Guy Fraser-Sampson, *Private Equity as an Asset Class* (New York: Wiley, 2007). An excellent book not primarily on finance but on the ways in which business practices and ethics are disseminated is Christopher D. McKenna, *The World's Newest Profession: Management Consulting in the Twentieth Century* (New York: Cambridge University Press, 2006).

Kevin Phillips mounts a savage indictment of American financial practices since the 1980s in *Bad Money: Reckless Finance, Failed Politics, and the Global Crisis of American Capitalism* (New York: Viking, 2008). Only slightly less critical are Charles R. Morris, *The Trillion Dollar Meltdown: Easy Money, High Rollers, and the Great Credit Crash* (New York: Public Affairs, 2008); Richard Brookstaber, *A Demon of Our Own Design: Markets, Hedge Funds, and the Perils of Financial Innovation* (New York: Wiley, 2007); John C. Bogle, *The Battle for the Soul of Capitalism* (New Haven, Conn.: Yale University Press, 2005); David Callahan, *The Cheating Culture: Why More Americans Are Doing Wrong to Get Ahead* (New York: Harcourt, 2004)—which goes beyond business into the worlds of sports and academics; and Robert H. Frank, *What Price the Moral High Ground?: Ethical Dilemmas in Competitive Environments* (Princeton, N.J.: Princeton University Press, 2004)—another book concerned with topics beyond business. These volumes are only a sample of what is already a large critical literature and one certain to become larger.

On the distribution of income, see the long and outstanding (as of 2008) entry in the online encyclopedia Wikipedia, "Income Inequality in the United States," which is full of tables, statistics, charts, and analyses based mostly on nonpartisan reports from federal agencies, especially the Bureau of the Census. A sample of the large number of good books on this subject includes *Class Matters* (New York: Times Books, 2005), a collection of 14 essays by staff members of the *New York Times*; David K. Shipler, *The Working Poor: Invisible in America* (New York: Vintage, 2005); Mark Robert Rank, *One Nation, Underprivileged: Why American Poverty Affects Us All* (New York: Oxford University Press, 2005); Sharon Hays, *Flat Broke with Children: Women in the Age of Welfare Reform* (New York: Oxford University Press, 2004); Thomas Frank, *One Market Under God: Extreme Capitalism, Market Populism, and the End of Economic Democracy* (New York: Anchor, 2001); Barbara Ehrenreich, *Nickel and Dimed: On (Not) Getting By in America* (New York: Metropolitan Books, 2001); and Robert H. Frank, *Falling Behind: How Rising Inequality Harms the Middle Class* (Berkeley: University of California Press, 2007). For additional sources about the skewed distribution of wealth and income, see the Selected Sources for Chapter Five above.

One major issue I have not discussed in this book is the unusual division of responsibility for social welfare in the United States between the government on the one hand and the private sector on the other. For an excellent discussion of that subject, especially as it applies to big business, see Jacob S. Hacker, *The Divided Welfare State: The Battle over Public and Private Social Benefits in the United States* (New York: Cambridge University Press, 2002).

## Selected Sources for Chapter Eight
## Information Technology

For excellent introductions, see Steven W. Usselman, "Computer and Communications Technology," *Encyclopedia of the United States in the Twentieth Century* (New York: Simon & Schuster, 1996), II, pp. 799–829; and Alfred D. Chandler, Jr., *Inventing the Electronic Century: The Epic Story of the Consumer Electronics and Computer Industries* (New York: Free Press, 2001). Other standard sources include JoAnne Yates, *Control Through Communication: The Rise of System in American Management* (Baltimore: Johns Hopkins University Press, 1989); and *Structuring the Information Age: Life Insurance and Technology in the Twentieth Century* (Baltimore: Johns Hopkins University Press, 2005); James W. Cortada, *Before the Computer: IBM, NCR, Burroughs, and Remington Rand and the Industry They Created, 1865–1956* (Princeton, N. J.: Princeton University Press, 1993); James R. Beniger, *The Control Revolution: Technical and Economic Origins of the Information Society* (Cambridge, Mass.: Harvard University Press, 1986); Ernest Braun and Stuart Macdonald, *Revolution in Miniature: The History and Impact of Semiconductor Electronics* (New York: Cambridge University Press, 1978); Arthur L. Norberg, *Computers and Commerce: A Study of Technology and Management at Eckert-Mauchly Computer Company, Engineering Research Associates, and Remington Rand, 1946–1957* (Cambridge, Mass.: MIT Press, 2005); Ross Knox Bassett, *To the Digital Age: Research Labs, Start-Up Companies, and the Rise of MOS Technology* (Baltimore: Johns Hopkins University Press, 2002); Kenneth Flamm, *Targeting the Computer: Government Support and International Competition* (Washington, D.C.: Brookings Institution, 1987); Flamm, *Creating the Computer: Government, Industry, and High Technology* (Washington, D.C.: Brookings Institution, 1988); James W. Cortada, *The Digital Hand,* 3 vols. (New York: Oxford University Press, 2003, 2005, 2007), which covers in detail the impact of computers on numerous industries as well as the public sector. On IBM, see Emerson W. Pugh, *Building IBM: Shaping an Industry and Its Technology* (Cambridge, Mass.:

MIT Press, 1995); and the extraordinary autobiography of IBM's second CEO, Thomas J. Watson, Jr. and Peter Petre, *Father, Son & Co.: My Life at IBM and Beyond* (New York: Bantam, 1990);

For other first-hand accounts, see David Packard, *The H-P Way: How Bill Hewlett and I Built Our Company* (New York: Harper-Business, 1995), an oddly disembodied book; the livelier work by Intel's Andrew S. Grove, *Only the Paranoid Survive: How to Exploit the Crisis Points that Challenge Every Company and Career* (New York: Currency Doubleday, 1996); and Bill Gates with Nathan Myhrvold and Peter Rinearson, *The Road Ahead* (New York: Penguin, 1996). Of many books on the leading software firm, see Randall E. Stross, *The Microsoft Way* (Reading, Mass.: Addison-Wesley, 1996); Michael A. Cusumano and Richard W. Selby, *Microsoft Secrets: How the World's Most Powerful Software Company Creates Technology, Shapes Markets, and Manages People* (New York: Free Press, 1995); and William H. Page and John E. Lopatka, *The Microsoft Case: Antitrust, High Technology, and Consumer Welfare* (Chicago: University of Chicago Press, 2007).

A quick overview of Silicon Valley may be found in a special 20-page survey by John Micklethwait, "Silicon Valley: The Valley of Money's Delight," *The Economist*, March 19, 1997. Carolyn Caddes, *Portraits of Success: Impressions of Silicon Valley Pioneers* (Palo Alto, Calif.: Tioga, 1986), is a pictures-with-text coverage of numerous participants in the creation of Silicon Valley firms, including not only engineers but also venture capitalists, lawyers, and others. See also the following standard works: Christopher Lécuyer, *Making Silicon Valley: Innovation and the Growth of High Tech, 1930–1970* (Cambridge, Mass: MIT Press, 2006); Leslie Berlin, *The Man Behind the Microchip: Robert Noyce and the Invention of Silicon Valley* (New York: Oxford University Press, 2005), which is informative on Fairchild Semiconductor and Intel as well as Noyce himself; and AnnaLee Saxenian, *Regional Advantage: Culture and Competition in Silicon Valley and Route 128* (Cambridge, Mass.: Harvard University Press, 1994), an insightful comparative study that contributes to the theoretical literature on industry clusters. A direct examination of this phenomenon as it relates to Silicon Valley is Stuart W. Leslie and Robert H. Kargon,

"Selling Silicon Valley: Frederick Terman's Model for Regional Advantage," *Business History Review,* 70 (Winter 1996).

The relationship between computerization and productivity is addressed in Shoshanna Zuboff, *In the Age of the Smart Machine* (New York: Basic Books, 1988); Daniel E. Sichel, *The Computer Revolution: An Economic Perspective* (Washington, D.C.: Brookings Institution Press, 1997); and Martin Campbell-Kelly, *From Airline Reservations to Sonic the Hedgehog: A History of the Software Industry* (Cambridge, Mass.: MIT Press, 2003). The course of information technology may be followed through current and back issues of periodicals such as *Wired, Internet World,* and *Datamation,* the latter of which provides continually updated statistical profiles of the computer industry.

Regarding the Internet, see Janet Abbate, *Inventing the Internet* (Cambridge, Mass.: MIT Press, 1999); Robert H. Reid, *Architects of the Web: 1,000 Days that Built the Future of Business* (New York: Wiley, 1997); Paul Ceruzzi, *Internet Alley: High Technology in Tysons Corner, 1945–2005* (Cambridge, Mass.: MIT Press, 2008); and William Aspray and Paul E. Ceruzzi, eds., *The Internet and American Business* (Cambridge, Mass.: MIT Press, 2008).

For analyses of venture capital, see the very thorough Paul A. Gompers and Joshua Lerner, *Venture Capital: The Money of Invention* (Boston: Harvard Business School Press, 2001); the practical reference book Andrew Metrick, *Venture Capital and the Finance of Innovation* (New York: Wiley, 2006); and the useful but uneven autobiography of the VC pioneer Tom Perkins, *Valley Boy: The Education of Tom Perkins* (New York: Gotham, 2007).

On the three companies analyzed in this chapter, a good starting place is their coverage in the full version of *Hoover's Reports.* Book-length studies include: for amazon.com, Robert Spector, *Amazon.com—Get Big Fast: Inside the Revolutionary Business Model That Changed The World* (New York: HarperCollins, 2001); James Marcus, *Amazonia: Five Years at the Epicenter of the Dot. Com Juggernaut* (New York: Norton, 2004); and the extremely critical Mike Daisey, *21 Dog Years* (New York: Free Press, 2002).

For eBay, the best book with which to start is Adam Cohen, *The Perfect Store: Inside eBay* (New York: Little, Brown, 2002).

Also useful is Ken Hills and Michael Petit with Nathan Epley, *Everyday eBay: Culture, Collecting and Desire* (London: Routledge, 2006), a collection of 19 essays that together comprise the first academic book on the company. See also Daniel Nissanoff, *FutureShop: How the New Auction Culture Will Revolutionize the Way We Buy, Sell and Get the Things We Really Want* (New York: Penguin, 2006), which uses social theory in predicting what its title asserts. Christopher Cihlar, *The Grilled Cheese Madonna and 99 Other of the Weirdest, Wackiest, Most Famous eBay Auctions Ever* (New York: Broadway Books, 2006), is entertaining as well as insightful. Several books warn against various kinds of fraud inherent in buying and selling through eBay, one of which is Michael Ford, *Scams & Scoundrels: Protect Yourself from the Dark Side of eBay* (Camarillo, Calif.: Elite Minds, 2007).

For Google, see David Vise and Mark Malseed, *The Google Story* (New York: Delacorte Press, 2005); and John Battelle's outstanding *The Search: How Google and Its Rivals Rewrote the Rules of Business and Transformed Our Culture* (New York: Portfolio, 2005), which is not only about Google but also nearly all other aspects of Internet companies and their culture.

On blogging as it relates to business, see Jeremy Wright, *Blog Marketing* (New York: McGraw-Hill, 2005); Robert Scoble and Shel Israel, *Naked Conversations: How Blogs Are Changing the Way Businesses Talk with Customers* (New York: Wiley, 2006); and Debbie Weil, *The Corporate Blogging Book: Absolutely Everything You Need to Know to Get It Right* (New York: Portfolio, 2006).

Almost none of the books listed in the Selected Sources for this chapter can possibly be fully up to date, because information technology is changing so fast. The sales and employment numbers listed in the text for Amazon.com, eBay, and Google continue to increase rapidly, and nobody can predict their future course.

The same point applies, though with less intensity, to this entire Bibliographical Essay. As full as the Essay may appear to be, new scholarship on all the topics covered in this book will continue to come forth, as both American business and interpretations of it persist in their patterns of relentless change.

# ACKNOWLEDGMENTS

For advice and assistance with this book, as with all my work, I am very deeply indebted to Susan McCraw. She is the most generous and intelligent person I've ever known.

During more than two decades at Harvard Business School, I have benefited immensely from the insights of students, colleagues, research associates, friends at both Harvard and other universities, and members of my own Business History Seminar. For assistance and advice with this book, I thank Sven Beckert, Jeffrey Bernstein, Laura Bureš, Bill Childs, Walter Friedman, Max Hall, David Moss, Rowena Olegario, Forest Reinhardt, Dick Rosenbloom, Jeff Strabone, Richard Tedlow, David Thomas, Peter Tufano, Dick Vietor, Felice Whittum, Mary Yeager, and the truly splendid reference staff at Harvard's Baker Library.

For any errors or infelicities in the book, I alone am responsible.

# INDEX

Notes are indicated by an "n" after the page number.

*American Business Since 1920: How It Worked,* Second Edition
Developmental editor and copy editor: Andrew J. Davidson
Production editor: Linda Gaio
Typesetter: Bruce Leckie
Proofreader: Claudia Siler
Indexer: Fred Liese
Printer: McNaughton & Gunn